THE STRAND

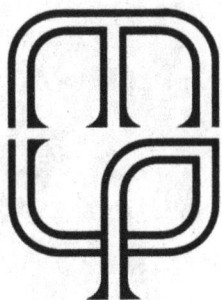

Manchester University Press

THE STRAND

A BIOGRAPHY

Geoff Browell *and* **Eileen Chanin**

MANCHESTER UNIVERSITY PRESS

Published by Manchester University Press
Oxford Road, Manchester, M13 9PL

www.manchesteruniversitypress.co.uk

British Library Cataloguing-in-Publication Data
A catalogue record for this book is available from the British Library

ISBN 978 1 5261 7911 1 hardback

First published 2025

The publisher has no responsibility for the persistence or accuracy of URLs for any external or third-party internet websites referred to in this book, and does not guarantee that any content on such websites is, or will remain, accurate or appropriate.

EU authorised representative for GPSR:
Easy Access System Europe, Mustamäe tee 50, 10621 Tallinn, Estonia
gpsr.requests@easproject.com

Typeset by R. J. Footring Ltd, Derby, UK

CONTENTS

PREFACE

This is our view of the Strand. While it offers tantalising glimpses into the essence of this remarkable street, it is not intended to be a comprehensive history but, rather, an introduction to the street and its life, including the lives and times of those who lived there and in its vicinity. Because there is a slice of history seen in every nook, in every corner of the Strand, there will always be other stories and other Strands.

We have adopted a simplified approach to names and all dates are New Style unless otherwise stated. Some quotations are abbreviated but, where appropriate, original spelling has been retained.

Currency has been converted to today's equivalent value.

The numbering of the buildings on the Strand has undergone considerable change over the past two centuries. Those given in the text are today's numbers, offered for the purpose of orientation to locations in past centuries.

INTRODUCTION

Life is change.
Nancy Price, *Into an Hour Glass*[1]

During early autumn, as in an equinox of old, the sinking sun shines down London's Strand, before hurriedly dipping below the horizon. Momentarily, on clear evenings, the street's shops, offices, hotels and theatres, traffic and pedestrians are bathed in an ethereal old gold. Light pours down this short, narrow, canyon road, reflecting off innumerable windows and leaving deep-purple shadows in the tributary streets. The Strand sits still, suspended in time.

This is its first twenty-first-century biography. Two thousand years of London's grand story have played out along this unique thoroughfare, from Roman road to the birthplace of broadcasting and the unravelling of the secret of the DNA double helix. Arguably, few streets have been more eventful and influential in the wider world, over such a long period. Stretching less than a mile along the Thames's northern shoreline, the Strand and its parishes comprise several connected but distinct villages, each with its own identity. East Strand is marked by Temple Bar and Fleet Street, the entrance to the City of London and the self-governing commercial heart of Greater London. West Strand comprises Charing Cross and the approach to Trafalgar Square, London's principal public space. The Strand's neighbourhood, to which this book also refers, then and now includes the maze of short roads to its south and north that connect it to the river and to Covent Garden, the former fruit and vegetable market now turned tourist attraction. The Strand was at the outset of London's post-Roman history the link connecting Westminster and the City of London and it remains the backbone of the capital. An archetype of urban advancement, it has today been redesigned with a new green park at its east end. It is ever-changing.

The Strand has worn many faces as power has shifted from Church to aristocracy and to commerce and law. It is where authority, tradition and ceremony have collided with non-conformity and experimentation, where extravagant wealth has sat alongside terrible deprivation. Yet its extraordinary life story has not been told for over a century – not since Beresford Chancellor published *The Annals of the Strand* in 1912. Then the street was experiencing one of its liveliest chapters and it had recently been hailed as the 'centre of the world'. Archaeological and other recent discoveries have now revealed still more about the street's past.[2]

A parade of personalities have dwelt or met their fate on the Strand. Books about the street have largely been written with their stories in mind, in the tradition of Thomas Pennant's memorialising of significant individuals associated with a place. This approach views the Strand as a passive and silent stage on which notable protagonists act out their celebrated roles. But a street is arguably an active player in its own history, its personality defined by its physical attributes, its location and form, the elements that lie beneath it and the morphology of the architecture that occupies it. According to proponents of psychogeography such as Iain Sinclair, its emotional impact is also important. The Strand, then, is less a passive witness to events, more the maker of its own story.

Scholarship published in the past century – not least the meticulous parish-by-parish *Survey of London* series, and Pevsner's *Buildings of England* – has greatly assisted in establishing the history of the buildings of the Strand and their relationship with near-neighbours such as Piccadilly Circus. Drawing on these studies and a wealth of sources – from archives, diaries and correspondence, journalism and fiction, art, film and photography – this biography seeks to answer the question: what has made and continues to make the Strand? What circumstances and events unique to the street have given it its character and played a part in shaping its history?

Numerous global cities can boast famous streets, for example the ancient Via Dolorosa in Jerusalem, which projects spiritual authority, or Wall Street in New York, a proclamation of the power of high finance. Other, European, cities reflect the grandeur of their heyday, like Unter den Linden in Berlin. Paris and its Champs-Élysées perhaps resemble most closely London and the Strand: both cities combined the national commercial, artistic and political centres of power of their respective countries in a single urban conurbation, and their principal thoroughfares consequently needed to be suitably impressive. Both France and the United Kingdom, too, assembled extensive global empires, and their imperial capitals and landmarks achieved disproportionate recognition far and wide. Streets from South Africa to Texas, New Zealand and India tried to emulate the fame of London's Strand and were named after it. Rival streets in London, including Oxford Street, Regent Street and Piccadilly, can also now lay claim to similar name recognition and are probably better known, not least in the United Kingdom. But only one street in London has historically and consistently projected its social, political and cultural influence over a span of more than a thousand years – the Strand. This is its story.[3]

Its prehistory represents an immense, barely conceivable span of experience shaped by cruel and impersonal geological forces. Their vast duration was described by pioneer geologists based on the Strand, including William Smith, who published the world's first national geological map, and Charles Darwin's contemporary Sir Charles Lyell, Professor of Geology at King's College London in east Strand and author of the influential *Principles of Geology* (1830–33). A deeper understanding of the origins of the world – and of London – began to emerge. The foundations of the Strand were fashioned by geology and by climate change, natural factors identified in the scholarship of pioneering twentieth-century authors of 'total history', for instance Fernand Braudel, who compiled comprehensive studies of the Mediterranean, and more recently in the work of scholars such as Peter Frankopan. The Strand – its aspect, pattern of settlement and ultimate purpose – was thus profoundly shaped by the power of its geography.[4]

Advances in field archaeology since the 1980s have transformed our understanding of Britain's prehistory and of Roman London and its riverside highway. Archaeological evidence points to the building of a road – which would one day become the Strand and Fleet Street – in the first century CE through a landscape of fields, farmsteads and burial grounds beyond the River Fleet, which then marked London's western perimeter. Its ultimate destination at that time remains unknown, though we might speculate that it followed the route of a more ancient pathway.

Our understanding of the early medieval precursor to the Strand (c. 600–900) has similarly been transformed by modern archaeology, revealing a bustling, multicultural market. This was then the principal road of the new settlement to the west of the old Roman city, adjacent to a beach used by flat-bottomed seagoing vessels. By the twelfth century it had acquired its modern name, derived from the Old English word for shoreline. The river remained the region's main artery of transport; the Strand's southern flank therefore exerted a profound influence on the street's history. To the east of the Strand lay the regenerated City of London, which had been reinhabited in the ninth century after centuries of abandonment following the end of Roman occupation. It grew wealthy from a trade in woollen cloth and it jealously guarded its new-found privileges. To its west was Westminster, built around a Benedictine abbey in the tenth century and a centre of religious, royal and legal power. As an 'extramural' suburb, the Strand was home to many dispossessed people seeking a living outside the rigid control of the City. Centuries later, it attracted European artisans sheltering from oppression and more recently theatrical players seeking greater freedom of expression. Its millennium-old status as a connection between the City and Westminster accelerated its urbanisation and from the thirteenth century it became a place of state processions, religious pageants, royal funerals and coronation celebrations: potent symbols of national thanksgiving and collective memory-making. It has remained so ever since, notably hosting the funeral corteges of war heroes Admiral Nelson in 1805 and the Duke of Wellington in 1852.

The English Reformation, a fundamental break from the authority of Rome, transformed the Strand into a centre of secular power. It grew rich from the Protestant ascendancy and from voyages of discovery to America, which opened up new markets and furnished remarkable imports of goods, people and ideas. The history of the mansions of its wealthy, such as Somerset House, has recently been described in exemplary detail in Manolo Guerci's magisterial *London's 'Golden Mile': The Great Houses of the Strand, 1550–1650*; these centres of new money and showcases for artistic treasures were bold statements of the power and prestige of their owners. In their shadow clustered engravers and print-makers, who promoted new institutions of art education and appreciation in the eighteenth century. A booming population bolstered by refugees from Catholic Europe brought important skills in the making of scientific instruments for navigation and astronomy, surveying and keeping time. The Strand was a place that cultivated – in its myriad workshops, retail premises, homes and warehouses – a variety of interconnected special skills of science, artisanship, artistry, print and performance. These flourished in the nineteenth and twentieth centuries, too, and included telegraphic technologies, the applied arts and theatre design. The Strand in effect became the craft quarter for a new 'West End' of town squares and smart terraces that were expressions of high society, conviviality and commercial energy reflective of London's new, global ambitions.[5]

Renaissance scholars sought to rediscover and reinvent the past, and the Strand's resident community of antiquarian 'Monuments Men', worried at the pace of change, strove to protect its manuscripts, books and buildings. Slowly, across two centuries, the Strand became aware of its past – and began to anticipate its future. It was celebrated in the wide distribution of high-quality prints by artists such as Thomas Bowles and Thomas Shepherd, and via the newspaper industry and, later, photography. This promoted, in thousands of pictures, postcards and souvenirs, a now familiar modern prospect of the Strand as a thoroughfare densely packed with horse-drawn and later motor buses and cabs, and cluttered with advertising and shop signs: prosperous, lively and buzzing with commercial and creative energy. Photographers, for instance Bedford Lemere with studios at 147 Strand, recorded fast-disappearing relics, not least late medieval timber streets – Holywell and Wych – at the eastern end of the Strand. This tension between progress and preservation remains integral to the Strand's story. Such visual records also introduce an important new set of sources for us to drawn upon, though often these were idealised or politically charged. What such images fail to convey, however, is the Strand's assault on the senses, the smells and sounds of its horses, taxi cabs and motor traffic and the accompanying cacophony of street hawkers, children, theatre folk, commuters and passers-through. This was an extraordinary highway of human life.

The story of this Strand and its inhabitants has been brought into focus by the growth since the 1990s of databases of contemporary records rich in millions of names, personalities and stories, the fruit of digitisation of newspapers, as well as state and parish records relating to rites of passage, taxation, trade, property and crime. Not least of these is the electronic *Proceedings of the Old Bailey* – a record of criminal trials from 1674 to 1913, which shines light on the lives of many ordinary local people. The Strand that these sources illustrate witnessed an explosion in sociability, inventiveness and curiosity, particularly new knowledge about the natural world shared in the fashionable coffee houses and dining clubs that sprang up in the district in the late eighteenth century, such as the Kit Cat, as well as in new political and debating bodies, for instance at the headquarters of the working-class London Corresponding Society. These were places of conversation, gossip and experiment. Impressive new subscription institutions such as William Shipley's Society for the Encouragement of the Arts, Manufactures and Commerce, founded in 1754 (which later became the Royal Society of Arts) and the Royal Academy of Arts, established in 1768, which relocated from Pall Mall to Old Somerset House in 1771, transformed the Strand into a place where art – its education, production and promotion – took centre stage.

The street's energy animated literary, musical and artistic geniuses (Dr Samuel Johnson, lexicographer and wit, who lived in a house nearby; composer George Frideric Handel), political leaders and scientists (e.g. Benjamin Franklin, who lived near Charing Cross, and was both), as well as eminent visitors, including the French philosopher Voltaire. This eighteenth-century Strand was diverse – living up to its medieval reputation for 'in-betweenness' – and an avenue on the edge of town. New, controversial, political ideas began to be shared in a world convulsed by the American War of Independence and the French Revolution. Around the Strand, people rich and poor – continental refugees, job seekers and servants in its many houses – could reinvent themselves, swap professions and identities and start anew. Debates about the causes of poverty, electoral reform, or the balance between freedom and censorship flourished among encyclopaedic minds. Letters and, later, telegrams connected its people with their contemporaries across the United Kingdom, mainland Europe and North America. Radicals and loyalists clashed between the last major domestic rebellion (in 1745) and the tumult of the 1840s in great meeting houses such as the Crown and Anchor, one of the street's many hostelries and taverns that mediated a conversation between the mob and the respectable classes. Others, including the Golden Cross coaching inn, from which Dickens's fictional Samuel Pickwick began his journey in *The Pickwick Papers*, were gathering places for people from far and wide. Charing Cross, where it resided, is now customarily regarded as the geographical centre of London, but at one time it was a crossroads of the mind.

An otherworldliness characterised this place. It was at one point the residence of the poet and artist William Blake, who in 1820 moved into a house adjacent to the Fountain Tavern near the present Coal Hole pub. The Strand had been his home and artistic playground from his days as a draughtsman and engraver at Henry Pars' drawing school at number 101 and William Hogarth's St Martin's Lane Academy, and the street was suffused with the power of his hallucinatory imagination. Blake was a follower of the Swedish philosopher and mystic Emanuel Swedenborg, who died in London in 1772. He was attracted to the philosopher's Neoplatonism, the belief that this world is but a ghostly representation of a deeper reality buried beneath and accessible only through art and dreams. He would no doubt have browsed the many print shops and bookshops in the Strand that sold Swedenborg's translated works, and the proximity of prosperity and deprivation that Blake encountered on the street fired his creativity and imagery. Doors away, in the Royal Academy, the painter John Martin, inspired by biblical prophecy, ancient mythology and the romantic turn, had unveiled the first of his immensely popular epic masterpieces, *Sadak in Search of the Waters of Oblivion*. In this and his later paintings, equally popular, for instance *Pandemonium* and *The Plains of Heaven*, the latter a part of his apocalyptic final triptych, Martin had truly glimpsed another world, great and terrible in scope. His friend Charles Wheatstone was an experimenter extraordinaire throughout the Strand's steam-powered era, and from it he bridged continents with his new telegraphic apparatus, rivalling Samuel Morse's, and invented the stereoscope, which allowed the public to view flat pictures in three dimensions. This was virtual reality, and it was magic by gaslight.[6]

Grinding poverty and conspicuous wealth sat cheek by jowl in the Strand during its time of greatest pomp and magnificence – the 200 years preceding the outbreak of the First World War in 1914. Grander public buildings and new spaces began to be erected in the 1770s, with Sir William Chambers's Somerset House, followed by the John Nash-inspired Trafalgar Square and National Gallery in the 1820s and 1830s. Waterloo Bridge opened in 1817 and necessitated large-scale clearances at the eastern end of the Strand. Such monumental engineering continued with the comparatively late arrival of the railways, notably Charing Cross Station, which opened in 1864. Joseph Bazalgette's Victoria Embankment, completed in 1870, was the product of the Metropolitan Board of Works, charged with London's modernisation. The Embankment housed part of an impressive new sewerage network designed to improve the river's water quality, and a roadway which it was hoped would relieve the Strand of its congestion.

From Charing Cross for a time trains ran to and from the Channel ports and brought a sophisticated clientele from Europe, and along with the District (underground) Railway from the 1870s attracted suburban travellers who commuted to new offices in the area. Theatre-goers used faster public transport to attend evening performances and enjoy pre-theatre meals in a new class of restaurant, such as Romano's, later the haunt of theatre celebrities (e.g. Marie Lloyd) and royalty (e.g. the future King Edward VII). Day trippers, meanwhile, enjoyed a hugely varied shopping experience. The street's diversity – also relevant to earlier Victorian London – is visible in John Tallis's famous shopfront *Street Views*, published in 1838–40, which featured for example, clockmakers (e.g. Dent, who later made Big Ben's timepiece) and print and paper sellers (e.g. the German Rudolph Ackermann's Repository at 96 Strand). Visitors stocked up on clothes at D'Oyley's Warehouse and tea at Twinings. The men's outfitters Thresher & Glenny was established in 1755 at the 'sign of the peacock' next to Somerset House, and it was awarded a royal warrant by King George III; impressed, Admiral Nelson bought his stockings there when he worked in the nearby Navy Office. Thresher & Glenny prospered by association with the growth of Britain's overseas territories made possible by its powerful naval fleet. It later became the preferred supplier to Edwardian army officers and civil servants making the passage to India, its catalogue boasting 'llama wool vests ... and fur rugs made from racoon, Japanese fox and opossum'.[7]

The Strand's theatricality, pageantry and pomp were exemplified by institutions such as the menagerie in Exeter Change, on its north side. A fashionable destination in Regency London, it even housed an Indian elephant that performed at the Theatre Royal, Drury Lane. During a visit, Lord Byron reported that the animal 'took off my hat – opened a door – trunked a whip – and behaved so well, that I wish he was my butler'. Sadly in 1826, driven mad by close confinement over more than a decade, the elephant went berserk and had to be shot. The Victorian Strand was home to a popular panorama featuring recreations of the world's natural and human landmarks, as well as a host of exhibitions and attractions, for example the Phrenological Museum at 367 Strand and the National Gallery of Practical Science on the north side of the multiple-glass-domed Lowther Arcade at Charing Cross. These palaces of precocious science bridged the era of the *Wunderkammer* and that of the public science museum; they made engineering and experimental philosophy fashionable and in the decades after the opening of the Great Exhibition in Hyde Park in 1851 drew a line between industrial potency and imperial success. They attracted a curious public hungry for knowledge, those disciples of the school of self-help espoused by bestselling authors such as Samuel Smiles. Through their windows could be observed various mechanical and electrical instruments, the engines of modernity and progress that powered a global empire.[8]

These public palaces of science competed with the theatres, which offered variety shows and burlesque, light comic operas and drama. They included the Adelphi (1819), Lyceum (rebuilt in 1834), Charing Cross Music Hall (1867), Vaudeville (1870) and the Savoy (1881). At the street's east end were the Olympic Pavilion (1806), the Globe and Opera Comique (1870 and 1868), which hosted Gilbert and Sullivan's phenomenally successful *HMS Pinafore*. The Tivoli music hall dominated south Strand. Other theatres included the Royal Charing Cross (1869), Terry's (1887), Aldwych (1905) and the pre-eminent Gaiety (1868). The larger theatres (notably the Gaiety and Tivoli) accommodated successful restaurants, confirming their status as centres of conviviality and hospitality. Most of the Strand's theatres – like its other buildings – were repeatedly replaced or served multiple purposes. The Strand itself had already been the fictional backdrop to numerous plays, including those of the Strand resident and Restoration playwright William Congreve.[9]

The Victorian and Edwardian Strand and Fleet Street hosted influential contemporary publications, notably the satirical *Punch*, founded in 1842 by the journalist and reformer Henry Mayhew, the campaigning *Morning Post*, where Charles Dickens began his career as a journalist, *The Economist*, founded in 1843 to seek the repeal of the Corn Laws, and the offices of John Chapman at 142 Strand, publishers of George Eliot and the subject of Rosemary Ashton's excellent history. The area's reforming and campaigning zeal (owing in part to a religious revival and high-minded philanthropy) was its hallmark throughout the nineteenth and early twentieth centuries. Huge crowds attended public meetings in Exeter Hall.[10]

The Strand Magazine, founded in 1891, published the Sherlock Holmes mysteries and celebrated what was now the Empire's glittering promenade and arguably the world's most famous thoroughfare. But its rear alleys and courtyards, overcrowded and insanitary, were home to the vast underclass of the poor and sick. The colourful maps compiled by the sociologist Charles Booth in the 1880s and 1890s depicted the homes of the street's well-to-do alongside those categorised as 'Poor', 'Very poor' and occasionally even 'Lowest class. Vicious. Semi criminal'.[11] Prostitution – much of it underage – had always been commonplace in the neighbourhood and from the 1750s even spawned an annual guidebook of sex workers, *Harris's List of Covent Garden Ladies*. This in-between place attracted outcasts or those deemed 'different', people such as the cross-dressing gay theatre-goers and scandalisers of polite society Ernest Boulton and Frederick Park, the erstwhile 'Fanny and Stella', who were acquitted of charges of sodomy in 1870.[12]

This was also a place where the fantastical and terrible were possible. Rudyard Kipling, briefly a tenant in Villiers Street, recalled it as being 'primitive and passionate in its habits and population'. One day, from his window, Kipling saw a man suddenly slit his throat in the street outside. His breast, wrote the author, 'turned dull red like a robin's'. Within minutes, an ambulance had removed his body and a boy had sluiced down the pavement. The incident seems otherwise to have gone largely unnoticed. The Strand throughout was a canvas of deformity and novelty, in which misery was transmuted into creative energy and progressive change; in the conspicuous display of its lurid hoardings, its hurdy-gurdy advertisements and its self-referencing music hall ditties, it basked in its own celebrity.[13]

Philosophers, artists, scientists and writers in the early twentieth century were enthralled by the mystery of time. Not least among them were Albert Einstein and the Frenchman Henri Bergson, who took opposing sides in separate lectures about its nature which were delivered a decade apart at King's College. Bergson

made the study of time his business, so much so that the best man
at his wedding was Marcel Proust, author of *Remembrance of Things
Past*. In Bergson's philosophy, perception and intuition shape the
passage and experience of time such that the distinctions between
past, present and future begin to dissolve. Like many of his contemporaries, he was drawn to the mysteries of the paranormal,
which it was believed might best be explained by reference to non-
linear time, and in 1913 he was elected President of the Society for
Psychical Research. Einstein, meanwhile, argued that time was
intrinsic to the geometry of the universe, of which he provided experimental proof in a lecture in the Strand in 1921. A century later,
Bergson's intuitive and Einstein's empirical approaches to time
remain unresolved.[14]

The pioneer sexologist Havelock Ellis, who lodged in the Strand,
explored the mysteries of reality in a different way, by ingesting
mescaline, a psychedelic drug used in traditional religious rites
in New Mexico. Under the light of a flickering gas jet, he reported
seeing a kaleidoscope of 'golden jewels studded with red and green
stones and ever changing and full of delight'. Colour adopted a new
vibrancy and 'a familiar noticeboard in the Strand with dark-blue
background was much more conspicuous and intensely blue than
usual'. The drug, he surmised, could facilitate access to higher
levels of consciousness, perhaps even 'a new artificial paradise' and
muse for poets and artists.[15]

The Strand's Victorian fogs no doubt swirled around the young
Vincent van Gogh, who worked at an international art dealership
in Bedford Street between 1874 and 1875. This was a stone's throw
from the birthplace a century before of the artist J. M. W. Turner,
in Maiden Lane, and mere doors from the stage entrance of the
Lyceum Theatre – the dramatic arena of the great actor Henry
Irving – where Bram Stoker, author of *Dracula*, would shortly
embark on a twenty-year career as business manager. Some twenty-
five years later, Beatrix Potter would meet her publishers in Bedford
Street with a jar of live frogs and new ideas, and Jeremy Fisher would
be born.[16] Van Gogh took inspiration from the prints displayed
weekly in the windows of the office of the *Illustrated London News*

and its rival *The Graphic*, also based in the Strand: 'The impressions I gained there on the spot were so strong that the drawings have remained clear and bright in my mind', he wrote. Turning right out of Bedford Street after leaving work, he would have encountered the setting sun, perhaps haloed luminously through the mists, just as Turner might have encountered it as a boy and when he exhibited at the Royal Academy.[17] Inspired by Turner, and the genius of the place, the French master Claude Monet, from his vantage point in rooms 510–11 and 610–11 of the Savoy Hotel, at the turn of the century produced a remarkable series of paintings of the Thames, Charing Cross Bridge and Waterloo Bridge – the Strand's Impressionist moment.[18]

New, fashionable accommodation such as the Savoy and Hotel Cecil were impressive landmarks of international high society, but could not wholly escape controversy, for example as the backdrop to the downfall of Oscar Wilde. The thoroughfare made its living from entertainment, idle amusement and conspicuous consumption, in its cafes and restaurants like Gatti's and Simpson's, host to roast beef and chess, and in its shops, brothels and theatres and amid the ceaseless pageant of traffic and relentless hive-hum of a curious humanity. Along its length, in time, new symbols of the Dominions such as Australia House were constructed within a handsome district set out by the London County Council: Kingsway and Aldwych. Meanwhile, statements of the democratic potential of commerce were made by the American Irving T. Bush, who sponsored a new complex (later called Bush House) that he intended to be a world trade centre.

Along the Strand, motor transport replaced horse-drawn carriages. Radio communications and the first broadcasts from the British Broadcasting Company (as it then was, before it became the Corporation, or BBC) began there in 1922, which soon included programmes by H. G. Wells and the playwright George Bernard Shaw – a noted Strand *habitué*. Theatre was a glittering highlight and remains so today.

The wars of the twentieth century left the Strand's physical fabric largely intact but, amid Britain's many postwar economic problems, from the 1970s it entered into a period of visible decline, just as Covent Garden and other parts of the West End became more popular. It lost many of its remaining distinctive family retail businesses. More recently, though, it has been improved through the provision of new art galleries and cultural centres such as the Courtauld Gallery, which has an exceptional collection of Impressionist and other art. Other recent proposed improvements have been rejected, for instance the 'garden bridge' at its eastern end, which would have spanned the Thames with flowers and offered a more direct connection to the Southbank's cultural attractions. In 2022, instead, a pedestrian park was set out south of Aldwych, evidence perhaps that the Strand is finding its feet again as a more attractive venue for tourists and visitors.

This Strand – with improvement beckoning – has been where we have worked and socialised for a long time, respectively as an archivist and as a historian of London. Across this span, the street has experienced many often-imperceptible alterations – to which we have borne witness, in its sights and sounds, in its outward appearance, in changes in buildings and in the eccentricities of its characters and their voices. The book was conceived many years ago in a spirit of curiosity and deep affection for the Strand. Our desire to understand its long story was sharpened when the COVID-19 pandemic stilled the seemingly eternal din of traffic. Then, as if in a dream, the deep past began slowly to seep into the street's spaces and, briefly, whispers of older times could be heard once again.

Come with us now, down the Strand.

CHAPTER 1

BEGINNINGS

And I remember like yesterday
The earliest Cockney who came my way
When he pushed through the forest that lined the Strand.
Rudyard Kipling, *The River's Tale*[1]

Strand means 'beach' in Old English, and this mile-long foreshore has always been defined by the presence of its ageless neighbour, Old Father Thames. Travelling back in time a million years, however, we encounter a very different landscape, one where the ground upon which the Strand will be built is yet to exist. Everything the street is to become, its prodigious potential shimmers in the future. The Thames then followed a more northerly course, flowing into a larger waterway called the Bytham River. Hauntingly discovered in the sands of its estuary valley on the Norfolk coast were the fossil footprints of a family of premodern humans who paddled here 800,000 years ago, the earliest evidence of hominin occupation in northern Europe.[2]

This London-to-be long ago was an immense plain between ridges of chalk to the north and south – the Chilterns and the Surrey Hills – built from the bed of temperate, shallow and languorous seas. Above this chalk lay the famous London clay, into which the tunnels of the London Underground would one day be sunk and from which the brick-built city would mushroom. Human-like species *Homo antecessor* and their successors *Homo heidelbergensis* began to occupy what was then a north-western promontory of Europe, habitation attested by a half-million-year-old campsite at Boxgrove, south of London. Here, generations of family groups gathered on the shores of an ancient lagoon to butcher rhino, bison and horse using skilfully worked flint hand axes.[3]

Climate change – cycles of ice ages and warmer periods triggered by the fluctuation of the Earth on its axis – transformed London and laid the foundations of the Strand. The cruellest of these ice ages, the so-called Anglian Glaciation, reached its maximum around 450,000 years ago, following millennia of cooling and the transformation, imperceptibly, of the flora of the proto-Thames Valley from green to grey. As if in a time-lapse, lush deciduous woodland progressively was replaced by birch and coniferous forest, followed by grassland then frozen tundra, scoured by hurricane winds off the ice shelf and blanketed by loess, the dust of ground-down mountains. In their most southerly ever advance, the Anglian glaciers which descended from the immense sheets that covered Scandinavia, Scotland and Wales, with their measureless caverns of ice, reached the valley of the Finchley Road at Swiss Cottage, just outside Sigmund Freud's house: they would have formed a sheer wall of blue and white, visible from the Strand.

The Thames adopted its present course, in its now familiar basin, following the retreat of the glaciers around 425,000 years ago. The Earth upon which the Strand was deposited was laid down during a renewed period of cooling between 375,000 and 130,000 years ago, then again during the last Ice Age, which reached its maximum 25,000 years ago. There followed times of fast-flowing meltwater streams, cold and frothy in icy spate, depositing the till shorn from the landscape by the ice to make a braided river. This broad body of water two and a half miles wide, resembling an inland delta, was cut into innumerable channels interspersed by higher islands of gravel terraces that accumulated progressively to deposit the gravel formations upon which the Strand was built. A slice through the ground would thus reveal a Victoria sponge cake-like base of chalk and clay, well drained gravel, a brick-earth of biscuity glacial detritus, then an icing of alluvial sand laid down during warmer periods of higher sea level, when the river began to meander and great silty marshlands rich in organic matter were deposited.[4]

This underlying prehistoric geology – together with the presence of the river – explains why the central London basin in general and the Strand in particular were attractive to human settlement: it made possible the creation of a prodigious underground aquifer and thus the appearance on the surface of springs from which fresh water might be drawn. Several of these were present in the vicinity of the Strand, including St Clement's Well, and would one day become a source of veneration by pre-Christian Londoners and their descendants. Then, as now, the Thames in its middle course was fed by numerous tributaries. These largely forgotten rivers, such as the Wandle and Effra to the south and Stamford Brook, Westbourne and Walbrook to the north, are integral to London's story but have progressively been buried or canalised. Such tributaries would make possible speedier navigation for early inhabitants in primitive dug-outs, and in larger rivers such as the Lea midstream eyots no doubt afforded prehistoric human settlers nocturnal protection from wolves and other predators. Their fishy waters, meanwhile, attracted animals which generations of peripatetic human hunters despatched and butchered using the flint clasts that they fossicked from the grit and pebble earth. Amid this watery world, the Strand came to be defined as the higher gravel escarpment between the valleys of the River Fleet to the east and the channel of the Tyburn in Westminster, marking the western perimeter of its curtilage (Tyburn in fact means 'boundary stream' in Old English).[5]

The post-Anglian landscape of the Thames Valley was an open and generous savannah of cold-loving plants, supporting mammoths, woolly rhinoceros, brown bears, leopards and the huge cave lion, which evolved independently of its African cousins. Short-faced hyenas, standing three feet high, hunted in fearsome packs. Other mammals that flourished included the English panda, which grew to twice the size of the red panda, as well as grazing animals (sheep, goats, deer) and wild pigs. Great flocks of waterfowl overwintered on the river's braid bars, a chilly prehistoric version of Okavango Delta spread out below the Strand. During colder parts of the climactic cycles, giant elk and grazing herds of migratory reindeer, horses and thunderous bison swept into Britain across the plains and river valleys of Doggerland to the east and the Channel Valley stretching to France in the south, low-lying areas that were exposed in these cool periods, when the sea level fell.[6]

An extraordinary collection of fossils was unearthed in 1957, during the construction of Uganda House in Trafalgar Square, from what we now know to be the warmest historic period before the present day – between 130,000 and 115,000 years ago. During this temperate time of high sea levels, Doggerland and the Channel Valley were inundated, and Britain once again became an island. Enjoying mild winters and dry summers, this veritable Eden supported a palette of exotic fauna reminiscent of parts of tropical Africa translated to an English country park. The meandering Thames supported bloats of hippopotami that basked in the swampy margins of the river, herds of straight-tusked elephants and prides of lions. Above, the brute beauty of a windhover and the dance of skylarks would have traced the velvet blue of the sky. Swampy sedges clung to the riverside, blurring into grassy parkland of yellow buttercup, mustard and marigold trampled by the herds of herbivores that it supported, before open scrub of hawthorn, sloe, maple, yew and dogwood, while great stands of deciduous oak, ash and hazel swept to the horizon, macaque monkeys swinging from their branches.[7]

The presence of pre-humans and humans has been intermittent over the past half million years, a fluctuation dependent on Britain's island status and a supportive climate. Stockier, more thick-set and muscular than modern humans, Neanderthals replaced *H. heidelbergensis*. They evolved around 450,000 years ago and ranged seasonally across the plains of Eurasia following herds of big game. Expert hunters, they used spears to bear down on large animals such as mammoths and rhinos, which they butchered and cooked over hearths fired with pine wood and coal. Skilled workers in stone, bone and antler, they appear to have been highly socially cooperative and may have spoken a primitive language. The presence of pigments shows that they understood art, while their burials hint at religious beliefs. They wore animal skins to protect against the cold and were well adapted to cooler northern latitudes.[8]

The earliest evidence of Neanderthals or proto-Neanderthals in Britain – the partial skull of a woman dating back 400,000 years – was discovered in 1935 in a quarry in Swanscombe in Kent. Further clues to their presence across the grassy plains and river valleys of the south, including the Thames Valley, come from palaeoliths – knapped flint knives, choppers, scrapers and axes and the chippings arising from their manufacture – extracted from gravel around upriver areas such as Heathrow and Eton. Neanderthals – like their predecessor species – are likely to have camped in the vicinity of the Strand, hunting animals (including the prehistoric cattle called aurochs) and foraging autumn fruits. Perhaps the most famous palaeolith hand axe – and the first ever to be identified as such – was excavated a stone's throw from the Strand, in Farringdon, by the apothecary John Conyers, in 1679. Some 350,000 years old, it was found next to the remains of an elephant.[9]

There is no evidence of pre-human species at all in Britain for some 150,000 years and Trafalgar Square's hippopotami would have wallowed undisturbed in their tropical idyll. Then, around 40,000 years ago, modern humans, *Homo sapiens*, began to arrive in Britain, following their dispersal out of Africa. They replaced but also interbred with the Neanderthals (modern humans of European and Asian descent share their genes). But with the cold embrace of another Ice Age 30,000 years ago, these early humans disappeared from Britain: their presence in the Strand was erased by the fury of the ice, followed by the flooding of the river. We know very little about them and can only speculate that the area supported tiny and transient populations, although their sophisticated culture is likely to have been similar to that which produced, for example, the cave paintings in the Lascaux network in the Dordogne, which dates back 17,000 years. In the absence of caves, they made use of makeshift timber bivouacs. We can picture a simple twilight fire by the still water's edge of the Strand on the cusp of an endless winter, the only illumination for a hundred miles. Amid the implacable blackness of the landscape of London-to-be, the portents of shooting stars and the shouts of wild beasts in the shadows, the family hunkered together in fear and apprehension. Around the protection of the fire's meagre warmth and amid an awareness of their fragile mortality they dreamed and sang stories.

Human beings returned to Britain around 12,000 years ago, when the Ice Age ended and sea levels rose. Doggerland and the Channel Valley were inundated, exacerbated by monumental submarine landslides at Storrega off the coast of Norway around 6200 BCE, which resulted in a succession of mega-tsunamis that swept the east coast. Britain thus became an island once again and adopted its modern coastline. Evidence of these so-called Mesolithic inhabitants of Britain – a timber hut, tools and ornaments in amber and bone – have been found at Star Carr in the Pickering Valley in North Yorkshire. Its finds included nearly two dozen head dresses made from the antlers of red deer. These resemble the skull caps once worn by Siberian shamans and native Americans during religious ceremonies to summon animal spirits and commune with the dead, in which they are believed to have entered altered states of consciousness facilitated by sleep depri-vation or the ingestion of hallucinogenic compounds. Perhaps similar practices would have been familiar to the prehistoric in-habitants of the Strand: Mesolithic remains have been recovered from the river valleys on the Lea at Broxbourne and Waltham Abbey, in the gravel eyots at Eton and near the Thames at Windsor and Uxbridge. The tips of hunting spears have been found at Battersea and Wandsworth, flint fragments in Southwark, bone axes in Hammersmith and Chelsea, and scrapers and knives from the Temple, Maiden Lane and Leicester Square, immediately adjacent to the Strand.[10]

Evidence of hearths and the detritus of flint tool manufac-ture called debitage has been excavated on the site of an ancient island on the south bank of the river adjacent to Waterloo Station opposite the Strand. This is a reminder of the strategic importance throughout the Mesolithic, Bronze and Iron Ages of the many reedy islands of the south bank. Resembling parts of the Norfolk Broads, they were used as places of refuge and ritual over immense periods of time; these camps must have persisted in the cultural memory of countless generations and over thousands of years. As

temperatures steadily rose, a country of moorland and pine resembling the uplands of Scotland and the Pennines was gradually
replaced by a deciduous wildwood of birch, oak, elm and lime, the
realm of the bear, boar, lynx and wolf. The people near the Strand
thus scavenged the course of the river, hunted, fowled and fished
in the boggy wetland scrummage of alder carr below Trafalgar
Square and the Fleet estuary, collected hazelnuts below the canopy
of the temperate woodlands, and forded the river and camped on
its braided islands to the south. This natural landscape – woodland
and wetland – no doubt had a deep ritual significance for the
foragers and hunters who inhabited this place.[11]

The practice of farming and husbandry of animals came to
Britain around 4000 BCE with new immigrants and their technologies, supplementing a hunter-gatherer way of life. The Neolithic
brought huge changes as populations began to subdivide the land
and more settled communities thus arose. Tombs for the dead were
constructed on sacred ground and more significant monuments
like Stonehenge were set out that required the mobilisation of
resources and people across hundreds of miles. Communities
settled the Thames Valley and began to clear the wildwood, notably
upstream at Stanwell, Staines and Runnymede. They constructed
round houses and avenues or cursus monuments used for burial
and collective rituals, no doubt accompanied by music, dancing and
feasting. Evidence of the presence of these folk around the Strand is
fleeting but small communities of settlers would undoubtedly have
cleared areas of forest there, while the river retained its spiritual
significance with ritual waterborne burial of the dead and votive
offerings to the gods with the deposit into the water of high-value
items such as axes.[12]

Another wave of immigrants began to arrive around 2500 BCE,
who largely replaced the existing population. They brought new
languages, more sophisticated farming practices and the secrets
of the manufacture of jewellery, tools and weapons made from
copper and bronze, an alloy of copper and tin. A growing population and new agriculture led to large-scale clearances locally, and
subdivision into family smallholdings surrounded by wooden

stockades, fields and boundary hedgerows. The plough began to be used in the area – there is evidence of their furrows in Southwark on the south bank opposite the Strand from around 1500 BCE – while rising river levels forced locals to adapt with makeshift wooden platforms for pedestrians and jetties for small canoes and other water traffic. Burial barrows for cremations were built on higher ground overlooking the river, highlighting its spiritual significance. The Bronze Age – the era of Minoan Crete – was one characterised by extensive import and export and cultural connections across Europe, including the distribution of tin, gold and silver from across the British Isles as far as the Mediterranean; in this the Thames highway played an important part.[13]

Celtic peoples and their distinctive ways of thinking began to colonise Iron Age Britain from mainland Europe around 600 BCE, and they would quickly have begun to cultivate the Thames Valley, including the Strand. Disparate populations, they occupied a swathe of Europe from Portugal to Turkey, united by a common language family, cultural habits and beliefs. The Celts were warlike, but they were also enthusiastic traders in luxuries sourced from far and wide and they forged beautiful jewellery, such as the magnificent gold torcs worn around the necks of high-status individuals, for which they are justifiably famous. Metalworkers in iron, a much more readily available and cheaper metal than bronze, they facilitated the development of small-scale industry. Their mercantile tendencies led to the adoption of coinage in Britain around 100 BCE and of close diplomatic and trade links with neighbours, notably the Gauls and the Romans. Several chieftains became the clients of the Romans, but the supposed support they provided to the rebellion against the Roman campaign in Gaul gave Julius Caesar the *casus belli* for armed intervention during his campaigns in Britain in 55 and 54 BCE.

The Celts were fiercely tribal and protected their local authority through fortified hilltop encampments that were dotted throughout the chalk downs of southern Britain. During the later Iron Age, they also projected their power from walled and gated regional centres of administration that the Romans dubbed *oppida*. These included Camulodunum (now known as Colchester), one time capital of the Trinovantes in modern Essex and Suffolk, and the power centre and royal mint of King Cunobeline, immortalised by Shakespeare as Cymbeline. There was also Verlamion (now known as St Albans) in modern Hertfordshire, the late-stage capital of the Catuvellauni. Together, the Trinovantes and the Catuvellauni were among the most powerful tribes on the north bank of the Thames and their *oppida*, like other regional centres, were later adopted by the Romans. There are no substantial physical remains of a Celtic *oppidum* preceding the foundation of Roman London in 43 CE, nor of a settlement on the Strand. Tantalisingly, though, its very name, Londinium – derived from older Celtic or pre-Celtic precursors and perhaps meaning the 'stronghold by the stream' – hints at a pre-history. There is indeed fragmentary evidence of late Iron Age settlement at Southwark, near the Fleet and at St Martin in the Fields, but this likely was only in the form of farmsteads or other small communities close to sources of water no doubt connected by narrow trackways, then little more than rural footpaths crossing meadows.

The river served as a boundary or crossroads separating the tribes to the north from those to the south and west, the Cantii, the Atrebates and the Regni. The river's northern shore – including the Strand – thus became the convenient meeting place and field of exchange for warriors, diplomats and merchants otherwise separated by the physical barrier of the Thames. This notion of the Strand as a frontier zone re-emerged during the Anglo-Saxon period, when it served as the border of several kingdoms, notably Wessex, Mercia and Kent (occupied by the East Saxons). To all concerned, it was the proximity of the Thames that mattered. As well as the principal artery for inland communication and trade in the south of the country, it was, to pre-Christians such as the Celts and the early Anglo-Saxons, a sacred river for a people who typically worshipped natural features (groves, springs, bodies of water) alongside a panoply of deities that included the antler-headed god Cernunnos and the god of healing, Belenus. Little wonder, then, that the Thames became the resting place for

FIGURE 1. The Waterloo Helmet, an Iron Age helmet recovered from the Thames near the Strand, showing that it was then a place of warfare and ritual. (British Museum)

votive offerings of martial ware that include elaborate iron sword scabbards with dragon motifs from Hammersmith, the magnificent Battersea Shield dredged up in 1857 during the construction of a bridge at Chelsea, and the Waterloo Helmet, recovered from the river opposite the Strand in 1868 (Figure 1).

During either the Bronze Age or the Iron Age the river acquired its name in a Celtic tongue, or in a language now lost; alternative theories for its meaning include 'the river which floods' or 'the dark river', but either way this name was adopted by the Romans in the form *Tamesis*.[14] The Romans invaded Britain in 43 CE, the armies of Emperor Claudius led by his general Aulus Plautius. After landing four legions comprising approximately 40,000 men, probably in Kent, Plautius met with fierce resistance from the local population, which sought to delay the Roman advance on the regional capital, Camulodunum. Thwarted by the barrier of the Thames estuary and the absence of an upstream bridge, the expeditionary force had to negotiate a safe route from Kent through the marshes south of the Thames in search of a suitable crossing. Such fords were likely connected on either bank by trackways like Watling Street, used by Iron Age tribes. Southwark would have presented the shortest and most advantageous such crossing place, perhaps aided by pontoon bridges, but it is also possible that the crossing was opposite Thorney Island, on the site of the present St Thomas' Hospital in Westminster. Less likely are crossings at Putney, where a moat in the former Bishop of London's palace on the north bank is suggestive of an invasion-era Roman encampment, and upstream at 'Old London', between Brentford and Isleworth on the confluence of the Rivers Thames and Brent, a site that has yielded numerous Bronze Age and Roman artefacts.

Recovered at low tide at the latter during engineering works in the nineteenth century were the remains of defensive wooden stakes driven into the northern bank of the river, perhaps to deter an amphibious assault. This defensive tactic of placing sharpened staves beneath the waterline was described by contemporary writers, including Caesar and Cassius Dio, and similar stakes are likely to have been used on the foreshore of the Strand to forestall a crossing at this point. Such defences and their opponents' guerilla tactics were temporarily successful in hindering the Romans; consequently, Claudius attended in person to lead his armies to victory. Legend says that he processed in triumph through Colchester seated on the back of a war elephant, and so it is tempting to imagine the stammering Emperor aloft on an armoured pachyderm lumbering ashore in the vicinity of the Strand. Both the Greek writer Polyaenus, probably writing about Caesar's campaign, and Dio on the history of Claudius's expedition describe the Romans' use in Britain of 'an animal till then unknown to the Britons ... mailed in scales of iron, with a tower on its back, on which archers and slingers were stationed'. However, regrettably there is no hard evidence to support the story of their use in battle in Britain and the logistical challenge of transporting the animals for up to forty-eight hours on a treacherous sea crossing and feeding them adequately even for a relatively short campaign makes their use highly improbable. More likely, it has been suggested, the term 'elephant' refers to Roman siege apparatus, since the Romans commonly gave nicknames to military equipment that resembled animals, for instance the *musculus* (mouse) and the *aries* (battering ram).[15]

The Romans – merchants and soldiers – then began to build a new town, called Londinium, and selected the tidal head as the place to locate their riverine port, as it made seaborne navigation easier. This is the furthest point upstream reached by salty tidal water, one that progressively moved upriver to the vicinity of the Strand during the Anglo-Saxon era and is now situated at Teddington. The presence of the Walbrook stream between higher ground – Cornhill and Ludgate – and numerous springs also made this a strategically advantageous position. Significantly, the river narrows at this point, enabling a timber bridge – London Bridge – to be constructed from the north to a series of marshy islands that now comprise Southwark. Good communications were vital to facilitate the rapid movement of troops, enable the transport of freight and support a sophisticated postal system called the *cursus publicus*, which operated in the more advanced provinces. It is likely that new roads began to be constructed by the army immediately after the successful invasion, connecting Londinium with Colchester and other Iron Age-era tribal *oppida* that the Romans adopted. A network was systematically developed by a corps of skilled surveyors, which linked the ports and major towns, and following the campaigns of Agricola and his successors in the north, a constellation of strategic military camps that ultimately supported the far-flung Hadrian's Wall.

The roads were built to common standards along a raised platform of soil called an *agger*, upon which was layered stone, gravel and mortar. They utilised sophisticated rainwater drainage comprising a considerable raised central portion with a steep camber to ditches on either side. Roman roads were thus costly engineering accomplishments of great strategic and commercial significance and not embarked upon frivolously. This is probably when the road we call the Strand first appears in history, the lesser of two highways west of Londinium likely constructed after the revolt of Boudicca in 60–61 CE and during the Flavian dynasty of the ambitious Emperor Vespasian and his sons. Although the Romans left a series of itineraries to calculate distances between their towns, notably the *Antonine Itinerary*, and a road map called the *Tabula Peutingeriana*, what is now the Strand, being of secondary importance, is omitted, and its Roman name, along with the names of other roads in the province, remains unknown. Writing in the 1950s, the preeminent scholar of Roman roads Ivan Margary argued persuasively that the Strand and Fleet Street complex comprised a single Roman highway, possibly built along a prehistoric path. Tantalisingly, the Tudor historian John Stow describes the excavation in the 1590s of stone and timber foundations around the church of St Dunstan in the West that potentially were the remains of this road, but confirmation of Margary's theory came only in 1988, during archaeological excavations near Ludgate Circus.[16]

Following the construction of London's defensive walls between 200 and 220 CE and the building of city gates, the more prominent of these two roads, designed for the movement of the legions, exited the city through Newgate. This followed the route now taken by High Holborn and Oxford Street to Pontes (Staines) and Calleva Atrebatum, one of most important strategic forts in the province, near Silchester in Hampshire. From there, the road then connected with Aquae Sulis (Bath). Part of this route is followed by the modern A40 road in London and north along Western Avenue, constructed in the 1930s. The original road ran further south, to connect with the ford at Old England (Brentford). Roman roads often followed the paths of ancient trackways, such as Watling Street from Kent to the north-west of Britain, via the Old Kent Road, Edgeware Road and the capital of the Iron Age, Catuvellauni, close to St Albans. It has been suggested, though with scant evidence, that before it was re-routed across the new London Bridge, Watling Street crossed the river at a ford likely at Thorney Island, on which Westminster Abbey and a royal palace would later be built. Evidence of Roman occupation – possibly a high-status villa – has been discovered there, including a boat and a rubbish pit beneath Downing Street, although the suggestion that it hosted a pagan temple dedicated to Apollo is probably apocryphal.

The second of the major routes west out of London was the Fleet Street–Strand highway, a straight road that exited the city at Ludgate Hill near the site of the present St Paul's Cathedral and crossed the Fleet to an unknown destination. Clearly, though, the road must have connected with *somewhere* or *something*. It is possible that this was Watling Street and its ford at Westminster and that the remains of a crossroads slumber beneath Buckingham Palace Gardens. The highway is likely to have continued westwards through Kensington, the King's Road in Chelsea, and Hammersmith, perhaps connecting yet undiscovered Roman riverside villas, and merged with the military road at the junction of Goldhawk Road and Chiswick High Road. This is the route later designated the A4, otherwise the Bath Road, from London to Staines.[17]

This combination of Fleet Street and the Strand, a trunk road, was probably around thirty feet wide, flanked by drainage channels and pedestrian walkways, with regular milestones, each one representing 1,000 paces of a soldier. Roman roads incorporated a variety of rest areas at intervals for refreshment, grazing for horses and board and lodging, called *mutations* and *mansions*. The first of these 'motorway service stations' was located a day's ride from London, although it is possible one or two smaller refreshment stops at short intervals were situated on the Strand. The new road would have stood out as an impressive engineering feat to the local British tribes and retired soldiers who lived in a countryside of smallholdings outside the city: it was probably elevated on a soil embankment, while its white cobbles and gravel metalling would have gleamed in the summer sun and blushed rose at dusk. Along its length moved livestock driven to slaughter in the city, cart loads of timber from the region's great stands of woodland, and couriers and tax collectors hurrying on foot or horseback to conduct official business. Merchants and businesspeople from the city's hinterland and travellers from the south-west could have used it as a shortcut to the great port of London, to its forum and numerous shops, or its many attractive entertainments, including baths and temples. Along its neighbouring river, visible from the road, were enslaved people who had been transported, perishable commodities and raw materials such as iron ore, while imports of Samian pottery, glass, silk and amphorae of wine flowed the other way. To the south of the road was London Fen, the area of marsh and bog west of the wide outlet of the Fleet. To its north, the highway was surrounded by market gardens that supplied the city with fresh produce, evidence of which has been uncovered in Drury Lane. The archaeological remains of more substantial structures, though, are absent, except half a mile to the north, in Holborn, on the military road. Instead, the length of the Strand is littered with fragments of discarded rubbish, pottery and coins rather than evidence of systematic urbanisation.[18]

The Strand district lay outside the boundaries of the city, to the west of Ludgate. Great change was no doubt visible to travellers approaching the city from this direction across more than 300 years of Roman occupation. The city's fortunes waxed and waned according to local exigencies and broader imperial history. Notably, it was rebranded Augusta in the fourth century before reverting to its old name. The city reached a peak in the mid-second century after it had superseded Colchester as the principal provincial city, before it entered a period of political turbulence and civil war which later saw the administration of the province subdivided.

While renewal preceded ultimate decline, its population peaking at around 60,000, throughout this time the city remained a cosmopolitan place, with migrants drawn from across the empire and a sizeable indigenous population of enslaved people or workers on the land, who retained their Welsh-like Brittonic language. Exciting, though small-scale, analysis of some burials has shown that between one-fifth and two-fifths were migrants from the Mediterranean and Africa. The presence of a large garrison of soldiers after the completion of the fort at Cripplegate c. 120 only added to this ethnic mix. Many different tongues would have been heard on the highways and in the public places and private homes of the city. The devastation wrought by the fires of the bloody Boudiccan revolt in 60–61

FIGURE 2. Bronze head of the Emperor Hadrian from London Bridge, c. 117–38 CE. Hadrian visited Londinium in 122. The statue from which the head came was probably cast to commemorate his visit and was one of many grand public monuments erected at this time. (British Museum)

that destroyed Londinium, and that which followed the visit of Emperor Hadrian in 122 (Figure 2) – must have been visible from the Strand, then probably packed with refugees and their moveable belongings, citizens, enslaved and formerly enslaved people, fleeing the disasters. In the words of the historian Tacitus, Boudica's rebels 'massacred, hanged, burned and crucified with headlong fury'. He estimated that 70,000 perished in Colchester, London and the other towns, but this is probably an exaggeration – the population of London was then only around 10,000 and many inhabitants are likely to have abandoned the town in advance.

Peace brought a major rebuilding programme of ramparts and a new port and bridge, warehouses, watermills and grain stores, alongside public buildings, including the forum (which housed civic administration), temples and baths. During this time, visitors to the market probably used the Strand to convey merchandise or foodstuffs. Tacitus attested to the city's importance as a trading centre, one that attracted merchants such as Metellus and Gratus, two names identified from among 92 on the 400 waterlogged wooden tablets recently recovered from the site of the Bloomberg building site along the Walbrook valley. The amphitheatre, too, would have drawn attendance from the wider London area, including the Strand. The latter was built as an earth-and-timber bank around 72 CE and rebuilt in stone in 120–22 to mark the visit of Hadrian. Accommodating around 7,000 spectators, it was probably mainly used for theatrical, ceremonial or civic purposes and, grimly, to stage the execution of prisoners.[19]

The Romans customarily buried their dead in oak coffins or interred their cremated remains in vessels in extramural cemeteries alongside roadways, and at a safe distance from the towns. The most famous, if monumental, example of this practice is the Appian Way, in Italy. Extensive evidence of Roman funeral urns and grave goods has for centuries been recovered below the suburbs surrounding the City of London. Spitalfields has yielded numerous Roman burials, and most recently a complete Roman funerary bed was discovered at Holborn Viaduct, preserved in the banks of the Fleet, at Aldgate along Ermine Street and in the west at Ludgate. Cemeteries sprang up along the Strand at the Savoy and Tavistock Place and along the Fleet, notably at Ship Lane. A Roman pavement and tiles and a defensive ditch were discovered during renovations to the crypt of St Bride's. The church, opposite Ship Lane, was dedicated to the Irish patron saint Bridget, a contemporary of St Patrick, who may have established a colony there in the sixth century. This was built atop an older building probably dating to the second century.

At the western end of the present Fleet Street–Strand, a sarcophagus and two other graves dating from the end of Roman rule, along with a large pottery kiln, were discovered in 2006–7 during the redevelopment of St Martin in the Fields. This cemetery was located on the edge of a complex of gravel quarries below Trafalgar Square, on the site of the prehistoric hippopotamus lagoons. The presence of this more substantial archaeology thus points to a more significant late-Roman presence in the Strand area that prefigures the development of the Saxon trading settlement of Lundenwic in the early seventh century, and to the ancient origins of both St Bride's and St Martin in the Fields. Roman burials and inhumations were common along the Strand and were often elaborate affairs accommodating funeral pyres or graves, offerings to the dead, feasting, processions and music. Grave sites along the Strand would have been melancholy places, potentially the haunts of ghostly revenants, and one can imagine the sense of relief felt by a lonesome traveller hurrying down this dusky avenue of the departed when at last the welcome lights of London were glimpsed.[20]

At the end of Roman rule in Britain, memory meets myth. Pressure on the province grew in the late fourth century from warlike tribes to the north, the Picts and Scots, and Saxons on its eastern flank, who, aided by the rebellion of the garrison on Hadrian's Wall, briefly invaded the province in 367–68. Ritualistic deposits of hordes of treasure and votive offerings became more common, suggesting that wealthy individuals were fleeing their homes in anticipation of returning at a later date. Beyond this, few facts are known. Rome, laid low by internecine warfare and with barbarians at its gates, its authority over far-flung provinces waning, recalled the tattered provincial legions. In 410, the youthful Emperor Honorius wrote 'letters to the cities in Britain urging them to take precautions on their own behalf'. The Romano-British people, singularly now, confronted the opportunistic reappearance of the border tribes, in the lamentable words of the monk Gildas, writing a century later, 'like worms which in the heat of the mid-day come forth from their holes'. A heartfelt appeal for renewed Roman military assistance (the 'Groans of the Britons'), probably addressed to Consul Aetius around 446, fell on deaf ears and shortly after the British King Vortigern, a 'proud tyrant', fatefully extended an invitation to the 'fierce and impious Saxons, a race hateful both to God and men, to repel the invasions of the northern nations'. These pioneer mercenaries settled at first in Thanet in Kent. Declared Gildas, 'nothing was ever so pernicious to our country, nothing was ever so unlucky'. So it was, according to the contemporary *Gallic Chronicle*, 'the British provinces ... are reduced to the power of the Saxons'.[21]

Gildas's account cannot be authenticated – his main purpose was to attribute the Anglo-Saxon invasion to divine punishment of the sins of the British, while the existence of Vortigern as a historical figure has been questioned. The speed and spread of the new arrivals also remain unclear, although the east–west distribution of Anglo-Saxon placenames can perhaps provide clues. It is likely that communities of mercenaries were already present in the province in small numbers during its maturity, to judge from the establishment from the third century of the so-called Saxon Shore, a line of coastal fortifications along the east and south coast, and lending weight to the argument that the invasions sprang from an earlier process of occasional settlement. According to the *Anglo-Saxon Chronicle*, the Britons were defeated in battle by the Saxons at Aylesford in 455 and Crayford in 457, in which no fewer than 4,000 were slain, causing the people of Kent to flee to the comparative protection of London. This is a tantalising clue to the continuation of Romano-British urban life in the capital, and the necessary population, economy, authority and taxation to maintain the Roman defensive bastions and walls. One can picture lines of refugees from Kent, warriors and civilians clutching meagre belongings, stumbling past St Martin's cemetery and trudging wearily down the Strand before taking the bridge across the Fleet. The abandonment of London, though, must have followed soon afterwards. The Strand fell silent, and then a darkness descended.[22]

CHAPTER 2

MEDIEVAL STRAND

An emporium for many nations who come to it by land and sea.

Venerable Bede, *The Ecclesiastical History of the English People* [1]

When Martin Biddle jumped aboard a bus from the Strand to St Pancras Station one autumn day in 1983, a flash of inspiration came upon him. The archaeologist's insight would solve a mystery that had puzzled experts for generations. Why had no meaningful evidence of human occupation postdating the withdrawal of the Roman legions in 410 CE ever been discovered below the streets of the City of London?

It had long been assumed from this absence of artefacts that Londinium had been abandoned when the country descended into an Arthurian Dark Age. Perhaps, it was argued, the population had fled to the comparative safety of the countryside, where they would be protected from the worst depredations of the Saxons. In any event, the city's grand public buildings – forum, baths, temples, amphitheatre, waterfront wharves and warehouses, bridge, triumphal arches, townhouses, shops and roads – were gradually reduced to a ghost town of rubble and decaying timber. London disappeared, swallowed by its own earth. Yet, some historical sources point to a contrasting story of urban continuity. The city is mentioned in contemporary land charters, and appears on coinage and notably in the pages of *The Ecclesiastical History of the English People*, whose author, Bede, describes London in 731 as 'an emporium for many nations who come to it by land and sea'. Nevertheless, there seemed to be no physical evidence of this tumbleweed town, Bede's Lundenwic. Where had it gone?

Biddle and colleagues (including Alan Vince) solved this riddle. One clue came from etymology. The name Aldwych was coined by the folklorist and founder of the Blue Plaque movement, Sir Laurence Gomme, when the district was laid out (at the east end of the Strand) by the London County Council in the early twentieth century. Its derivation was 'Old Wic', meaning market, and is mentioned as early as the thirteenth century; Wych Street was one of the historic roads demolished during redevelopment. Another clue came from the elevated aspect that Biddle noticed on his bus ride. The Strand comprised higher ground above a lengthy shoreline ideal for landing small boats. Thirdly, and definitively, came a wealth of archaeology from more than seventy sites excavated from the 1980s around Covent Garden, including Jubilee Hall, the London Transport Museum, the Royal Opera House and the National Gallery. These studies unearthed abundant evidence that early Anglo-Saxon London once lay beneath the Strand.[2]

Lundenwic was part of a network of emporia or trading towns that stretched across northern Europe. That network included Ipswich and Southampton, the Frankish Dorestad, located near modern Utrecht in the Netherlands, and Quentovic, on the northern coast of France. Focusing on commerce, and home to farmers and artisans, these towns were commonly situated along coastal trade routes, on greenfield sites under aristocratic or royal patronage, and often in the shadow of old Roman towns. Their infrastructure was resolutely commercial, comprising quays, warehouses and market halls. They flourished between the seventh and the ninth centuries, until the piratical Vikings interrupted their lucrative trade.

Lundenwic was situated at the contested frontier of four of the seven competing territories into which mid-Anglo-Saxon England was divided, the Heptarchy. It enjoyed excellent transport connections via the Thames, Strand and the *mickle herepath* or large army street to the north, latterly Oxford Street. It was a town where representatives of the neighbouring kingdoms of the East Saxons (in Kent) and West Saxons (in Mercia) could conduct commerce in relative amity. In practice, however, it is likely that Mercia, which

emerged during the seventh and eighth centuries as the most
powerful kingdom in the island, sought to harness the potential
of a new town. It is thought that Lundenwic was founded by the
ambitious Christian King Wulfhere, who reigned between 658
and 675: timber from riverside revetments from Buckingham
Street at Charing Cross has been dated to 672 and the settlement
is mentioned in Kentish laws from around 680. Wulfhere's successors, Aethelbald (716–57), Offa (757–96) and Coenwulf (796–821),
were also notable patrons, and it is feasible that the entire town
comprised a single royal estate, as it is described on local coins
as 'vicus regis' or the 'King's village'. It is probable, in any event,
that Coenwulf maintained a royal palace, possibly on the Strand.
The extensive distribution of coinage, likely minted near St Paul's
and modelled on that of the powerful Merovingian dynasty on the
continent, additionally points to the comparatively high status
accorded to this community. The Church also took a close interest
in its success, acquiring plots of land and negotiating lucrative
exemptions from tolls on shipping; beneficiaries included the
Bishops of Hereford and Worcester and even the Abbey of St Denis
in Paris.[3]

The new town was built outside the protection of the Roman
walls, a pattern not uncommon in the Anglo-Saxon world.
Superstition likely played a part in this decision, a fear perhaps
that the haunted and abandoned city was cursed by the ghosts
of the past and was best left undisturbed. After all, mysterious
and tangible material evidence of Roman Britain still littered
the British landscape (its marble and limestone were routinely
scavenged as building materials). London was no exception,
becoming a quarry of memories and myths. The special spiritual
significance accorded to the faded glory of Roman monuments
is the subject of the surviving fragments of a melancholy eighth-
century elegy, *The Ruin*. Like the traveller in Shelley's 'Ozymandias',
the poem surveys the decaying wreckage of a once-great city, the
magnificent hot springs in Bath, where 'the city buildings fell
apart, the works of giants crumble'. Towers tumbled, roofs ruined,
ceilings agape, its buildings were 'torn and collapsed and eaten up

by age' – a metaphor for the futility of earthly ambition of its 'dead departed master-builders'. In the shadow of London's two highest points, Ludgate and Cornhill, and below a daunting circuit of walls and defensive towers already 400 years old, the inhabitants of Lundenwic would perhaps in this spirit have surveyed from afar the colossal wreck, boundless and bare, of the Roman amphitheatre, and of the collapsed basilica and forum, once the largest north of the Alps. At dusk and silhouetted against a darkling sky, these ruins would undoubtedly have exerted a powerful hold over the imaginations of the new settlers.[4]

Lundenwic inherited an overgrown but still impressive Fleet Street–Strand thoroughfare. The waterfront hosted an open-air market called the port of London, 'where ships come to land ... on the southern side of the public way'.[5] To its east, the missionary Bishop Mellitus, under the protection of the Kentish King Aethelbald, had erected the first St Paul's Cathedral – then a modest timber building – on Ludgate Hill in 604. Mellitus was a follower of Augustine, whose mission from Pope Gregory the Great in 597 sought to convert the pagan Anglo-Saxons to Roman Christianity. He built his St Paul's perhaps on ancient foundations of faith – a possible fourth-century basilica close to the latter-day Tower of London. The succession of Bishops of London stretches back at least to Restitutus, who attended the Church's Council of Arles in 314. St Paul's remained the devotional heart of London until the tenth century, when the Benedictine abbey at Westminster was dedicated to St Peter. A short distance from St Paul's, across the Fleet, lay the church of St Bride's, built in the sixth century on Roman foundations. At Lundenwic's western limit, another imperial structure would become the church of St Martin in the Fields, surrounded by burial grounds from the fifth century, from which have been recovered grave goods, including an early seventh-century gold disc brooch.

Lundenwic sat on the western end of the axis of these familiar landmarks. Geography, too, played an important part in its situation – the Strand was the first dry and elevated land west of the London Fen, and it was close to the ford at Westminster, a necessary crossing point when a decaying London Bridge became impassable. Significantly, too, this was now the furthest point upstream reached by tidal waters and thus navigable by seagoing vessels. Given that the ruined riverside Roman docks were unusable, Saxon boats (dug-outs for short journeys and shallow-draught or flat-keeled plank vessels) were able to load and unload their cargo on the beach or transfer it to smaller boats to be transported upstream into the heart of England. The road above would have been crowded with timber warehouses from which a swarm of ginnels, resembling the narrow passages called 'scores' and 'rows' that survive in coastal towns such as Lowestoft and Great Yarmouth, descended steeply to the shoreline market.[6]

Lundenwic was relatively small, with a population of perhaps 9,000 in the mid-eighth century, in an area approximately half that of the old Roman city, a space that now encompasses the National Gallery, Leicester Square and Covent Garden. Its boundaries were delineated by the Strand in the south, Trafalgar Square in the west, Long Acre in the north and Kingsway and Arundel Street in the east. There is fragmentary evidence from deposited glassware and a grant of a property called Ceolmuningchaga to the Bishop of Worcester that the settlement extended to Hare Court in Fleet Street, but it is probable that the eastern limit was a stream below Milford Lane. The new town was built on fallow grassland and marshy sedge on the river's edge between two cemeteries near Long Acre and St Martin's. It is likely that new roads were laid perpendicular to the Strand, including the precursor to Drury Lane. Around 100 properties along them have been excavated. These small rectangular houses were made from wattle and daub, with earthen floors and oak shingle roofs and rear yards for the keeping of poultry, cattle and sheep. There is evidence of a piggery and butchery near the Opera House, and it is likely horse breeding and falconry were practised.

Londoners subsisted on a diet of meat, peas and beans supplemented by the seasonal bounty of crab apples, strawberries, blackberries and elderberries. Both ocean fish (cod, herring, haddock) and freshwater fish (eel and pike) were also a staple. Locals also foraged botanicals such as horehound, nettle and dandelion, kale, beet and mallow. Bread was ubiquitous, its flour milled from wheat, barley, rye, acorns and hazelnuts using German quern stones, and cakes were baked from poppy and fennel seeds. The preferred cooking method was stewing, likely in communal cauldrons, with food served up in pottery vessels sourced from Suffolk, alongside wine and ale in pitchers imported from France and Belgium. The settlement was alive with busy craft industries, including carpentry and the carving of bone and antler, and, to judge from the widespread distribution of loom weights first recovered from below the Savoy by the archaeologist Sir Mortimer Wheeler, textile manufacture using wool or flax was ubiquitous. These items of clothing were dyed with red madder and worn alongside leather and hides prepared locally.[7]

Lundenwic was busy and cosmopolitan. A babble of languages would have been heard as Frisian and Frankish traders and sailors haggled with local Anglo-Saxons surrounded by numerous itinerants and enslaved people. The town also attracted the wealthy and powerful, who established a church called the West Minster nearby on Thorney Island, which began to rival St Paul's. A densely populated urban community, its poor sanitation led to outbreaks of infectious disease, notably a devastating bubonic plague that spread from the continent in 664. Ominously dubbed 'the great mortality', it coincided with the establishment of the new town. Heralded by the ill omens of a spring solar eclipse and summer storms, the disease, we are told by the Venerable Bede, depopulated the British Isles, 'a sudden pestilence raging far and wide with fierce destruction'. Adding to this apocalyptic backdrop, and in a town with scattered smithies, ovens and open hearths, serious fires were common, with no fewer than three between 764 and 802.[8]

Lundenwic, along with other emporia across the Baltic and North Seas, entered a period of economic decline from the late eighth century, coinciding with the emergence of the Vikings. They were peerless enslavers, traders, explorers, merchants and marauders from Scandinavia, and their influence extended across northern Europe and North America. In 789, seeking plunder, the first of their ships, according to the Anglo-Saxon Chronicle, 'came to the land of the English'. Then, in 793, a year accompanied by a great famine and 'dire portents ... immense whirlwinds and flashes of lightning', the raiders destroyed the famous monastery of Lindisfarne in Northumbria. The event – interpreted as a terrible signal of God's punishment of the collective sins of the people – sent shockwaves throughout Christian Europe. The scholar monk Alcuin, resident at the Frankish court of Charlemagne, called for repentance for the numerous 'fornications, adulteries and incest [that] have poured over the land'. What should be expected for other places, he warned, when the divine judgement had not spared this holy place?[9]

Alcuin's words proved prophetical, as eventually the Vikings turned their attention to targets further south, striking Wessex some fifteen times between 840 and 853, while Lundenwic experienced a terrible slaughter in 842 and another brazen attack in 851. The arrival of the Vikings, splashing ashore on Strand beach, must have left an indelible impression among the town's already dwindling population. Likely warned of the approach of their boats, locals may have fled inland; alternatively, if the enemy landed in the dead of night, families may have been wakened by the cries of the watch and the screams of their neighbours. Thus, with fire and fear, the Vikings pillaged the Strand. Worse still was to come. In 865, Danish forces, reconstituted as an army of conquest, the Great Heathen Army, spread out from the east coast in search of loot and land. The next year, this formidable horde of warriors and settlers captured York; in 870 they martyred the East Anglian King, Edmund, and conquered his kingdom. That army overwintered in London in 871–72. The whereabouts of its camp is unknown, although it is probable that it lay between Lundenwic and the old city, and that St Clement 'Danes' church is a distant echo of this ancient association. The camp was relatively short-lived – the Viking presence persisting for perhaps fifteen years – but we know from descriptions of similar sites in northern Europe that these makeshift towns supported flourishing local industries, including smelting, woodcraft and boat repair, alongside leisure activities such as drinking and gaming. The London camp must have cast a long shadow over its hinterland, with raiding parties sent out to provision the army and to capture people to enslave.[10]

The Scandinavians fell upon the great kingdoms in Northumbria, Mercia and East Anglia and then turned their fury on Wessex. Alfred, King of the West Saxons, rallied their defence, beginning with the fortification of dozens of towns throughout their heartlands. These *burhs*, or boroughs, were no more than a day's ride from each other, allowing for swift reinforcement, and included Alfred's capital, Winchester, as well as Oxford, Chichester and Exeter. The ancient walls of old London, too, began to be refortified as the population sought protection against the river-borne invaders. Alfred achieved a famous victory over the Danes at Edington in 878, and concluded a treaty with their leader, Guthrum, but this peace was uneasy, as the 'green line' between Danelaw and English territory lay only a few miles east of the Strand, on the Lea. London thus remained a contested space and it was perhaps inevitable that a serious clash should ensue, and it did so in 883. In 886, the *Anglo-Saxon Chronicle* records, Alfred reoccupied the ancient city, when he rechristened it Lundenburh. He instituted the repair of its walls, as well the building of new roads and wharves at Queenhithe, near St Paul's, thus ending the Strand's recent monopoly on handling river traffic; haltingly, the local economy began to revive.[11]

Alfred the Great died in 899. Between 959 and 975, the youthful and energetic English King Edgar sought to re-establish the power and prestige of the Church, emulating Alfred's devotion to a scholarly and religious renaissance that might serve as both a unifying cultural project and a bulwark to heathenism. In 959, he founded Westminster Abbey, and endowed it with a huge local estate comprising most of the area now occupied by the City of Westminster, including the Strand. This territory encompassed Bulunga Fen, where the Tyburn flowed into the Thames (Millbank), the fields of Cowfold (Green Park and Half Moon Lane), the military road, the old timber church of St Andrew in Holborn and the Fleet. Its southern boundary comprised the Strand and

Thames, whence it returned to its starting point. The Strand is described in contemporary charters as Akemannestraete, the road to Acemannesceaster, an Old English name for Bath, the town where Edgar was consecrated in 973. It followed its current course, then took a sharp right angle north at a hamlet on the bend in the river called *cierring*, or 'charing' – the Anglo-Saxon word for 'turn', along Haymarket, west along Piccadilly and crossing the Westbourne stream at the 'knight's bridge'. Fortnum & Mason, the Ritz and even Harrods, had they been transported back to this time, would thus have been proud Strand businesses.[12]

The Strand was categorised in a mid-tenth-century charter as a 'waste place', and even at the time of the compilation in 1086 of the Norman inventories of landholdings called the Domesday Book it remained comparatively rural and undeveloped: the manor of Westminster lists nineteen villeins and forty-two cottars (both classes of serf), and twenty-five houses belonging to knights or Abbey staff. The Conquest in 1066 changed the course of history, for instance introducing Norman French as the language of law and government and instigating wholesale transfers in the ownership of land. England became part of a wider continental empire centred on France, which expanded dramatically after the accession in 1154 of Henry II, the first Plantagenet King of England. Continental wars – and campaigns in Ireland and Scotland – were expensive and this drove the rapid development of Westminster as a financial and legal centre. Thomas Becket's biographer William Fitzstephen, writing a century after Domesday, described the Strand as a 'populous suburb' connecting a prosperous Westminster with the City. The first historical mention of the 'Stronde' as a road is recorded from this period – 1185 – but its status as a suburb proved enduringly ambiguous and tensioned. The Strand fell between competing jurisdictions: Middlesex, the priory of Westminster, the diocese of London and a City increasingly jealous and protective of its urban privileges, reluctant to become directly responsible for suburban government, laws and trade, but periodically countenancing intervention and interference borne out of fear and envy, a pattern repeated until the twentieth century.[13]

Westminster and the Strand began to grow in tandem after Edward the Confessor, who reigned from 1042 until 1066, replaced the Saxon church with a stone-built abbey in the Romanesque style and started work on a new royal palace; its centrepiece would be Westminster Hall, erected by William Rufus (William II, who reigned 1087–1100). Edward was canonised in 1161 and his cult became popular during the long reign of Henry III (1216–72), who translated his mortal remains to a new shrine in 1269. This served as a devotional focus for growing numbers of Westminster pilgrims. A fair – which attracted the crowds – was held every October in the shadow of the Abbey, on the anniversary of his translation; it expanded to a two-week affair, when all other shops in the city were closed by royal command. Royal justice and administration had begun to be centralised in this Westminster complex under Henry II in the twelfth century and Henry III continued this in the thirteenth; notably, Westminster hosted the Courts of Exchequer, Common Pleas and King's Bench, as it proved infeasible for the growing body of government archives to continue to move around with the king on his travels. This concentration of administration brought with it an influx of office holders and clerks attached to the royal household. The growth of Parliament, which began to meet almost annually during the thirteenth century to raise taxes for Henry III's wars, and a comprehensive rebuilding of the Abbey that attracted craft workers and traders, similarly greatly increased the local population.[14]

The Abbey, the principal landowner, benefited from speculative property ventures catering for these new residents – by 1407 its rentals totalled 188 inns, tenements and shops. Earlier, in 1385, it had expanded its portfolio of shops along a 200-foot frontage at Charing Cross, including twelve let out for between 5 shillings and 9 shillings per annum. One of these shops was later leased to the bakers Thomas and Alice Haket, typical of local tenants, and the area attracted diverse trades, including builders, tailors, cordwainers, brewers and cutlers, as well as numerous brothels, for which the area was notorious. Westminster and the Strand also became home to dozens of alehouses, taverns and inns, selling wine, ale and

food sourced from local allotments, notably the fertile gardens of
the Pied Friars between the Strand and the Westminster convent's
garden. The poet Thomas Hoccleve, who lodged in Chester's Inn in
east Strand and walked to work in Westminster, complained of the
daily temptation presented to him by 'the outward signe of Bachus
and his lure'. The short stretch of the neighbouring King's Road
(Whitehall) between Tothill Street and Charing Cross illustrates
his point, as it was home to no fewer than fifty-eight pubs in the
mid-fifteenth century. The authorities complained that unauthor-
ised dining tables and chairs from cookhouses were blocking the
highways and in 1585 sought to limit the number of taverns in the
parish of St Margaret's to a maximum of sixty.[15]

Alongside the development of Westminster as a political and
religious centre, the tenth to the twelfth centuries also marked
the establishment of the parochial system of Church government,
one that for a thousand years would provide for the cure of parish-
ioners' souls. Parishes accounted for the rhythm of everyday life,
from birth to marriage and death, and oversaw the observance
of a packed calendar of spiritual observance of holy days, Church
festivals and days of fasting and thanksgiving. The Strand's
parishes reflected the intense religiosity of medieval society, and
they profoundly shaped life in the Strand. To the west was the huge
parish of St Margaret's, covering Westminster and St James; to the
north, across intervening fields, lay the parishes of St Giles and
St Andrew's. Several new churches had been consecrated at the east
end of the Strand before the Norman Conquest, which suggests
the population had grown following Edgar's reformation. The
presence of St Clement's, dedicated to the patron saint of mariners,
hints at some seafaring association in that church's early history;
a Viking Danish cemetery is believed to have existed during the
reign of King Cnut, where the body of his son and claimant to
the throne, Harold Harefoot, was possibly interred in 1040. Its
neighbour was St Mary's, erected on land granted to the Bishop of
Worcester by the King of Mercia in 857 on the western approach to
Strand Bridge. This carried the road over a small stream associated
with Cock and Pye ditch, a watercourse that rose in St Giles, which

still bubbles beneath the basement of King's College London. An ancient stone cross also sat in this spot from the thirteenth century, beneath which Middlesex legal assizes were held. St Giles's most famous incumbent was Thomas Becket, martyred under the orders of Henry II in 1170. St Dunstan in the West, situated just east of the Strand, was dedicated to the Archbishop of Canterbury and co-architect of Edgar's reforms, who was canonised in 1029. The Church of the Holy Innocents, meanwhile, is believed to have existed for two centuries west of St Mary's, until it fell into dereliction. St Martin in the Fields in west Strand is first mentioned in records around 1180; its parish was in existence from at least 1200. Its eastern boundary was Ivy Lane, halfway down the Strand. These medieval parishes were joined by the Chapel of the Savoy Hospital, dedicated in the reign of Henry VII, and St Paul's Covent Garden, consecrated in the seventeenth century.[16]

The late medieval period shaped the fundamental character of the Strand. A bustling thoroughfare now connected the commercial centre of the City with courtly and religious life in Westminster. Its buildings took on a grander quality, not least in the aftermath of the devastating City fires of 1135 and 1212, the former extending as far as St Clement Danes. A series of building codes were introduced to improve safety, including the removal of thatched roofs, stone-built construction and a raising of the height of pentices, the overhanging first storeys of buildings, which were a fire hazard. It is unclear how far these measures were successful or how far they were enforceable in the suburbs: most of the Strand's tenements remained timber-built throughout the seventeenth century.[17]

The Strand became a place of civic pride and pageantry, one of London's chief processional routes; it accommodated royal rites of passage, peace treaties, the annual perambulation of the Lord Mayor swearing allegiance to the crown and even the promenading of condemned traitors, including William 'Braveheart' Wallace in 1305. The events of 13 October 1247, the feast of Edward the Confessor, were not untypical: the procession of Henry III from St Paul's to the Abbey bedecked 'with symbols, crosses and lighted candles' and in the presence of the nation's principal magnates and

prelates. Clad in sackcloth, and beneath his four-cornered coronation canopy, he carried aloft a crystal goblet containing perhaps the
ultimate holy relic, drops of the blood of Christ preserved from His
crucifixion, the recent gift of the Patriarch of Jerusalem. The King
was greeted by the extraordinary sight of the Abbey's more than
100 monks lined up outside Durham House, 'tearfully singing and
exulting'. This was a remarkable *coup de théâtre*, an expression of
personal and public piety that cemented the King's authority and
enhanced national pride.[18]

During the thirteenth century, the population of the Strand
boomed, and new housing burgeoned. The fourteenth century,
however, saw the appearance of three of the four horsemen of the
apocalypse: famine, war and pestilence. The Great Famine (1315–17)
afflicted large swathes of Europe, caused by cold winters and wet
summers that heralded the start of the so-called Little Ice Age, a
period that persisted until the seventeenth century. Widespread
crop failure led to a trebling of the price of wheat and other commodities and the spectre of mass starvation: up to 10 per cent of
some local populations died, and the bodies of the dead littered the
streets.

The Black Death, probably bubonic plague, reached London late
in 1348. It claimed the lives of as many as 60 per cent of Londoners,
which profoundly transformed the city and its suburbs. Emergency
cemeteries quickly filled up with victims, and the work of the
courts, local government and Church ground to a halt as officials
and clergy succumbed to the disease. Hospitals struggled to cope,
and the activities of the City's many trades were interrupted by
a large drop in the number of apprentices. Galloping inflation
followed a surge in wages as the labour market contracted, leading
to ill-starred government price controls called the Ordinance of
Labourers. The psychological impact was profound – the numbers
of orphans and widows surged, as the pestilence disproportion-
ally affected younger men. A second outbreak in 1361 is believed to
have killed some 34 per cent of the population of London, many
of them children, and it was followed by further outbreaks in 1368
and 1375. Shorn of businesses and residents, one-third of the City's

buildings remained empty, and this no doubt extended to parts
of the Strand, lending it an air of desertion. New sumptuary laws
were also enacted for fear that extravagant fashions had attracted
God's wrath; and the surviving inhabitants of the Strand were thus
more sombrely attired.[19]

The Strand was often dirty, noisy and foul: open sewers ran
along St Martin's Lane and garderobes discharged directly into
the river, prompting a proclamation against the 'throwing of
rushes, dung, refuse, and other filth and harmful things into the
bed [of the river]'. The Great Conduit lay along the length of the
Strand and Fleet Street. Built in 1245 to deliver fresh water from
Marylebone to London, it was also connected to individual homes
in the Strand. According to John Stow, this was 'the first sweet
water that was conveyed by pipes of lead underground to ... the
citie from Padington. It was castellated with stone and cesterned in
lead.' Public health took on a new importance after the Black Death:
Edward III and Richard II sought to suppress abattoirs on the Fleet
whose effluent occasioned 'grievous corruption and filth', and the
City appointed its first sanitation officer in 1385, called the Serjeant
of the Channel, to keep roads clean. Wealthy new residents in the
Strand petitioned the authorities to improve the highway and in
1315 Edward II signed an ordinance to pave it. The results were
unsatisfactory, as such was the depth of mud that in 1353 a commissioner was appointed to lay a new pavement along its length at the
expense of residents. Two hundred years later, though, the Strand
was still described as being 'full of pits and sloughs, very perilous
and noisome' and 'in many places thereof very jeopardous to all
people passing and repassing ... on horseback as on foot'.[20]

New public buildings and monuments were raised in the Strand
during the thirteenth and early fourteenth centuries. Temple Bar
was erected in the 1290s, marking the western boundary of the
City. At first simply a chain across the highway, it was replaced by
a wooden structure, then a monumental stone archway that served
as the grand showcase of royal entrances into the City. The Royal
Mews occupied the area to the north and west of the Strand, under-
neath the present National Gallery, and housed the crown's falcons

(horses were stabled in Bloomsbury). The Mews were refashioned to accommodate horses (their hay was traded in the nearby Haymarket) and in the aftermath of a dreadful fire in 1547 they were rebuilt at a cost of £8,000 (more than £2 million today). The west end of the Strand acquired its defining statement in 1294 with the erection of a giant stone monument, the last of twelve crosses built to mark the route from Lincolnshire to Westminster of the body of King Edward I's wife, Eleanor of Castile. The huge Charing Cross, as it became known, dominated west Strand at the junction of the King's Street (Whitehall), St Martin's Lane and the Strand until its destruction by the Puritans in 1647. The landmark was situated where the equestrian statue of King Charles I now stands guard over Whitehall.[21]

Savoy Palace towered over mid-Strand. It was first erected by Peter, Count of Savoy, uncle to Henry III's wife, Eleanor, around 1263. This monumental structure was designed to impress (in 1293 it received a licence to crenelate its walls) and was greatly extended by Henry, 1st Duke of Lancaster and his son-in-law, John of Gaunt, Edward III's fourth son and reputedly the richest man in the kingdom after the King. It was renowned for 'its beauty and grandeur [as] the fairest house in the kingdom'; it had a complex of courtyards, a chapel, stables and a river gate in which the business of state was conducted. It served as the place of imprisonment of King John of France following his capture at the Battle of Poitiers in 1356. The Palace housed a retinue of 150 knights, a large household staff and numerous clerks, who included the poet Geoffrey Chaucer (he is purported to have written *The Canterbury Tales* there) (Figure 3). Its extensive pleasure gardens were renowned for their roses, including apocryphally the red rose of Provence, which became the emblem of the House of Lancaster in the War of the Roses. Disaster struck in 1381 when the Palace was targeted by rebels led by Wat Tyler, protesting against the hated Poll Tax, for which they blamed Gaunt. They destroyed its luxurious contents, including its gold and silver plate and jewels, and even used Gaunt's archery jacket for target practice. The Palace was then set on fire and blown up using gunpowder from the stores,

FIGURE 3. Portrait of Geoffrey Chaucer, from the poem *Regement of Princes* by Thomas Hoccleve, fifteenth century. Both writers lived and worked in the Strand in the late fourteenth century. (British Library Archive/Bridgeman Images. British Library Harl 4866 f.88)

inadvertently killing thirty-two of the rioters. The surviving buildings were turned into a prison before a hospital was founded there by Henry VII.[22]

At the junction of the present Northumberland Avenue and Trafalgar Square, opposite the Mews, was the Priory of St Mary Rounceval, endowed in 1235 as the London cell of a wealthy abbey in the Pyrenees. It provided hospitality, rest and medical treatment to pilgrims to the shrine of Edward at Westminster Abbey, and its buildings included a gatehouse, chapel and alms house surrounded by gardens where a variety of giant vegetable called the Rounceval pea was cultivated. Typically, such institutions – and there were at least thirteen similar priory hospitals in London – were relatively small scale and intended for short stays. St Mary's kept only nine beds and allocated a penny for each patient. Despite substantial landholdings and royal patronage, its fortunes dipped in the wake of the Black Death. It therefore sought to supplement its income by participating in the notorious practice of the sale of indulgences, that is, the granting of remittances from divine punishment in return for money or prayer. The practice would later bring the Church into disrepute, but it was criticised even in the fourteenth century. Rounceval played a prominent part in this scandal and inspired Chaucer to create the satirical character of the 'gentile Pardoner of Rouncival' in *The Canterbury Tales*. After the resumption of the Hundred Years' War, which excited patriotic sensibilities, the property was ransacked in 1381 by anti-Poll Tax rioters and nearby Savoy Palace was burnt down. It was eventually reinvented as a charitable religious guild supporting local poor before finally being suppressed by Henry VIII, who used its stones in the building of Whitehall Palace in the 1530s.[23]

St Mary's was one of several religious communities near the Strand. Other examples included St Katherine's Hermitage, also founded in the reign of Henry III, on a yard called Scotland, the Carmelite friary of Whitefriars in Fleet Street, the Dominican friary at Blackfriars and leper hospitals in St James and St Giles. The Knights Templar dominated the eastern approaches of the Strand. This wealthy military order of warrior monks was founded around 1120 to protect pilgrimages to Jerusalem. Its first preceptory in England was in Holborn, which it soon outgrew, and so it relocated under the patronage of Henry II in the 1150s to a new complex adjacent to the river. A north–south road that later became known as Chancery Lane was laid through the fields that the knights used for military practice. At the heart of their headquarters was a new round church modelled on the Church of the Holy Sepulchre in Jerusalem and consecrated in 1185. The Templars quickly acquired a reputation as money men on account of their extensive international networks, which permitted cash to be moved across borders, and the security of their places of deposit at a time of lawlessness. They thus gained political power that reached its height in the thirteenth century, when London's Temple became a *de facto* treasury for the crown and a place of important meetings and decision-making under King John and King Henry III. Amid growing unpopularity, the order was violently suppressed in 1314 and the status of the Temple as the strongbox of the Strand ended abruptly.[24]

In 1232, Henry III founded the Domus Conversorum or 'House of Converts' as a place of refuge for Jews who had converted to Christianity, as in doing so their estates were rendered forfeit. Generously endowed, it also relied on the levy of a special poll tax on Jewish people to provide bed, board and spiritual sustenance to its residents. It was popular: in the words of the chronicler Matthew Paris, 'large numbers of converts gathered therein and being baptized, were instructed in the laws of the Christians in a praise-worthy manner'. When Edward I expelled the Jews from England in 1290, however, the supply of new converts dwindled until only one remained, Claricia of Exeter. She died in 1356. Between 1331 and 1608, the Domus hosted some new arrivals, such as Johanna and her daughter Alice, who took up residence in 1409 and remained until their deaths, forty and forty-two years later. In 1377, the office of its Master of Converts was merged with the Master of the Rolls, the senior legal officer who preserved the parchment records of the Court of Chancery. The Master of the Rolls thereafter lived in the house and the records in his care were stored in the chapel. This Rolls Chapel comprised the nucleus of a national archives, which survived the demolition of the rest of the buildings and the construction around it of a new Public Record Office, which was conceived following the destruction of Parliament in the fire of 1834. This opened in 1856, to a design by Sir James Pennethorne, and brought the records of government together under one roof. A replacement chapel opened in 1902 to house important archives, until the Public Record Office transferred to Kew in 1997. The building is now a library.[25]

The east end of the Strand began to attract communities of lawyers in the thirteenth century, prompted by a prohibition on the clergy practising law and a series of statutes requiring legal education to be conducted beyond the bounds of the City. The Inns of Court – Lincoln's Inn, the Middle Temple, Inner Temple and Gray's Inn – served a dual purpose as places of legal training and mutuality for the medieval forerunners of barristers and solicitors. The Middle Temple and Inner Temple were established on the Strand and Fleet Street on land leased from the Templars' successors, the Hospitallers; Gray's Inn and Lincoln's Inn were to their north. Each Inn of Court was affiliated with one or more smaller institutions, called the Inns of Chancery. Numbering at least eight, and originating in the fourteenth century, several were clustered at the east end of the Strand, namely Clifford's Inn, Lyon's Inn, New Inn, Clement's Inn and Strand Inn, which would later be demolished to make way for Somerset House. Initially home to Chancery clerks employed to write legal writs, they soon became preparatory schools for barristers, who were expected to transfer to the senior Inns of Court on the completion of their studies. Eventually they were repurposed as academies for the training of solicitors.[26]

The medieval Strand was lined with grand south-facing mansions, the urban residences of the country's bishops, who made the road a centre of political power. The Reformation witnessed the transfer of their ownership to lay courtiers at the heart of Tudor and Stuart government, but the houses remained defining landmarks of the Strand for 400 years, until in the aftermath of the English Civil War, in the late seventeenth century, they were replaced by handsome town houses and new roads. The most easterly of these residences was the house belonging to the Bishops of Exeter, beginning with the ill-fated Walter de Stapledon in 1324, who was later beheaded by rioters and his body buried outside his half-finished palace by St Clement Danes. The largest episcopal palace on the Strand – once the site of Arundel House and now 180 Studios – belonged to the Bishop of Bath and Wells and was first recorded as granted to Bishop Jocelyn in 1228; latter residents included Cardinal Wolsey. To its west were several smaller houses, the inns of the dioceses of Coventry, Lichfield and Chester, Worcester, and Llandaff, followed by the homes of the Bishops of Carlisle and Durham, located halfway down the Strand. Durham House was a substantial property with a chapel and hall and a fortified river frontage, as shown in later illustrations; at one time it was the temporary home of Anne Boleyn. The Bishops of Norwich, meanwhile, occupied a smaller plot to the west, the future York House.[27]

The mansions – each a complex of buildings set in extensive grounds – served as domestic residences, offices and places of entertainment. They were approached through modest gatehouses (similar to those in Oxford and Cambridge colleges) and via landing stages on the river. The buildings generally comprised a great hall, a solar or private living quarters, and service areas, including kitchens and brewhouses, surrounded by kitchen gardens and orchards. The properties were often let out to lay tenants when bishops were out of public office, but each also owned rows of oak-built tenements or 'rents' on the Strand, generally let to wealthy tenants, with shops and other businesses occupying ground-floor rooms. Income from tenements was substantial: in the case of the diocese of Carlisle, 6 per cent of the annual income of the entire diocese. Some premises were put to practical use. In 1486, for example, a John Holgrave took out a twenty-year lease on le Floure de Luyce, four cottages and a garden in the parishes of St Mary's and St Clement Danes. In 1489, the same tenement appears to have been assigned to one James Atkinson as a small brewery, although the buildings were described as in 'great ruyne and decaie'.[28]

The medieval period, then, profoundly shaped the history of the Strand, as the time when its name, dimensions and parish boundaries were established. It was now a suburb that connected political power with the rising commercial energies of the City, a showy throughfare and place of procession and ritual. Its growth was accelerated by the evolution of English identity and the institutions of statehood – a national Church, law courts and Parliament – and the centralisation of a previously peripatetic royal court at Westminster following the Norman Conquest. Large

public buildings and the houses of the great and the good began to
shape the physical appearance of the Strand – now a long, narrow,
west-facing medieval street with churches at either end, lined with
shops, residential tenements, inns and grand mansions, and the
home of nobility, clergy, lawyers, clerks, shopkeepers and craft
workers. But the Strand was now to face momentous change.

CHAPTER 3

EARLY MODERN STRAND

The high streate of Westminster, comunly called the Stronde.
Tudor indenture[1]

The artist Wenceslas Hollar, weighed down by the tools of his trade, scrambled to the top of St Saviour's Church in London's Southwark. Overlooking the south bank of the Thames, the church's tower afforded a bird's-eye perspective of the city. The Prague-born Hollar was in this spring of 1642 some thirty-five years of age, but he had already completed six years' service as engraver to Thomas Howard, Earl of Arundel, the most renowned art collector in the country. Following the Great Fire in 1666, he would cannily market 'before and after' views of the city and successfully petition to be made honorary Royal Scenographer.[2]

The panorama that Hollar sketched on that spring day, the *Long View of London*, comprises six plates depicting the view from London Bridge to Whitehall Palace. The river is foregrounded; dotted with small boats belonging to an estimated 40,000 watermen, it was still the main highway for passengers and freight in a capital with one bridge and congested highways. The river was also the venue for occasional frost fairs, when its shallow waters froze over – 1608 and 1683–84 were especially harsh winters. Then, the Strand and its neighbourhood – and its sports, entertainment, food and drink – broke free of its urban straitjacket and spilled onto a broad riverscape. In composing his panorama, Hollar drew upon surveyors such as Ralph Agas, associated with a famous view of London in 1561, and cartographers George Braun and Franz Hogenburg, who published a map of London in the 1570s

(Map 1). These depicted the Strand at the start of Elizabeth I's reign as a rural suburb with grazing pasture to the north and a parade of shark-toothed gables and courtyards with rear allotments. In contrast, Hollar's etching of the Strand is both monumental and sweeping, showcasing the arc of grand riverside landmarks for which the suburb was now famous – Temple, Arundel, Somerset House, Savoy – and illustrating the remarkable development of the district in the century since Agas and his contemporaries.[3]

Hollar lived at a time of revolutionary change. Outward-facing, literate, curious, the Strand became a bullish proving ground for modernity, when scientific method and witch-burning occupied the same intellectual space. Momentous changes in society and belief, driven by the technologies of printing and navigation, spanned little more than four long lifetimes. Religious absolutism divided families, and grave and learned divines anticipated the apocalypse in thunderous pulpit sermons. Across Europe, the Protestant Reformation, from its origins with Martin Luther in 1517, challenged the precepts of the Church, dissolving age-old authority. It split the light of faith into a rainbow spectrum and threw the pieces up in the air, upturning the spiritual lives of millions. Henry VIII's Dissolution of the Monasteries transferred the wealth of the great religious houses to a Protestant landed elite inspired by a nationalist belief in England's providential exceptionalism. A building boom ensued, and the West End was born. This revolution in faith was fuelled by mass publishing and a growth of literacy that began to democratise access to knowledge, releasing urgent, heterodox – and sometimes frightening – new creative energies. Books, ballads and broadsheets, calendars and chapbooks – theology, history, geography, medicine and drama – poured forth from the presses in St Paul's, Fleet Street and the Strand, from printers such as Robert Waldegrave at Somerset House, Richard Gammon by Exeter House and Thomas Horseman near York House. Shortly, this district was to become the nerve centre of a global newspaper and publishing industry.[4]

Hollar and his contemporaries embodied a humanist intellectual curiosity and spirit of rigorous enquiry stimulated by a

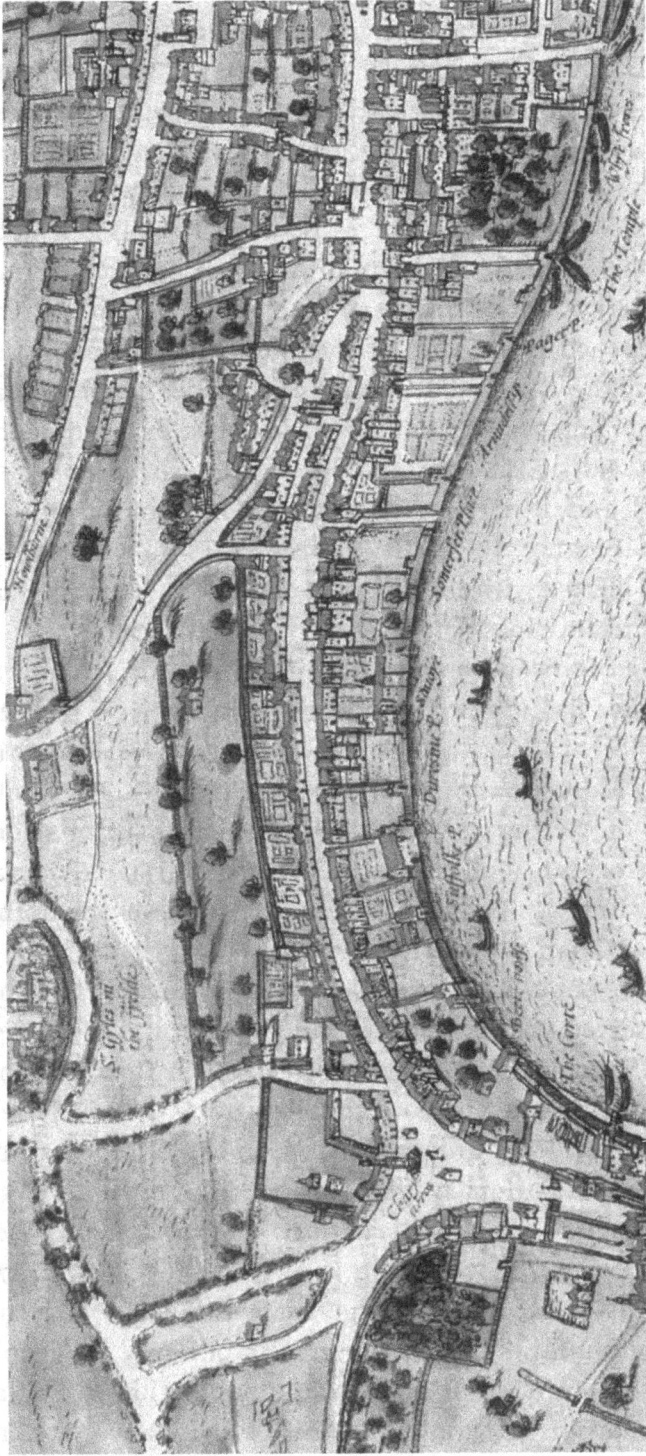

MAP 1. Detail from a hand-coloured bird's-eye view of London, c. 1572, by Georg Braun and Franz Hogenburg, from *Civitates Orbis Terrarum*, a multi-volume set of maps of European cities, published 1572–1617. Detail of the Elizabethan Strand amid a still predominantly rural setting. (Folger Shakespeare Library MAP 229985.1, image 4551)

desire to celebrate national economic, intellectual and human potential. The term 'chorography' came into general use at this time to describe a new literary genre that fused authentic historical research with fieldwork and maps. It was exemplified by the publication in 1586 of *Britannia* by William Camden, Headmaster of Westminster School, and the work of his pupil Sir Robert Cotton, founder of the first Society of Antiquaries, whose famous library was briefly housed in the Strand. From 1600, new trade routes were opened up to the Americas and Asia by mercantile houses, notably the East India Company; these led to the remarkable and unseen perspectives that were published by cartographers and globe-makers in the Strand. The street boasted embassies, exotic visitors and itinerant artisans drawn from Europe and further afield – France, the Netherlands, Spain, Italy, Turkey and Africa – and it buzzed with the prospect of new opportunities, tales of adventure and anticipation of loot.[5]

At the centre of this excitement was the talismanic explorer and writer, Sir Walter Raleigh, whose home was in Durham House on the Strand. There, in 1584, he hosted two Native American chiefs, Wanchese and Manteo, who stayed for nine months. The visitors were the talk of the town, and Raleigh and his man of science, Thomas Harriot, set about trying to learn their language and customs; they introduced them to society and observed them canoeing on the Thames.[6]

Domestically, popular maps, plans and perspectives such as Hollar's also served as the first A–Z guides, essential for navigating the capital's crooked and creaking streets. John Stow, a freeman of the Merchant Taylor's Company, published in 1598 his *Survey of London*, which provided a unique window on the Elizabethan city. In the midst of revolutionary change, and despite the terrifying outbreaks of plague that periodically scythed down its denizens, London's population rose from 60,000 in 1500 to 600,000 in 1700, surpassing Paris to become the largest city in Europe, driven by buoyant internal migration and the growth of newly burgeoning suburbs like the Strand. One-sixth of the population of England resided in London at some time in their lives and many more knew

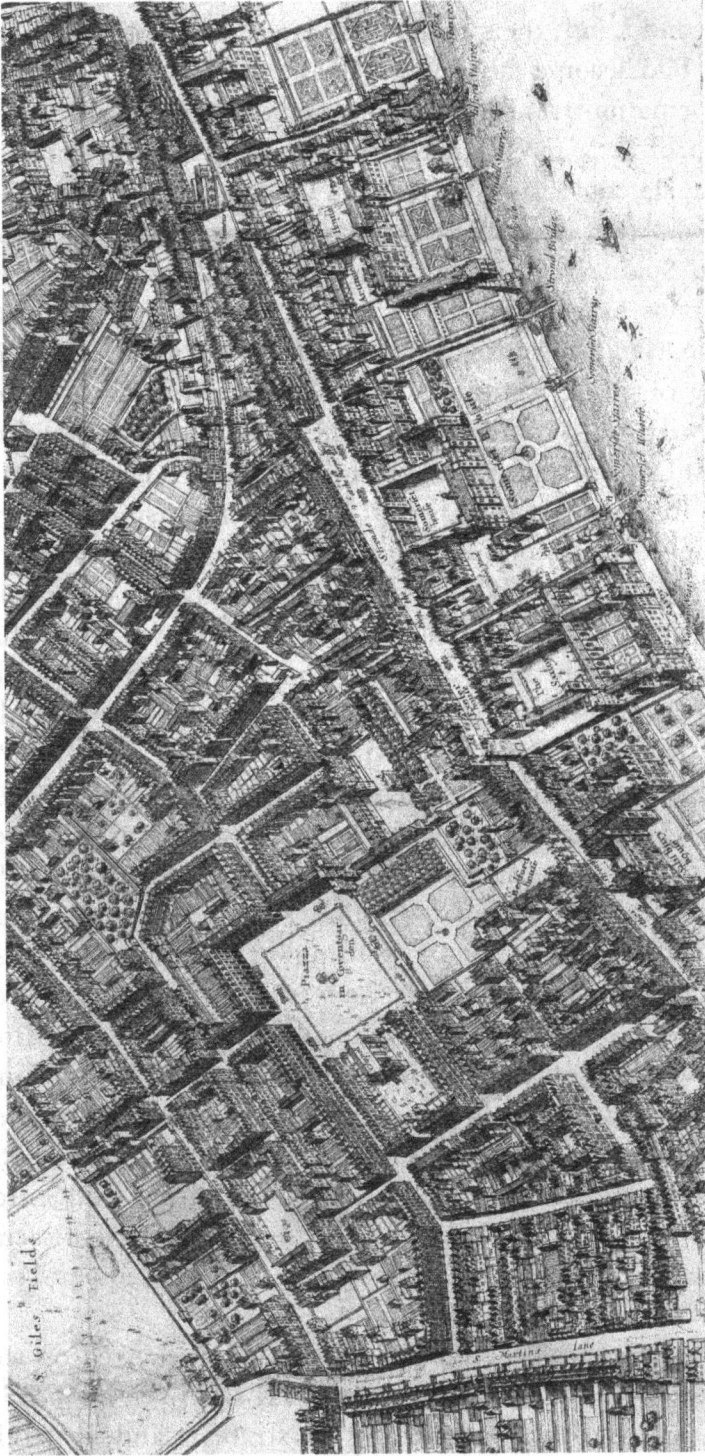

Map 2. Detail from a rare proof sheet for Wenceslaus Hollar's incomplete *Map of London and Westminster*, c. 1660, depicting a bird's-eye view of the Strand area, including its mansions and gardens, tenements and river stairs. The maypole and Church of St Mary's have yet to be re-erected. (Folger Shakespeare Library ART264–511, image 22302)

about it second hand: then, as now, its landmarks, stories, sights and sounds had become the property of all.[7]

The Reformation transformed the Strand, beginning with the suppression of St Mary Rounceval at Charing Cross, completed by 1544, and its conversion into 'divers tenements', occupied by a mix of widows and, later, wealthy tenants such as Charles I's ambassador to Spain, Sir Francis Cottington, and Lionel Empres, at whose house lodged foreign visitors to the Restoration court. The Reformation thus provided an unrivalled opportunity for the making of quick fortunes.[8] The transformation of the area continued with the bulldozing in 1548 of St Mary's by Edward Seymour, 1st Duke of Somerset, Lord Protector to his nephew, King Edward VI, to make way for his new Renaissance-inspired palace, Somerset House. Short of building materials, Somerset scavenged the church, evidently with no concern for the dignity of burials. A near contemporary wrote that 'the bones of many ... were cast up and carried into the fields'.[9] Not content with the wholesale destruction of the one historic building, and in a hunt for materials, Somerset ordered the pulling down of the steeple of St John's, Smithfield, and macabrely the demolition of the charnel house adjacent to St Paul's Cathedral, which scattered 500 tonnes of bones belonging to thousands of London's dead across Finsbury Fields.[10]

Somerset never lived in his new home. Having made numerous powerful enemies in his rapid rise to power, including Princess Mary and her Catholic supporters, he was detained in the Tower in 1549. The very public destruction of church property, including St Mary's, added weight to contemporary accounts of his vaulting ambitions, the Elizabethan historian John Hayward declaring they were 'in a high degree impious, so did they draw with them both open dislike from men and much secret revenge from God'. Later writers, too, were quick to draw links between his apparent sacrilegious desecration of Church property and his subsequent trial and execution in January 1552.[11]

Political violence and factional politics – often centred on the royal succession or religion – were never far from the surface in the Strand at this time, underlining its strategic and symbolic importance at the heart of the nation. In 1554, Sir Thomas Wyatt organised an abortive coup against Queen Mary, fearing that her proposed marriage to the future King Philip II of Spain would lead to the suppression of Protestantism. Wyatt's supporters from Kent numbered several thousand armed with pikes and bills, but the uprising was swiftly put down by Mary's soldiers. A pair of gallows erected at the site of their ignominious last stand beside Charing Cross despatched the surviving leaders.[12]

Eleven mighty mansions – the fruit of the Reformation – lined the Strand from Essex House in the east to Northumberland House in the west, the latter being only house that survived into the era of photography, although it was then demolished in 1874. Inspired by royal patrons, including Charles I, they transformed the Strand into a 'museum mile' that showcased the finest antiquities and modern art, a brilliant swagger of power, refinement and diplomacy. Leading nobles at the heart of the Protestant government met and deliberated here during a long cold – and hot – war with Catholic Europe. The street was also home to royalty, including no fewer than three Queens of England (Map 2).

The Strand became a centre for scholarship. The Inns of Court at its east end, blessed with encyclopaedic libraries and curricula befitting England's 'third universitie', were augmented by the fine libraries of rare books and manuscripts of the noble mansions. Contemporary stars of the European artistic firmament such as Peter Paul Rubens and Anthony van Dyck were commissioned as statements of owners' power and prestige, education and refinement. Households employed the best European curatorial and artistic talent: painters, engravers, musicians and historians emblematic of a new cosmopolitanism. This street-long arthouse thus became a showy and symbolic backdrop to grand entertainments, masques and state conferences; the Treaty of London, for example, which ended the long war with Spain, was negotiated in Somerset House in 1604. Championed by the philosopher and statesman Francis Bacon, who was born, lived and died in the Strand under Queen Elizabeth and King James I, new ideas about science also began to take root, while John Locke, tutor to the Earl of Shaftesbury there, began to reflect deeply on the preferred organisation of civil society, ideas that were translated to America.[13]

High culture flourished at the home of Elizabeth I's favourite,
the soldier and stateman the Earl of Leicester. Arguably the most
powerful, albeit controversial, courtier in the realm, he was also
one of its foremost patrons, who sponsored the royal miniaturist Nicholas Hilliard as well as the first licensed company of
theatrical players, Leicester's Men. In 1569, he rebuilt the former
episcopal palace of the Bishops of Exeter by the 'shore of silver-
streaming Thames'. The house enabled him to display his many
treasures, which included Hilliard's limnings, commissions from
the Venetian Paul Veronese and Mark Gheeraedts's *Portrait of
Queen Elizabeth I at Wanstead Palace*. Perhaps the ultimate symbol
of wealth in grand residences was fine tapestries. Leicester's were
fabricated at the Sheldon works in Warwickshire and inspired by
designs from the Low Countries. Four of the best, commissioned
around 1585, took pride of place in a new banqueting house on the
banks of the river.[14]

Leicester's home became a centre for European humanist scholarship. A steadfast Protestant, he sponsored numerous Puritan
religious texts. His client group reflected his religious preoccupations; it included Elizabeth's chief spymaster, Francis Walsingham,
to whom he was related by marriage, and his family's tutor, the
royal astronomer and occultist Dr John Dee. Leicester's nephew
and confidant, the courtier and poet Sir Philip Sidney, lived there
almost until his untimely death in 1586 aged only thirty-one. It is
likely that Sidney wrote *A Defence of Poetry* there in 1580, an influential critical text that inspired Romantic-era poets such as Shelley
and Wordsworth.[15]

The brilliant court of Leicester ended with his death in 1588,
whereupon he was succeeded by his stepson, Robert Devereux,
2nd Earl of Essex. Devereux was Elizabeth's favourite during her
dotage but he fell out of favour and in February 1601 plotted to
overthrow his political opponents, led by Robert Cecil. The tumult
centred on Leicester's former home, now called Essex House, which
was equipped, it was said, with 'all manner of warlike provisions'.

There, in a dramatic escalation of hostilities, royal emissaries sent to negotiate were instead taken hostage. Charing Cross was barricaded to protect Westminster and the house was besieged. The insurrection was quickly suppressed, and following a short trial, at which he protested his innocence, Essex lost his head at the Tower only two weeks later.[16]

William Cecil, 1st Baron Burghley, and his younger son, Robert Cecil, Earl of Salisbury, together bestrode English affairs of state from Elizabeth's accession in 1558 until Robert's death in 1612. William built Cecil House (renamed Burghley House after he was elevated to the peerage) on the north side of the Strand in 1560, on the present site of the Strand Palace Hotel. It was inherited by his elder son, Thomas, Earl of Exeter, but demolished in 1676 to make way for a shopping arcade called Exeter Change. Its frontage projected into the Strand, narrowing it dramatically – a distinctive if unwelcome feature of the road until the 1830s. Burghley House boasted mod cons, including a tennis court and bowling alley with a private entrance on the Strand. Here William Cecil raised his family, entertained guests and conducted state business, including meetings of the Privy Council. It provided working space for his secretary and amanuensis, his nephew Hugh Alington, who was assisted by a team of clerks. They worked tirelessly drafting correspondence and issuing orders dealing with local and national emergencies, including war, trade, plague and national security. This work required a meticulous eye and a versatile and trustworthy bureaucracy. The Cecil family's home in the Strand and their country residences (Theobalds in Hertfordshire and Burghley House near Stamford) were also places of soft power for them, and cemented their status through lavish or intimate entertainment, including banquets, masques and the reception of royal visitors.[17]

Cecil was Master of the Court of Wards, supervising guardianship of the orphaned sons of the nobility, including the direction of their distinctively Protestant curriculum of education. His library became a place of reformed scholarly industry, a forge for Reformation statecraft countering Catholic revanchism. The Strand supported a team of scholar-tutors, linguists, antiquarians

and propagandists, in this Elizabethan nationalist project. Such
men included Arthur Golding, English translator of the edition
of Ovid's *Metamorphosis* consulted by Shakespeare, and John Hart,
Cecil's Secretary in the Court of Wards and advocate for the reform
of English spelling. Laurence Nowell lived in the house and tutored
the young Earl of Oxford, poet, courtier and sometime candidate
for authorship of Shakespeare's plays. A seminal character in the
revival of the Anglo-Saxon language, Nowell owned the surviving
manuscript of the epic poem *Beowulf* and one can perhaps picture
him scurrying through the Strand gatehouse clutching the price-
less codex. Nowell was a prominent cartographer of the British
Isles, which catered to Cecil's love of maps. Cecil also sponsored
the surveyor John Norden, who published a famous map of London
in 1623 called *A Guide for Countrymen*. Cecil and his son used
such maps to promote a more cohesive sense of British national
identity – as Protestant, progressive and patriotic – especially after
the union of the crowns of England and Scotland in 1603.[18]

Robert Cecil succeeded his father as Elizabeth's, then James I's,
chief advisor. In 1599, he commissioned a new home on the south
side of the Strand, comprising two neighbouring properties. The
smaller one was let out to wealthy families, including the Earls of
Devonshire, and, as such, later became home to the family's tutor,
the philosopher Thomas Hobbes, author of *Leviathan*. The houses
had been built on the former stables of Durham House and a
complex of lucrative tenements called Durham Rents. Robert used
strong-arm tactics to acquire the land from the Bishop of Durham
and then hastily evicted the sitting tenant, Sir Walter Raleigh.

Like his father, Robert was a man of culture without ostentation,
with an eye for the eccentric: it is said that he kept a pet parrot,
which, after feeding, 'was want to settle in a gentlewoman's ruff all
day'. His house became a treasure trove of paintings, tapestries and
maps but was also a place where the music and song integral to the
personal and professional life of a cultivated Renaissance courtier
flourished. Transcending confessional differences, Robert was a
dedicatee of the famous Roman Catholic composer and lutenist
John Dowland, and his library catalogue lists 'diverse books of

musicke and songes'. Unusually for the time, he employed full-time musicians and apprentices to entertain dignitaries and educate his young wards, including the Queen's lutenist and composer Robert Hales and the celebrated Irish harpist Cormack MacDermott.[19]

Aletheia Howard and her husband, Thomas, 14th Earl of Arundel, were leading art collectors and connoisseurs, famous for their extended diplomatic and cultural expeditions to the continent, which are among the earliest documented 'Grand Tours'. They used her inherited wealth – she was the granddaughter of the famous Bess of Hardwick – to acquire the finest treasures for their homes, including Arundel House in east Strand. These were arranged in splendour in a building designed by the architect Inigo Jones and surrounded by new Italianate gardens, affording perambulating family and visiting 'high society' gentle perfumed respite from London's poisonous air. Arundel House was a signature of the revived fortunes of the Howard family, suitable for a premier nobleman and diplomat, its collections a reminder that the public expression of education and learning was a statement of wealth, taste and power.[20]

Aletheia was an intimate in the court of Anne of Denmark, located in the former Somerset House; she performed in court masques and was chief mourner at Anne's funeral in 1619. A noted hostess, her parties in the Strand were legendary. One, thrown for the Venetian ambassador, deployed a full-sized gondola as its showpiece. Her influence as a patron of the arts was pervasive and as an author she is credited with one of the earliest scientific publications written by a woman, the medicinal *Natura exenterata* ('Nature unbowelled'). Her husband (Figure 4) was also an esteemed and educated patron, one who 'doth ... expose these jewells of art to publicke view in the Academie of Arundell House'. There he assembled a peerless library overseen by the learned German philologist Francis Junius and patronised the historian Robert Cotton. He was also a friend of the greatest legal mind of his generation, John Selden. The royal physician, William Harvey, who discovered the circulation of blood, was his personal doctor and accompanied Howard on a continental mission in 1636. A democratic

FIGURE 4. Thomas Howard, 14th Earl of Arundel, by Daniel Mytens, *c.* 1618. The diplomat, patron, connoisseur and collector, Thomas Howard is shown in his house, after it had been remodelled by the architect Inigo Jones; he points to his famous collection of marble antiquities, some examples of which are now preserved in the Ashmolean Museum in Oxford. (© National Portrait Gallery, London)

host, Howard cultivated a wide appreciation of his collections, by commissioning facsimile editions of his art from Hollar for the enjoyment of the reading public.

The treasures of Arundel House were renowned: paintings, rare medals, cameos and valuable books, and the most exquisite examples of Greek and Roman sculpture, whose rarity was praised by Rubens when he visited England in 1629 to paint the Banqueting House ceiling in Whitehall. A gallery displayed the drawings and engravings of Leonardo da Vinci, Hans Holbein and Albrecht Dürer. The collection of paintings included seventeen Raphaels, Holbein's dramatic narrative masterpieces *The Triumph of Poverty* and *The Triumph of Riches*, mythologies by Titian, portraits by Tintoretto and landscapes by Bruegel.[21]

Inigo Jones redesigned the garden with terraces and balustrades, stone archways, and bowers that served as a setting for some of the marbles (Figure 5). Jones used perspective to draw the eye south, across the river to the Surrey Hills, which would at times shimmer dreamlike in the distance; the garden thus became an extension of the picture gallery, hinted at in two famous portraits, painted in 1618, of the Earl and Countess by the Flemish master Daniel Mytens. The garden was renowned throughout Europe and impressed visitors such as the German art critic Joachim Sandrart, while the polymathic Francis Bacon declared it a perfect restoration of the classical world. The outbreak of the Civil War and Arundel's exile and death in 1646 ended this brief idyll. The diarist John Evelyn, bemoaning the damage to the statues inflicted by soldiers billeted at the house, arranged for their transfer to the University of Oxford. They remain on public display to this day in the Ashmolean Museum.[22]

Gardens like Arundel's became fashionable in the seventeenth century, modelled on Italian and French designs with classical imprimatur, and featuring innovations such as terracing, grottos, allegorical statuary, and elaborate water features. The Strand nobility nurtured talented gardeners; for instance, John Rose, reputedly the first person to cultivate the pineapple in England, was apprenticed in Leicester's garden. The area also became known

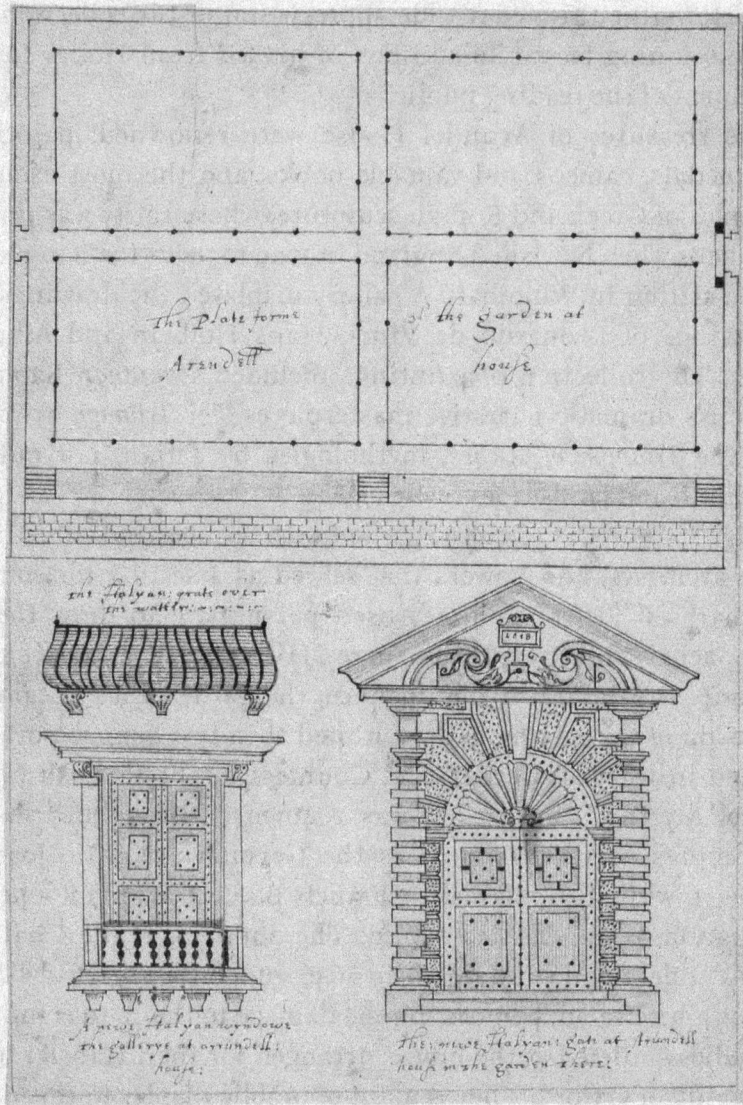

the plate forme   of the garden at
Arundell   house

the Italyan grate over
the watter ...

A newe Italyan window
the gallerye at arundell;
house:

The newe Italyan gate at Arundell
house in the garden there:

Figure 5. Arundel House, Strand, London: survey plan of the garden with details of an 'Italyan' gate, window and gateway, designed by Inigo Jones. Sketch by John Smythson, architect, c. 1618. Thomas Howard and his wife Alethea commissioned architect Inigo Jones to redesign Arundel House on the Strand, including its garden. The architect and stonemason John Smythson, visiting London, produced sketches of Jones's fashionable Italianate designs, along with other Strand buildings, including the New Exchange. (RIBA Collections)

for the sale of plants and seeds, notably Edward Fuller's shop at the sign of the Three Crowns and Naked Boy at Strand Bridge, which sold vegetables (such as 'Colly Flower'), flowers (the 'African Marygold') and exotic imports (the 'Broad-leav'd Mirtle of Portugal' and the 'Three leav'd Virginian Bladder-Nut').[23]

William Cecil employed the best-qualified staff to supervise his gardens, notably the celebrated herbalist John Gerard, who also kept his own garden in nearby Holborn and one adjacent to Somerset House. A beautiful colour plan of London's Burghley House, believed to be the oldest surviving example for an English garden, depicts an orchard, a private space for quiet contemplation and formal parterre gardens with low hedging and lawns leading from an Italian-style loggia. A banqueting house and an artificial hill or snail mount were provided for the entertainment of guests, who could gaze across the Elysian fields of 'Convent Garden' to the hills in Hampstead. An impressive brick wall enclosed the garden, which backed onto the estate of the Earl of Bedford, with a private gate for the Queen and other dignitaries, away from prying eyes of the Strand.[24]

Robert Cecil was also a keen garden innovator at his various homes, including Salisbury House in the Strand. He was among the first people to cultivate oranges in England and employed perhaps the most famous gardener of his day, John Tradescant the Elder, who, with his son, assembled the Ark, a famous garden and cabinet of curiosities in Lambeth, which the public entered through an archway made from the ribs of a whale. Tradescant returned from plant-buying expeditions in Paris and Brussels ladened with pomegranates, orange trees, willows and fruit trees. He remodelled Salisbury House in 1610 with new gravel walks, a kitchen garden with onions and radishes and cloches for melons, and planted lilacs, cherries, jasmine, clematis and roses around new arbours and a pergola.[25]

One of the most famous gardens in the Strand was that of Somerset House, the home of James I's consort, Anne of Denmark (it was renamed Denmark House during her residence). In 1609, the frontage was redesigned in neoclassical style and the garden improved by Simon Basil and William Goodrowse, who introduced raised terracing, a shady avenue of trees leading to the river and an orangery and banqueting house. The centrepiece was a vast fountain by the accomplished French garden designer Salomon de Caus, inspired by his visits to Italian gardens, for instance the Medici villa, Pratolino, outside Florence. In 1615, de Caus published the two-volume *Les Raisons des Forces Mouvantes*, which advocated the use of aquatic engineering in gardens, prefiguring Capability Brown by a century. His younger brother Isaac was also a familiar face on the Strand as a client of the Earl of Bedford and a designer of the new Covent Garden in the 1630s. The Denmark House fountain was thirty feet high and eighty feet wide; it comprised a huge rocky recreation of Mount Parnassus in Greece, a cavern containing the nine muses, and four streams of water representing the great rivers of England, surmounted by a gilded statue of Pegasus. It is unclear whether the fountain's water was drawn from the Thames – de Caus built a pumping station that is visible in contemporary drawings – or an underground spring: accounts mention a 'Great Cesterne over the Strand Lane which serveth the new Fountaine with water'. Much later, in 1776, it is likely the cistern was re-purposed to supply a new public bath with its entrance on Surrey Street, a road developed in the late seventeenth century following the demolition of Arundel House. This was advertised as a 'Roman Bath' and is mentioned in Dickens's *David Copperfield*. The bath survives under the care of the National Trust.[26]

Perhaps no other mansion exemplifies the fickle fortunes of the district's noble landlords as York House in west Strand, the former inn of the Bishops of Norwich. This dilapidated medieval mansion was renamed when Elizabeth I granted it to the then Archbishop of York. It was later home to Sir Francis Bacon and then George Villiers, James I's dashing young favourite, who had risen rapidly from relatively humble origins to become one of the most powerful men in the realm. In 1624, Villiers, now Duke of Buckingham and aged a mere thirty-one, began transforming the house and gardens. Occupying the most elevated point on the Strand on a strategic bend in the river, in panoramic proximity to the seats of national legal, courtly and religious power, Westminster Hall, Whitehall and Lambeth Palaces, this flourish of aesthetics, high society, diplomatic showmanship and political one-upmanship was conjured up and set down in under two years. The house, it was expected, would cement Buckingham's precocious reputation as a man of lofty taste and critical discernment. He employed as curator of his collections and factotum the Dutch miniaturist and occasional architect Sir Balthasar Gerbier. He masterminded improvement works to showcase the magnificent collections he assembled, which it was expected would rival Arundel's and would serve as a canvas to sumptuous entertainments (e.g. masques) designed to further Buckingham's political ambitions. Rubens's signature painted ceiling, *The Apotheosis of the Duke of Buckingham*, was one of seventeen by that master, among 330 in total scattered throughout the painterly penthouse. Gerbier's grand rebuilding plans were only partially realised as, sensationally, his unpopular master was assassinated in 1628. Today, the only surviving portion is the water gate situated in Embankment Gardens. Variously attributed to Gerbier, Inigo Jones or Nicholas Stone, master mason on the Banqueting House, it gives some impression of the real or proposed grandeur of the whole house.[27]

The New Exchange exemplified the growing commercial vigour of the Strand across the seventeenth century. Situated on the site of the former stables and gatehouse of Durham House, and intended to rival the Royal Exchange, it was a home to upmarket traders and retailers. Styled 'Britain's Borse' by King James I in a nod to Antwerp's famous exchange, its construction cost its promoter, Sir Robert Cecil, the princely sum of £10,760 (about £1.5 million today). It took a team of 250 builders and masons from the West Midlands a year to erect using 520 tons of stone salvaged from St Augustine's monastery in Canterbury. The Exchange remained a prominent Strand landmark until its demolition in 1737.[28]

The Exchange was opened by King James to great fanfare in April 1609, amid 'pleasant speeches, gifts and ingenious devices'. An extravagant masque was commissioned for the occasion entitled *Entertainment at Britain's Burse*. Composed by locally born

Ben Jonson, superstar playwright and the artistic contemporary of Shakespeare, its costumes and elaborate stage design were the responsibility of the young Inigo Jones. The two men cooperated closely, though quarrelled often, in the production of numerous masques, including *Entertainment at Salisbury House* in May 1608, to celebrate Robert Cecil's appointment as Lord Treasurer, and performed in its magnificent, gilded library adjacent to the construction works on the New Exchange. *Britain's Burse* featured players from the theatre company Children of the Queen's Revels, accompanied by musicians and singers, and promoted the new Virginia Company, in which Cecil was an investor. Innovatively, it used one of the shops and its expensive stock of fashionable imported Chinese porcelain as a backdrop; some of the many luxury items on sale included 'umbrellas, sundials ... ostrich eggs, birds of paradise ... flowers of silk, mosaic fishes ... waxen fruit ... [and] fine cages for birds...'. Automata meanwhile indulged Cecil's taste for mechanical inventiveness and included figures of the sun and moon and a singing statue of Apollo.[29]

The Exchange boasted a handsome façade surmounted by statues of the apostles. Its gilded interior comprised a two-storey galleried arcade, 201 feet long; its constituent shops, numbering 150 in its heyday, operated from small self-contained wooden stalls resembling a covered market. This luxury shopping experience was strictly regulated. Tenants were expected to be people of 'reputable vocation', begging and pickpocketing were discouraged and, considerately, a private room was set aside where disobedient servants might be whipped without disturbing shoppers. A bathroom, or 'pissing place', was installed and fines were levied for throwing out of the windows 'any piss or other noisome thing'.[30]

The Exchange sought to be commercially competitive, with lengthy opening hours and lower rents than its rival Royal Exchange. The Venetian ambassador confidently predicted it would 'bring in immense revenue', while the Lord Mayor warned it would disadvantage the City. Its popularity soared following the development of Covent Garden and after the Great Fire in 1666 that laid waste to the Square Mile, helped by municipal improvements such as public seating and the paving of the Strand. The diarist Samuel Pepys reported in 1668 that trade was booming, one shop-keeper telling him 'Retail trade is so great here, and better than it was in London, that they believe they shall not return, nor the city be ever so great for retail as heretofore'. Many guild members relocated there in new occupations, including Nathaniel Barsham, who ran a chandlery shop in 1614, and former cloth-workers Rich Davyes, a confectioner in 1641, and Giddeon Jematt, a cabinet-maker in 1668.[31]

Other notable occupants included the Edinburgh-born jeweller to James I George Heriot, whose fortune made there was bequeathed to charities in his home city. Heriot-Watt University, founded in the nineteenth century, recalls his generosity. The Exchange was home to literary types, too, notably the bookseller and stationer Thomas Walkley, who, drawing on his working association with Shakespeare's company of players, the King's Men, published in 1622 the first quarto edition of *Othello*. Henry Herringman's shop became popular after the Great Fire destroyed business rivals. He was perhaps the first modern wholesale bookseller in London. Significantly, also, he was responsible for launching the career of the famous poet John Dryden, who worked with him as an editorial assistant throughout the 1660s and 1670s. Samuel Pepys was a regular visitor there when shopping in the Exchange with his wife to view the latest fashions on Doll Stacey's stall or enjoying takeaway lunches of ox tongue and curds and cream, washed down by a cup of whey from the milk bar in the cellars.[32]

The cloth trade predominated. It was mostly run by women seamstresses, milliners and up-market mantua-makers such as Anne Redford, who rented a shop for £6 per annum, and sold fabrics, fashion and haberdashery to wealthy customers from the court in nearby St James's Palace and Whitehall. Moralisers warned against the loose morals of so-called 'Exchange-women', one de-claring that 'thy shops with pretty wenches swarm/Which for thy custom are a kind of charm/To idle gallants'. In 1648, Parliament investigated complaints from tenants of sexual harassment com-mitted by 'Sundry Debaucht Gentry'. The Exchange was a favourite nudge-nudge, wink-wink setting for plays written by Restoration dramatists; examples including Congreve's *Old Batchelor* and a whole scene in William Wycherley's explicit *The Country Wife*, where it is the sexual playground for the libidinous antihero, Horner. It was a target for violence – cabbies fighting over fares – and crime, most noteworthy being the murder committed in 1653 by Don Pantaleone Sa, the brother of the Portuguese ambassador. The defendant had his diplomatic immunity revoked by the Chief Justice and he was hanged at Tower Hill in July 1654.[33]

The New Exchange was one example of the rapid growth in local business driven by those keen to escape the restrictive guild regulation of the City. Workshops were set up by skilled artisans from the Low Countries and Germany that manufactured precision mathematical instruments used in architectural and agricultural surveying, navigation and warfare. These included clocks, sundials, astrolabes and compendia (a type of pocket organiser), thermometers, barometers and telescopes. English craftspeople and their apprentices soon appeared. These included royal appointees such as Bartholomew Newsam, based near Somerset House (fl. 1568–93), Elias Allen, at St Clement's (fl. 1607–53), and Francis Clewitt, of the Blue Bell at Charing Cross (fl. 1672). Instrument-makers were often also talented book-engravers, and this interdependency flourished in Fleet Street and the Strand. Mathematicians and skilled artisans also began working closely together to publish science manuals intended for a general readership, written by the likes of Leonard Digges, Hugh Plat and William Cecil's man, William Bourne.[34]

This burgeoning of local business attracted the eye of entrepreneurs such as the Earls of Bedford, who consequently began to develop Covent Garden in the 1630s, and John Holles, Earl of Clare, who was granted market rights in 1657 in the parish of St Clement Danes, and opened one of London's largest meat markets (it even housed a kosher butcher that supplied Jewish customers). The market lent its name to Butcher's Row, which, along with Wych Street, Holywell Street and Middle Row, occupied the site of the present-day Aldwych, a complex of extremely narrow, almost unpassable, lanes of Elizabethan and Jacobean timber-framed houses

that survived until the late nineteenth century and on account of
their impassibility were known to wary cab drivers as the 'Straights
of St Clements'. Crowded, anonymous, gloomy and mazy, they
became infamous as the place where the Gunpowder Plot conspira-
tors met in 1605.

The Plot was emblematic of the divisive religious upheavals
that characterised Tudor and Stuart England, which comprised
Protestant majority and Roman Catholic minority populations,
and the growth of purist forms of worship, pejoratively labelled
Puritanism. Religious doctrine and belief stirred bitter and
violent passions, expressed in war with England's neighbours and
in the matter of the royal succession, brought to the fore under
Elizabeth I and in the Glorious Revolution of 1688. Providence took
on a fresh significance from the 1550s and became the worldview
of generations who lived and worked in the Strand. A vast literature arose cataloguing the 'theatre of God's judgements' in history,
in current affairs and in personal lives, the last giving birth to
the diary as a record of personal piety. Perhaps the most public
example of this divine intervention was the defeat of the Spanish
Armada in 1588. This was made possible, so it was widely believed,
by a sudden and unexpected change in the direction of the wind,
which blew Spanish ships off course. On Sunday 24 November,
Queen Elizabeth gave thanks for the victory, when she rode in an
open carriage from Somerset House to St Paul's, accompanied by
music by the renowned composer William Byrd, and returned to
the Strand by torchlight. The following morning, the street was
decked with blue broadcloth as a backdrop to a military parade;
the windows and road thronged with well-wishers applauding the
Queen's progress.[35]

The overt patriotic Protestantism of Elizabeth's reign faded
during the reign of Charles I, notably under the ecclesiastical
policies of his Archbishop of Canterbury, William Laud; nevertheless, the conspicuously foreign art and fashions of the Strand
nobility began to arouse suspicion that the corridors of power were
being infiltrated by Roman Catholics. Catholic chapels at Savoy
Chapel and the French embassy in Durham House attracted a

sizeable local congregation of resident French people but were also, more worryingly for the authorities, the 'daily Resort of multitudes of English Subjects of more than a hundred at once to Masse'. Much more politically damaging was the apparent toleration of Roman Catholic practices by the unpopular though devout Queen Henrietta Maria, symbolised by the building of a beautiful private chapel at Somerset House under the care of French Capuchin friars. This was erected to grand designs by Inigo Jones and was magnificently appointed with a painted ceiling of the Assumption and a Rubens altarpiece of the crucifixion. It opened on 8 December 1635 – the Feast of the Immaculate Conception – accompanied by a public Mass sung by an invisible choir. The chapel remained open for three days to accommodate the crowds of visitors: a novel attraction to London's Catholic community – many of whom congregated around the Strand – and who were otherwise denied the legal right to worship.[36]

The 1630s witnessed growing religious controversy, not least surrounding the imprisonment and exemplary punishment of the Puritan controversialists Henry Burton, John Bastwick and William Prynne. The last's condemnation of masques and their actresses, whom he accused of debauchery, was widely held to be a thinly veiled allusion to Henrietta Maria, her retinue and her religion. Prynne was sentenced to life imprisonment for his impertinence and had his ears cropped and his books burned. In 1634, King Charles ordered the Inns of Court, of which the lawyer Prynne was a member, to demonstrate their loyalty by staging a masque at Whitehall called *The Triumph of Peace*. This cost a staggering £21,000 (£2.5 million in today's money) and was preceded by a torch-lit procession down the Strand. The case became a *cause célèbre* that galvanised popular dissatisfaction with Charles I; the prisoners' release in 1640 was a cause of huge public celebrations – they were greeted by cheering crowds and handed sprigs of rosemary for remembrance.[37]

London took the side of Parliament in the Civil War, which broke out in 1642 and which engulfed the whole of the British Isles. It spanned a decade and was arguably the most calamitous conflict in modern British history: it claimed the lives of some 3 per cent of the population – both civilians and combatants – through sword, siege, plague and famine, twice as many proportionally as were lost during both World Wars. The war sundered families, ruined towns, destroyed fortunes and left a wake of people wounded, maimed and disabled, not least among Strand residents, such as Staffordshire-born Richard Dawson, who served two years in Clonmel in Ireland and was awarded an annual pension of twenty shillings, or impoverished war widow Alice Lunn of Charing Cross, whose late husband John, formerly landlord of the Red Lion pub, had been 'a Souldier & a Great Sufferer for his Majesty King Charles the First of ever glorious memory'. The Strand mansions and their contents belonging to the King's supporters either were sequestrated and turned over to official use or, in the case of the Savoy and Burghley House chapel, became a place of refuge for dispossessed Catholics. Henrietta Maria's chapel was vandalised by Parliament's Henry Marten, a Puritan with an eye for the ladies whom the King had once described as a 'whoremaster'. Somerset House then became a principal barracks for Parliamentarian soldiers and an auction house for the sale of the royal art collection to raise public funds. The Strand's houses and their contents never recovered from the damage inflicted upon them during the Civil War and Interregnum which followed the execution of Charles I at Whitehall but a short distance from the Strand. Oliver Cromwell lay in state in Somerset House after his death in 1658, but soon after, the republican cause began to disintegrate. Cromwell's war, though, had accelerated the growth of a newly fashionable 'West End' of shops, businesses and smart town squares towards which the Strand was now orientated.[38]

King Charles II returned to Britain in triumph in May 1660, when he bound its wounds with declarations of tolerance and plumped up its pillows with youthful, self-confident swagger. The diarist Thomas Rugge bore witness to the monumental parade along the Strand that accompanied his entry into Westminster, troops of soldiers, merchants, sheriffs, aldermen and Lord Mayor, trumpeters in blue livery and silver lace, a dreamy ribbon of joyous red, velvet black, green and gold, and 'such shouting as the oldest man alive never heard the like'. The route was strewn with flowers and rich carpets and cushions hung from its windows accompanying cheering crowds, fireworks, music and bonfires. Charles's coronation – symbolically arranged for St George's Day, 23 April 1661 – was preceded by a grand procession from the Tower of London to Whitehall through four triumphant arches depicting the kingdoms, the royal family and classical themes. Along its route, fountains of wine replaced water and the acclamations of the King's subjects rang out.[39]

The procession passed the newly re-erected maypole at Strand Bridge. The country's tallest, it would become a familiar rendez-vous that attracted a murmuration of artists, writers, makers, the wealthy, witty and indigent. This spot had long been a place of public celebration and punishment, home to an ancient stone cross and one of London's busiest pillories. In 1625 a former naval captain, John Bailey, founded a new business in its shadow – the world's first taxi rank. It was wildly successful and undercut the watermen, who lobbied in vain against it.[40]

A maypole some 100 feet high resided here until 1644, when, in the midst of Civil War, it was removed on the orders of Parliament. Like Charing Cross, destroyed three years later, to its opponents it represented an idolatrous remnant of England's pagan past and a lightning rod for God's displeasure. The abolition of Christmas and Mayday, the closing of theatres and the whitewashing of churches were seen to be Parliament's patriotic way to make things right with God. A few years later a new Coronation maypole was erected, some 134 feet high; this was masterminded by the Duke of York (the future King James II). The Navy transported the mast-like pole upriver in two sections, supported by 'numerous multitudes of people thronging the streets'. Its ceremonial dedication was attended by Morris dancers in purple scarves and garlands of fresh flowers amid the beat of drums. Lanterns hung from it on dark nights and four golden royal crowns were placed around its circumference. It was surmounted by a golden weather-vane from which a purple streamer fluttered. It is questionable, however, given its exceptional height, that the maypole was ever used for its intended purpose. Progressively shortened by storms, the surviving stump finally disappeared in 1721, when Sir Isaac Newton transported it to Wanstead 'to use this glass upon, in astronomical observations'.[41]

The Great Fire of London, which broke out the night of 2 September 1666 in Pudding Lane at the end of a long dry summer, steadily devoured the City across some three days. All routes out of London – by road and river – witnessed a monumental caravan of evacuees, 'every creature coming away loaden with goods to save, and here and there sicke people carried away in beds. Extraordinary good goods carried in carts and on backs'. Tent cities in Highbury and Moorfields accommodated an estimated 200,000 Londoners, and churches, chapels and schools became makeshift shelters. The Duke of York took command of operations, and whole streets were demolished to create firebreaks, in vain as the fire poured down Fleet Street, consuming its timber tenements. However, fortuitously, the winds slackened and the fire, 'meeting with brick buildings', lost its potency at Temple. A spectator in the Strand, surveying its aftermath, would have been confronted with a moonscape of smoking ruins stretching from St Clement Danes to the Tower. The Strand had escaped disaster – either by good fortune or providence. Now it began to pick up the pieces, and it provided a home to the City's many displaced institutions, notably the Royal Society, in Arundel House.[42]

The Fire transformed London's physiognomy by levelling an estimated 13,500 properties, St Paul's Cathedral and eighty-seven parish churches, the Guildhall, the Royal Exchange and some fifty-two livery halls. Radical designs for the new City were proposed by Sir Christopher Wren, Sir John Evelyn and Sir Robert Hooke. A new breed of builders and developers, in the teeth of opposition from the City and government, came forward to meet a pressing demand for housing in London's western suburbs, which were booming from the near-permanent relocation of businesses after the Fire and the peace dividend from the end of war with the Dutch in 1674.

Typical of these new entrepreneurs was Nicholas Barbon. His father, the radical political leader Praise-God Barebone, owned the Lock and Key on Fleet Street, one of the last properties to be destroyed by the fire. Barbon had experienced at first hand the impact of the disaster and he quickly found his vocation in London's fertile property market. He purchased and demolished old properties and erected new terraced streets, beginning in east Strand with Crane Court, latterly the home of the Royal Society. Controversially, he demolished Essex House in the 1670s, replacing it with a new road, Essex Street, and nearby New Court, Garden Court and Devereux Court. The famous Grecian Coffee House relocated to the Devereux Court; in the 1690s and early eighteenth century it became a renowned meeting place for Whig politicians and influential members of the Royal Society, including Sir Isaac Newton, who once dissected a dolphin there. The Earl of Exeter obtained a licence to build on the site of his house on the north side of the Strand in 1673, which he leased to Barbon, who developed there the Exeter Change, 'in the style of a palace, adorned with many columns, large doorways and distinguished by decorations and statues'. Two new roads, Exeter Street and Burleigh Street, were built off the Strand.[43]

The Restoration period thus witnessed the demolition or re-development of most of the Strand's great houses, which never recovered from the damage inflicted by the English Civil War on the wealth and prestige of their owners (Figure 6). In addition to Essex House and Exeter House, the remnants of Durham House were pulled down in 1660, York House in 1672, Salisbury House in 1673, Arundel House in 1678 and Worcester House in 1694. Hungerford House – the London residence of the Earl of Hungerford, below what is now Charing Cross Station – was destroyed by fire in 1679 and replaced by a market. A mix of speculative building and new and fashionable properties appeared along virgin streets that marked the localities' former associations in their names, such as Villiers Street and Buckingham Street. The Strand's frontage diversified with taverns and shops, including the Golden Lion, White Lion and King's Head. The district to the

FIGURE 6. Detail from *The Strand in its Antient State, Anno 1547, the Strand and its Neighbourhood, Anno 1700*. Etching and line engraving by an unknown artist published by John Boydell, *c.* 1820. This half of the illustration re-imagines east Strand in 1700. The mighty maypole is clearly visible in the background. (Yale Center for British Art; Yale University Art Gallery Collection, B1998.14.834)

south also became home to famous men of letters and artists such as Samuel Pepys and Sir Godfrey Kneller.

Perhaps the most consequential development, though, was the opening by Thomas Killigrew of the new Theatre Royal in 1663, a stone's throw from the Strand. Theatres – indoor and outdoor – had existed from the 1570s, most famously on the periphery of the City on the south bank of the river, at Shoreditch and Blackfriars, but also in Drury Lane, where the Cockpit – an indoor arena – was opened in 1616. It briefly survived into the Restoration as the Phoenix (it had been burnt down by rioting apprentices in 1617) and was raided by the authorities when theatres were suppressed by the government. The Theatre Royal, however, was the first modern licensed theatre permitted to show serious drama and was the progenitor of the many theatres that now characterise the Strand and West End. Along with its rival in Lincoln's Inn Fields called Lisle's Tennis Court, it pioneered the use of moveable sets and other innovations, especially after it reopened in new premises in Drury Lane in 1674. Its popularity was assured by its royal patronage, talented dramatists such as Dryden and famous players such as the actress and royal mistress Nell Gwynne. The Theatre Royal typified the remodelling of the Strand as a destination for entertainment, pleasure and commerce at a time when London's centre of gravity was moving westwards, towards the court, and with the development of fashionable new districts, for instance Piccadilly. Still greater change lay ahead.[44]

CHAPTER 4

EIGHTEENTH-CENTURY STRAND

From Charing Cross we turn'd up towards the Strand, at the Entrance of which, I observ'd an Ancient Stone Fabrick, in the Front of it I beheld, with satisfaction, the handy-work of our Forefathers, in whose sully'd Antiquity I could discern, much more Beauty than my Genius can discover in any Modern Building.

Edward Ward, 1699[1]

[Improvement] can be no where pointed out with so much propriety as in the Strand, which from being dark, dirty and inconvenient, is become splendid, elegant, and in respect of what it was before, magnificent.

John Gwynn, 1766[2]

In the early morning of 13 August 1739, at about four o'clock, a fire broke out at the house of a stationer in the Strand and destroyed it, along with the house of the milliner next door. News reports said it did great damage to Mr Sisson, mathematical instrument-maker at the corner of the Beaufort Buildings.[3]

Jonathan Sisson was among the specialists who were centred on the Strand and whose work reflected the course of the speculative and probing age in which they lived. Situated in the middle of its south side, they experienced many changes throughout the 1700s as the Strand evolved into a greater thoroughfare in a more urbanised 'New London'.

To his good fortune that August, Jonathan Sisson's solidly built brick building withstood the scourge of the fire that consumed the adjacent timber-fronted buildings remaining from earlier days. Beaufort Buildings stood in a cul-de-sac on the high ridge of the Strand's southern slopes (at roughly 96 Strand, near where the Savoy Hotel presently stands). Located opposite the block between

Southampton and Burleigh Streets adjoining the open piazza of Covent Garden, they were among the newer premises of red brick with outer walls more than two feet thick that were reshaping the street and adjacent district during this building boom.

They were built by Henry Somerset, 3rd Marquis of Worcester and 1st Duke of Beaufort in the early 1680s over the place of his riverside mansion, Worcester House. Estates like it fell to pressures for more housing after the Great Fire, when new structures were erected hurriedly. Seizing this opportunity, the aristocracy undertook developments west of the City and speculated in building over the string of grand houses on the north bank of the river in order to realise the greater profits to be made from developing streets of townhouses and tenements. In the years up to 1720, the Strand saw itself becoming built up as never before, with the construction of many-storeyed dwellings. In time, their mixed occupancy transformed the Strand into the high street of what London guidebooks called 'the most flourishing city in Europe, and chiefest Emporium, or Town of Trade in the whole World'.[4]

By 1750, London was a city with 676,000 individuals, its population swelling to 900,000 in 1801.[5] With this growth, it also experienced artistic, economic, literary, scientific and political advancement that followed the establishment of the United Kingdom of Great Britain on 1 May 1707. As its capital, London expanded into a metropolis of unmatched attraction. Union created Europe's largest free trade area. London, as the main centre for Britain's trade and dominant market for its products, was the lodestone which attracted many people, Britons (like Sisson) and foreigners alike.

The Act for the Rebuilding of the City of London (1667), introduced after the Great Fire, stipulated building to 'Better Regulation, Uniformity and Gracefulness'. Structural standards were enforced regarding ceiling height, wall thickness, piping and guttering, and the use of wattle or lath and plaster; there were also standards for brick, tile and glass. The aim was to prevent the irregular building practices of the past – particularly building with combustible façade materials. Surveyors were appointed to ensure these necessary regulations were observed.

Advertisements in July 1728 promoted surveying and mapping to new standards and greater exactness than before, due entirely 'upon the Improvements made on the Theodolite, and [that] is the sole Invention of Mr. Jonathan Sisson'.[6] In the following year, Sisson was appointed Mathematical Instrument-Maker to Frederick, Prince of Wales. Instrument-makers (who specialised in making equipment for fundamental measurements) were among the era's celebrities, none more so than those in the most exacting part of the trade: measuring instruments for surveyors, navigators and astronomers. In a golden age of exploration, the new natural philosophy – science, as we know it today – was taking off and British breakthroughs that were led by new endeavours in astronomy would transform knowledge of the globe and of the natural world.

Jonathan Sisson built and sold barometers, wall quadrants and other instruments (Figure 7). His son, Jeremiah, continued his business, and supplied the Board of Ordnance; the Astronomer Royal, Nevil Maskelyne, supported him.[7] Observatories Europe-wide bought valuable theodolites, sextants and telescopes from their workshop.

The Sissons constructed a roof-top observatory which the architect Thomas Sandby captured in an illustration. His water-colour (now at the British Museum) shows the frame used to support a telescope and its steps, rising among the chimney tops above the Strand.[8] From this vantage point, ideally perched over the curve in the river, the Sissons could observe the city's ribboning length beside the river, with the vista of the Surrey Hills beyond its southern shore, as well as changes in their neighbourhood. Wren's new domed St Paul's Cathedral, its rebuilding declared complete on Christmas Day 1711, exemplified the power of measurement and calculation, and signalled a new era.

When candlelight was for many the principal light of a winter's day, the Sissons's Strand workshop was among those that established the high reputation for precision instrument-making that the London trade enjoyed. With Britain ahead of European competitors in its manufacturing ability, compatriots working nearby (including John Bird, John and Peter Dollond, Jesse Ramsden, John

FIGURE 7. Trade card of Jonathan Sisson, at the Sphere, the Corner of Beaufort Buildings, in the Strand, London. The sophistication of this trade card eloquently advertises Sisson's success from his observatory and workshop in Beaufort Buildings. (© The Board of Trustees of the Science Museum)

and Edward Troughton) upheld the Sissons's hard-won leadership in optics and the manufacture of accurate instruments of measurement. John Bird worked in Sisson's workshop before he established his own laboratory in 1745, in nearby York Buildings, some 240 feet westward on the Strand. He also tested the instruments that he made from the roof of his quarters: the first brass mural quadrant of eight-foot radius for the Greenwich Royal Observatory and the first marine sextant (which revolutionised navigation).

Steps away from the Sissons, John Dollond and his son Peter traded from their shop at the Golden Spectacles and Sea Quadrant, near Exeter Change in the Strand. Inventive opticians, they developed and perfected refractive lenses and brought the achromatic lens successfully to the market. The first telescope to be encased in a mahogany tube, 'a Dollond' was in high demand; Captain James Cook relied on several of Dollond instruments on his second voyage of exploration to the Pacific.[9] Optician to the Duke of York in 1763, Peter Dollond's trade card and bill papers show that his workshop made most kinds of optical and astronomical instrument, including the refracting telescopes that they invented and produced.[10]

In improving standards of measurement and computation from their workshops, innovators like them established the Strand as a hub of knowledge and innovation, their instruments raising to an unprecedented level the standing of Strand-side expertise within Europe's scientifically minded communities. Accurate charting and mapping were essential to successful exploration, trade and diplomacy; in the competition for instruments that enabled this accuracy, the elevated status of its instrument-makers drew eminent scholars and customers to the Strand. Jérôme Lalande, upon his appointment to the chair of astronomy in the Collège de France in 1762, came to the Sisson workshop and to the Royal Society. In 1786, Thomas Jefferson, future President of the United States, bought from Dollond on his only visit to London.[11]

This success endorsed John Dryden's hope that 'Among the asserters of free reason's claim, the English are not the least in worth or fame'.[12] Inquisitive minds among members (like Dryden) of the now seven decades-old Royal Society, many of them devout Christians, were stepping into the world of modern scepticism and secularism. They met post-Fire at Arundel House, and after its demolition they continued assembling on the Strand's eastern end. The Strand flourished from discoveries disseminated at the Society's assemblies (Lalande included in 1763) and ideas circulating in informal discussions that its members held in neighbouring circles that stimulated and expanded outlooks. Proud of this inventive 'Strand of Ideas', the author and lexicographer Dr Samuel Johnson considered more learning and science were to be found within its ten-mile radius than 'in all the rest of the kingdom'.[13] Its mathematically minded craftspeople imagined and assembled state-of-the-art instruments that stretched understanding of the world. Their steady approach to measurement and order contrasted with the disorderly nature of their snug Strandside surroundings in a crossroad location wedged between the two cities of London and Westminster.

Structures that expressed the regulatory forces of both these cities hemmed the under-a-mile-long quarter where these independently minded denizens hived. Temple Bar, bounding its east, was the Strand's portal to the City of London, and connected the City to its most direct route to Westminster. Wren's ornamental stone arch, built in 1672 of stones largely taken from older City buildings, replaced the razed wooden gatehouse that previously marked this approach. Wren's gateway, at its centre fourteen feet wide between its piers, barely passable for a double line of teams, impeded all trying to squeeze through it.[14] It slowed and inconvenienced pedestrians wending through its customary jumble of vehicles (post-chaises, loaded drays and handcarts, hackneycoaches, faster chariots) beside beasts herded to Clare Market for butchering. From the perspective of the Strand, Temple Bar increasingly came to be regarded as serving no purpose but to preserve the City burghers' privileges and prerogatives.

Dominating its western boundary, the seventeenth-century Northumberland House, the London residence of the Percy family, expressed dynastic privilege. Considered London's largest and most magnificent palace in 1821, its 150 rooms occupied riverside grounds at Charing Cross within its Strand façade, a wall 162 feet long, and three storeys high, with taller turreted towers at each end.[15] Frances Seymour, 7th Duchess of Somerset, when renovating it in 1750, attempted to make its street frontage 'look less like a prison' (as she wrote to a friend).[16] Its Strand-front balustrade once carried the ducal name. Atop the parapet of its gate went the Percy family emblem – the stiff-tailed Northumberland lion, six feet high, just under twelve feet long, cast in lead.

Placed before it, from 1675, on a Portland stone pedestal, Hubert Le Sueur's more modestly scaled equestrian statue of Charles I viewed Whitehall. Coaches reaching London at this point lumbered into the Golden Cross Tavern and Coach-house, opposite the statue and the ducal frontage. As depicted by Canaletto in 1752, then later by Thomas Bowles and other artists, passengers alighting at the Strand's western entry could glimpse buildings of irregular scale and detail that immediately flanked the street, such as the commercial premises beside the coaching tavern and those adjacent to Northumberland House (Figure 8).

On the street (judging from their observations), gentry and beggary met, stray dogs roamed, hawkers touted wares, cast-off cart or wagon wheels and timber planks lay abandoned. Ongoing makeover was a condition of the Strand. Remodelling and construction of buildings brought inconvenience to the street and its tributaries, wrought by excavations, rubble, scaffolding, wagons ferrying materials, and related noise. At the foot of the statue crowds took part in the punishment of those put in the pillory.

The Strand's three churches also defined its importance in the early decades of the century: St Clement Danes at its eastern end, St Martin in the Fields at its west end and St Mary le Strand standing between them. All three were newly constructed where earlier churches had stood. Together they adorned the street, flagged its length, met its urgent need with its increased population for extra church accommodation and marked its altering character as it was redeveloped. The Sissons, belonging to the parish of St Clement Danes, could appreciate Wren's rebuilt church

FIGURE 8. Thomas Bowles, *A View of Northumberland House, Charing Cross*. Engraving. The western entrance to the Strand. This aspect reproduces a 1752 painting by Canaletto, after whom many artists produced their versions of this popular view. (Yale Center for British Art, Paul Mellon Collection)

of 1682, which assumed greater prominence when architect James Gibbs elevated its spire in 1719.[17] The royal church of St Martin in the Fields (also by Gibbs, built from 1722 and consecrated on 20 October 1726) capped the importance of the Strand.

Landmarks such as these mattered when buildings on streets were not yet numbered. Addresses were tied to known monuments or events or described in general terms. For instance, Bull Inn Court (a seven-foot-wide alleyway off north-side Strand – where number 408 is today – leading to Maiden Lane) is listed in a 1772 guide as 'in the Strand, so called from being built where the Bull Inn formerly stood; which some Years since fell down, and kill'd 5 or 6 People in their Beds, besides hurting some others'.[18] Such a localised geography reflects the parochial nature of the communities in which residents lived. The mazy routes to their premises in the former villages of Charing, St Clement's and the Strand retained their largely medieval nature. Parishes were key in administrating essential services such as poor relief, and parish-based watchmen protected property. Painted and carved signboards overhanging the street identified premises, swinging from metal frames and creaking in the wind. Many of Hogarth's prints, such as *The Times of Day: Noon* (1738) and *Beer Street* (1751), show how ubiquitous these were.

Primarily for fire protection, the Metropolitan Buildings Act in 1774 graded buildings into classes and standardised further the structure of façades and limited exterior timber elements. Prominent constructions were not allowed to stand more than thirty-one feet (or three storeys) above ground. Among these were public buildings (churches, meeting houses, banks, barns), sizeable houses (with a ground floor larger than 900 square feet) and factories.[19] These new rules generally resulted in street frontages presenting a more unified appearance. Signboards endangered pedestrians upon falling and therefore were outlawed unless displayed flat up against the owner's wall; regardless, many continued in use.

The Sissons and Dollonds were two of the many families of Strand-side specialists operating businesses whose trade and shops gave the neighbourhood its vitality. They increasingly established interconnections among other specialists in their enterprising activities. In a world governed by systems of privilege and exclusion, when business custom came as much from patronage and association as from expertise, they worked with apprentices and craftspeople, and negotiated with one another to make work that necessarily engaged exact skills across different fields (as were involved in making books, to give one example). Their families united in business partnerships in their trade. Their combined achievements within an increasingly competitive market contributed to the Strand's fame.

Music-seller, engraver and instrument-maker John Walsh traded from the Golden Harp and Hoboy in Katherine Street off the Strand from about 1690. Appointed Musical-Instrument-Maker-in-Ordinary to William III in 1692, Walsh became the principal English music publisher of the early eighteenth century and was followed in 1736 by his son, also John. One of only three of his fourteen siblings to survive infancy, he succeeded his father as musical instrument-maker to the King. For over seventy years, the Walshes were influential, mass publishing music, largely by pewter-plate engraving, issuing more than 2,200 separate pieces. They introduced George Frideric Handel to the London public as an instrumental composer, and advertised their publications of his new music in the *Daily Courant*.[20]

Handel redefined the profession of musician beyond the work of serving a royal patron during his long English career. In the opera winter season of 1711, the London public came to know him as performer, director and composer with his directing of the performances of *Rinaldo* from the harpsichord (the songs for which John Walsh the Elder published). His display of arias, duets and orchestral effects with this first Italian opera written for the London stage (while catering to Baroque taste for spectacular stage effects) catapulted the young Handel to fame. *The Spectator* described this debut as being 'filled with Thunder and Lightening, Illuminations, and Fireworks; which the Audience may look upon without catching Cold, and indeed without much Danger of being burnt; for there are several engines filled with Water, and ready to play at a Minute's Warning, in case any such Accident should happen'.[21] Though lauded the Orpheus of the age, Handel found that the London public lacked interest in Italian opera, it being unfamiliar to them.

Music rang from the Strand's taverns, alehouses frequented by journeymen weavers, music clubs and occasionally its coffee houses. The Academy of Vocal and Ancient Music was established in 1726 to revive ancient church music. Aristocratic amateurs and eminent professionals (as well as Hogarth) featured among the Academy's sixty-nine members, with Handel playing; they met fortnightly till 1784 at the Crown and Anchor Tavern (opposite St Clement Danes – Figure 9). It housed many concerts performed by several societies. Playing there is thought to have first inspired Handel to bring oratorios to the stage. Here, on 23 February 1732, the Master of the Children of the Chapel Royal gave the first of three private

FIGURE 9. J. Maurer, *A perspective view of St Clement Church in the Strand.* Etching with engraving, 1753. The Crown and Anchor on the corner of Arundel Street in east Strand (right), opposite St Clement Danes Church, was a popular meeting place for musical clubs, scientists, the literati and political radicals. (Lewis Walpole Library)

performances of *Esther*. This was Handel's first oratorio in English and the first oratorio heard in England. Skilfully composing new music while adjusting to public preference, he introduced a form of composition that (his first biographer judged) was more suited 'to the native gravity and solidity of the English' than Italian opera.[22] So successful was the response that Handel was asked to give further performances of *Esther* in May. Six were presented at the King's Theatre, the first of its public performances that Handel gave. English tenor John Beard, who while still a boy had sung in Handel's *Esther*, won immediate success on his operatic début as Silvio in *Il pastor fido* with Handel's Covent Garden company in 1734. In their long association up to the 1750s, Beard sang more parts under the composer's direction than any other singer. Beard took a leading role in every one of Handel's English oratorios, odes and musical dramas (except *The Choice of Hercules*, which has no tenor part), including many first performances.

To the Strand came Johann (John) Christian Bach in 1762. He moved to London where German immigrant craft workers were developing the pianoforte, which he championed. When the Mozarts visited London in 1764–65, Bach (a lifelong player and teacher of keyboard instruments) improvised duets on the harpsichord with the eight-year-old composer Wolfgang, who subsequently always acknowledged Bach's influence. Bach performed the first solo on the piano in public in London in 1768.[23] London's expansion underpinned this cosmopolitan activity.

Hanoverian London was wealthy and bustling but unable to keep pace with its ever-growing population and uneven development. Visiting Prussian author Johann Wilhelm von Archenholz remarked on its incongruous disparity due to the rapid growth beyond the City, especially shoreside of the Thames, '[which] consists of old houses, the streets are narrow, dark and ill-paved.... The contrast between this and the west end is astonishing; the houses here are mostly new and elegant; the squares are superb, the streets are straight and open'.[24]

Villiers Street (off the Strand's western end) was built after 1675 over the demolished riverside mansion of York House. The York

FIGURE 10. *View of the stairs at York Buildings,' in the Strand, with the water works & a distant prospect of Westminster Bridge c. 1740.* A promenade lined with trees next to the River Thames, looking towards the York Buildings Waterworks and the tower of the steam engine on the right, with the York Watergate in front; on the left is the river with Westminster Bridge in the distance. Etching with engraving. (Lewis Walpole Library)

Building Waterworks at its riverside end (Figure 10) supplied water to about 2,500 houses. Destroyed by fire twice within six years, the waterworks were incorporated by an Act of Parliament (1691–92) and rebuilt with an engineering landmark. In 1712, its 100-foot-high water tower was the first in London to use atmospheric pressure generated by steam power to pump river-drawn water to higher quarters. In an industrialising age, this ingenious system (devised by Thomas Newcomen initially to pump water from deep-cut collieries) was reputedly London's first true steam engine. Foreign visitors (e.g. Swiss travel writer, César-François de Saussure, in England in 1725–29) marvelled at this curiosity, prominent on the riverfront, which was known as the York Buildings Dragon.[25]

Strand-side households paid for water which reached them for three hours daily through small lead pipes stemming from a large oakwood street-laid pipe. Those unable to afford this drew water from street-side pumps and wells. By 1731, the 'Dragon' seems to have produced more fumes than power; John Bird, living on Villiers Street, fell ill from the noxious air.[26] Respiratory illness was common: many reports testify to the need to escape the foul air that settled in the narrow streets and close courts, blackening buildings, furnishings, clothing. Pierre-Jean Grosley, in London in 1765, described the corrosive smoke-laden vapours and black rain that coal-burning produced:

> [The smoke] being loaded with terrestrial particles and rolling in a thick, heavy atmosphere forms a cloud which the sun pervades but rarely; a cloud which, recoiling back upon itself, suffers the sun to break out only now and then, which casual appearance procures the Londoners a few of what they call 'glorious days'.[27]

Negative aspects of metropolitan growth surrounded the Sissons and their contemporaries in toxic air, unsightly sprawl, filth and poverty. With enterprising Strand, the street of inspiration and creation that they and Samuel Johnson relished, went disorderly Strand: unruly, squalid, and dangerous.

The Strand's troublesomeness became as notorious as its renown for cosmopolitan shine and sociability. Its shops, de Saussure thought, were among Europe's finest, where passersby could look at the choicest merchandise from the four quarters of the globe. 'A stranger might spend whole days, without ever feeling bored, examining these wonderful goods.' But he found the streets were unpleasantly full, either of dust or of mud. 'This arises from the quantity of houses that are continually being built, and also from the large number of coaches and chariots rolling in the streets day and night.'[28] He was cruelly shaken in coaches, the roadways torn up by the narrow wheels of heavily loaded wagons and carts, many hauling coal and building materials up the Strand's northern flanks from riverside wharves, destroying and obstructing main connections.

With people largely getting about by foot, poet and playwright John Gay abhorred the way 'the rough Pavement wounds the yielding Tread; Where not a Post protects the narrow Space' (i.e. safeguarding pedestrians from vehicles).[29] Gay loathed the Strand in the hot dusty summer, the discomfort caused by the filth that tumbled through it in heavy downpours, the hurry that barricaded its passage, let alone thievery and its other dangers. Tread it with caution, and beware its impatient throng, he warned.

Social critic William Hogarth vividly pictured the complexity of Strand-side existence. Scenes from his series depicting four times of day reflect prosperous New Strand, where all sorts, from high and low life, overlap and privacy is minimal. We see the elites, the middling sorts, the industrious poor and the low-life types rubbing shoulders in Hogarth's depictions (as they also do in the novels of Daniel Defoe and Henry Fielding). Wealth and poverty coexisted with associated evils, particularly in the crime waves of the 1720s and 1750s, when de Saussure reported that criminal activity seemed undeterred by the frequent public executions – up to fifteen individuals hanged every six weeks.[30]

Fresh-faced country girls made up the largest number of arrivals from rural villages seeking employment (their wages in agricultural work had fallen in depressed rural regions).[31] The fate that befell some of these women concerned journalist Richard Steele, who wrote of one, 'it is not to be doubted but after she has been long enough a prey to lust she will be delivered over to famine' (or forced into crime from mere necessity).[32] Eyeing the gangs, prostitutes and reprobates of the street, satirist Edward (Ned) Ward pitied those who were brought to beggary by sexual licence, as at a brothel in the New Exchange, where nine-year-old girls were 'made as Ripe in Thought before they are out of their Hanging-Sleeves, as a Country Wench is at Five and Twenty'.[33] Newspaper reports and accounts of trials in the *Proceedings of the Old Bailey* note the perils inherent on the Strand, as could only be expected from its incessant human tide in which many were caught in the struggle to survive in an unequal society.

Many visitors reported the hostility shown to foreigners. Grosley, elected to the Royal Society in 1766, found workers engaged in street-side occupations (porters, chairmen, day-labourers) to be 'as insolent a rabble as can be met with in countries without law or police'; and de Saussure sounded warnings about the mob's disregard for authority, being particularly wild on holiday occasions.[34]

The elite were fair game. Thieves cut the braces of the coach of Mary Seymour, Duchess of Somerset, while passing through the Strand and, pretending to help her out, pocketed her gold watch and jewellery.[35] On 3 July 1749, a riot erupted at neighbouring brothels, one The Star on the Strand, and over successive nights riots spread widely. The authorities delivered rough justice as a warning to the mob: twenty-three-year-old Bozavern Pelez, a provincially raised innocent, was made an example of and hanged. In response, crowds who wished that he be pardoned, defying authorities, paid for and attended his burial at St Clement Danes.

Looking east, a portico resembling a classical temple gave entry to the 'New Church' of St Mary le Strand (see Figure 11 below). The small Baroque church was one of the first to be built under the Fifty Churches Act of 1710, when erected between 1714 and 1717 to the design of James Gibbs. Jewel-like at its island site mid-Strand, its Italianate style signalled a new approach to the streetscape. This was timely because parts of this area had fallen into dilapidation, with ruinous buildings needing reconditioning.

Somerset House, facing St Mary's southern side, mouldered in poor condition: its irregular wings jumbled in various Tudor and Stuart styles, its inner courtyard appeared antiquated. A rickety tenement encroached against its eastern end; propped up across Strand Lane, with timbers fastened into the ruins of a wall belonging to the crumbling palace, it blocked access to the river.[36] This typified the unsightly jerry buildings and shanties that sprang up despite Parliament passing rafts of Building Acts. Savoy Hospital, to its west, having fallen into dereliction, served as a barracks to the City garrison and a prison for deserters. It remained so until demolished for developments associated with the construction of Waterloo Bridge (1816–20).

The Strand itself was irregular, being of different widths. It was thirty feet six inches wide just mere paces west of St Mary's, between Burleigh and Katherine Streets, where Exeter Change over-reached into and narrowed the road.[37] St Mary's bottlenecked the Strand at its northern side, restricting wheeled passage, encumbering traffic. It overshadowed tenements opposite its northern side and was built up against those continuing eastward at Holywell Street to St Clement Danes. Small casement windows dimly lit the low-ceilinged rooms with raw rough beams in these tipsily stacked wooden buildings (some dating from before Hollar's days). They cramped space, confined the air and rendered the tight and darkened access in their passages increasingly filthy. Others pressed together into a block behind St Mary le Strand, to hide St Clement Danes from view. Wheeled vehicles mostly passed St Mary's along its southern side. Passage by St Clement Danes could be made only at that church's southern side, to the short distance to Temple Bar (see Figure 9).

With St Mary's situated amid decaying 'old Strand', artist Thomas Bowles idealised it in 1753 as the Strand's finest and largest edifice, grander than any surrounding building, the highlight of Stow's 'broad street' that served Londoners as their processional 'avenue', and improving it (Figure 11). Bowles, responsible for many eighteenth-century city views, perhaps reflected a new sentiment gaining currency, with increasing interest taken in remedying the

FIGURE 11. Thomas Bowles, *A View of Somerset House with St Mary's Church in the Strand London.* Engraving, 1753. This view, looking down east Strand with St Mary's Church and Somerset House (to the right), is an idealised portrait of the street to celebrate the new church alongside the old palace. (Yale Center for British Art, Paul Mellon Collection)

wretched conditions, miserable buildings and continued incon-
veniences experienced on the Strand when, by mid-century, such
improvement proved slow to materialise.

Detail in Bowles's illustration (Figure 11) shows how unmatched
are the church and its surrounding streetscape. The buildings are
disparate, irregular, many bearing overhanging signboards, some
with fronts of enclosed wooden balconies jutting over the street.
The coherence aimed at in the Building Acts is absent. Iron rails
fence the church off from the street and a watch house (built earlier)
standing before it suspends whatever gracious impression Gibbs
may have intended – 'Can any thing be more indecent, absurd
and tasteless, than the placing a paltry brick watch-house directly
in front of the New-Church in the Strand?', railed architect John
Gwynn.[38] In 1766, Gwynn published his London and Westminster
Improved, with a foreword written by his friend Dr Samuel Johnson,
who advocated in future building 'the utility and advantage of
Publick Magnificence ... wherein the good of the community is so
essentially concerned ... that regularity, convenience and propriety,
may hereafter take place of unskilfulness and disorder'.[39]

To Gwynn, the deeply rooted popular prejudice about London
being the 'finest city in the world' blinded most from seeing and
considering its defects. He urged that London needed 'publick improvements', with proper rather than piecemeal attention given to
building. He equated what Johnson called 'Publick Magnificence'
with public benefit. By improving public convenience, through
better roads and buildings, health benefits and thus prosperity
would follow.

With the Strand's commercial activities among its principal
attractions and market trading always regulated to some extent,
Thomas Twining (a freeman of the Weavers' Company) could enjoy
virtual monopoly or at least privileged trading rights. Formerly apprenticed to an East India merchant, he aimed to make a special
feature of tea (popular in London from around 1650), which he
supplied.[40] In 1706, he opened at the sign of the Golden Lyon in
Devereux Court, near the Temple. His son Daniel had joined in the
business by 1710 (as, later, did his grandson Richard). From their

Coffee House they sold 'all Sorts of fine Teas, Coffee, Chocolate, Cocoa-Nuts, Sago, and Snuff: Also true German Spaw, Pyrmont, Bath and Bristol [mineral] Waters, Arrack, Brandy, &c.'[41]

The printeries, bookshops and coffee houses in the vicinity of St Clement Danes to Temple Bar were popular. Coffee houses in the narrow dog-leg alley that housed Twinings included the Grecian Coffee House, where Royal Society members Sir Isaac Newton, Edmund Halley and Hans Sloane met alongside medical men. At the coffee house next door, Thomas Birch, historian and Secretary of the Royal Society (and a coffee-mill-maker's son), met eminent lawyers. Birch spent time with Jérôme Lalande, whose diary noted they also remained at Rawthmell's Coffee House in Henrietta Street (by Covent Garden) till 9.30 p.m. on Saturday 19 March 1763. The following evening, Lalande went to nearby Slaughter Coffee House, St Martin's Lane, favoured by the leading artists of the time. He noted in his customary matter-of-fact manner: 'I had four or five cups of tea there. It cost 10 d' (at a time when 30 d might have bought a day's skilled labour).[42]

Patrons at coffee houses and taverns dotted along the Strand and in its offshoots mixed in conversation in an informal environment in which new ideas germinated. In this Strand-side mix, thoughts about the public good took ground. In hand with the more solidly built fabric emerging on the street (such as the new church of St Mary le Strand), social affiliations made on it were altering perceptions. Sentiments were evolving in the course of the increasing specialisation of abilities at work within its community. The entrenched system of privilege based on property and customary rights paled in this age of new measures, which included the adoption of the Gregorian calendar in 1752, arguments about borough-mongering among the factional Whig ministry, and the independence of the legislatures of the American colonies declared in 1776. As Samuel Johnson said:

Now learning itself is a trade. A man goes to a bookseller, and gets what he can. We have done with patronage.... With patronage, what flattery! what falsehood! When a man is in equilibrio, he throws truth among the multitude, and lets them take it as they please; in patronage, he must say what pleases his patron, and it is an equal chance whether that be truth or falsehood.[43]

The Strand's many coffee houses, where different networks intersected, were unofficial knowledge bourses: heaven to speculative investors and tipsters alike, those stock-jobbing, as well as those after political gossip and debate (when parliamentary reporting was suppressed), or others after more philosophical discussion. And this when 'information' abounded on the street with the growth of a popular press, as occurred from 1695 once the Parliament revoked the government's right to review and censor print prior to publication. Periodicals such as those of Joseph Addison and Richard Steele flourished with the end of licensing (respectively *Tatler*, published tri-weekly between 1709 and 1711, and *The Spectator*, issued daily between 1711 and 1712).

The Spectator sought to bring knowledge out of its exclusive enclaves and sourced information from coffee houses and tea tables. These meeting places of daily life became the libraries and colleges from which information expanded. 'Learning' became a popular movement. César-François de Saussure saw how well attended coffee houses were, where the gazettes and other public papers were the greatest attraction to so many. He noted:

> All Englishmen are great newsmongers. Workmen habitually begin the day by going to coffee-rooms in order to read the latest news. I have often seen shoeblacks and other persons of that class club together to purchase a farthing paper ... some coffee-houses are a resort for learned scholars and for wits; others are the resort of dandies or of politicians or again of professional newsmongers.[44]

Strand publishing entrepreneur John Bell began the *Morning Post* in 1772 among his other ventures, which included a circulating library. Fourteen dailies were being published in London by 1790, including the *Morning Chronicle* (from 1769) and *The Times* (from 1788).

On Bow Street, one of the newer streets veering northwards from the Strand, resided notable 'Gentlemen of Honour and Abilities'. Publisher Jacob Tonson, theatrical manager John Rich (Handel's

one-time theatrical partner), barrister and novelist Henry Fielding
and his blind half-brother, the magistrate John Fielding, were
among those who wished for an end to the thefts committed
daily. They challenged the growing immorality seen in the neighbourhood. They wished 'to see the Strand and Places adjacent, as
decently inhabited as any other Part of his Majesty's Dominions'.[45]
Evolving among them was a sharpening sense of community
responsibility. They envisaged improved street lighting, watch
arrangements and law enforcement. Concerned about violence
and exploitation, close-knit Strand residents like them, who were
connected by commercial interests, sentiment and public spirit,
sought to make the Strand a centre of society.[46]

In February 1750, John Fielding, with Henry Fielding and
others, opened the Universal Register Office opposite Cecil Street
in the Strand, which aimed 'to bring the World … together into
one Place'.[47] Wanting to promote independence and relieve want,
they faced the intractable task of solving poverty and crime. Their
difficulty was working within the regulatory order of the day.
Taking example from parish practice, Henry Fielding applied the
voluntary principle to the task. Six volunteer 'thief-takers' began a
community policing of sorts with a uniformed detective force who
pocketed reward money paid upon convictions at the nearby Bow
Street Magistrate's Court, at which Fielding presided. Becoming
the third magistrate in 1754, John Fielding had by 1772 centralised
crime detection from Bow Street.

Artist William Shipley held related views about public benefit.
Artists studying under him at Beaufort Buildings included Richard
Cosway, William Hodges and Joseph Nollekens. Of a singular
mind, like Fielding, Shipley took a practical view to fostering endeavours in the 'Arts & Sciences'. On 22 March 1754, with other
co-founders meeting at Rawthmell's Coffee House, Shipley established the Society for the Encouragement of the Arts, Manufactures
and Commerce. It raised money by subscription to offer prizes for
demonstrations of skill and ingenuity in a heterogeneous range
of categories, many of them connected to specific trades and
manufacturing. The Society's office was at Denmark Hall (opposite

Beaufort Buildings), where members met on Wednesday evenings and held their exhibitions. Robert Dodsley, eminent publisher, bookseller and writer, commended Shipley's Society for its instantaneous success:

> The public spirit of this age is perhaps in no instance more remarkably shewn than in the flourishing condition of this valuable Society, whose sole object is the improvement of the polite and commercial arts in all their various branches, by exciting industry and emulation amongst all who can be moved either by honorary or pecuniary rewards.[48]

Within seven years the Society had over 1,000 members, many of whom were thought to be of the 'greatest quality and fortune', and was able to award prizes of nearly £2,000 per annum (£500,000 in today's money). Engraver John Boydell, working nearby at the Globe, near Durham Yard, joined the Society and from 1760 published engravings of the paintings that won its major prizes. It later became known as the Royal Society for the Arts, and Boydell became London's most famous print-dealer.

The undisciplined aristocracy had by mid-century largely relocated to homes in West London, where building boomed in the 1760s and 1770s, and there also began a busy time of building and refurbishing on the Strand. Steps taken to improve its safety began when in 1751 the vestry of St Clement Danes obliged those whose houses adjoined the street to hang out lights at their doors from end of light till midnight, under penalty of being fined. Further improvement followed with the Westminster Paving Act in 1762. Some sections of the Strand were newly laid with dark-coloured whinstone paving (a difficult material to work with, as it is so hard), which was paid for by public money.[49] Adjacent streets either side of the Strand (e.g. Norfolk and Holywell Streets) were similarly paved, where three-quarters of their residents paid the cost.[50]

In 1765 measures were taken to number individual addresses. New buildings called Adelphi, begun in July 1768, were built between the Strand and the river, over what was Durham Yard. A speculative project of the Adam brothers, they built this

development of twenty-four imposing terrace houses on top of
an embankment of arches. They made the houses level from the
Strand and set apart from the traffic of the waterside wharves and
warehouses loading and unloading vessels on the embankment.
John Gwynn, two years beforehand, had pointed out how the
situation of the Savoy was low and damp, and recommended that
a vaulted basement storey be made into extensive warehouses.[51]
Several other places between the Strand and the Thames might be
advantageously laid out in the same manner, he suggested.

The former Tudor and Stuart royal palace of Somerset House
was demolished in 1775 to make way for a huge courtyard building
for public offices, built in 1776–1801. Its up-scaled Strand frontage
on its north wing was refashioned into a classical expression (with
columns, balustrade and sculptural flourish, and a handsome
vaulted vestibule at its entry). It brought a new order of French-
inspired magnificence to the Strand. Extending 135 feet, with a
depth of 61 feet, the whole stood seven storeys high with two wings,
each 40 feet wide and 42 feet deep. The best materials were used:
it was faced with Portland stone; its roof covered with copper, lead
and Westmorland slate; Russian timber was used within. With the
completion of its south wing, it became London's most monumental building other than St Paul's and the Abbey. It added grandeur
to the riverfront as well.

The Royal Academy of Arts (established December 1768) moved
into New Somerset House's north wing at its Strand frontage from
1779. On 1 May 1780, the Academy opened its twelfth annual exhibition, the first to be held in the newly fashionable Somerset
House. Where once the elites promenaded its riverside garden,
now they rushed for the stairway to the Royal Academy exhibition
room (where the Academy's annual exhibition was held for the
next half century). Other learned societies also moved in: the Royal
Society from 1780, the Society of Antiquaries from 1781. The Royal
Navy and the Stamp and Inland Revenue Office occupied the
riverside wing in 1789. Somerset House epitomised the Strand's
new character as an administrative, business and ongoing sociable
centre.

Having harboured foremost cartographers and artists in the seventeenth century, the Strand became a printmaking centre in the eighteenth century. Boydell's fame as an art entrepreneur created a European market for English engravers and their prints, and brought Sophie von La Roche, Germany's first female novelist, to his shop on 28 September 1786. Its stock impressed her, but its location became the greater attraction: 'The shop is on the Strand, one of the city's most populous thoroughfares, and has a view either side'. As she saw it, the Strand itself was an exhibition of sorts from which much could be learned. She offers insight into how impressionable the street was and how lively were its *habitués*:

Here again I was struck by the excellent arrangement and system which the love of gain and the national good taste have combined in producing, particularly in the elegant dressing of large shop-windows, not merely in order to ornament the streets and lure purchasers, but to make known the thousands of inventions and ideas, and spread good taste about, for the excellent pavements made for pedestrians enable crowds of people to stop and inspect the new exhibits. Many a genius is assuredly awakened in this way; many a labour improved by competition, while many people enjoy the pleasure of seeing something fresh – besides gaining an idea of the scope of human ability and industry. I stayed inside for some time so as to watch the expressions of those outside: to a number of them Voltaire's statement – that they stare without seeing anything – certainly applied; but I really saw a great many reflective faces, interestedly pointing out this or that object to the rest.[52]

In theatrical productions, literature, pamphlets and visual attacks on the establishment, the pens of the day's masters of satire aimed sharply at failures of the government. Their sentiment un-doubtedly reflected coffee-house talk. Republican sentiment was inspired in the populace by politician John Wilkes, who pitted himself against King and Parliament. He successfully challenged the suppression of parliamentary reporting. Strong support for Wilkes on the part of lower-middle-class and artisan voters, and of the unenfranchised 'mob', presented an ominous challenge to the old oligarchical order. A memorandum from Sir John Fielding

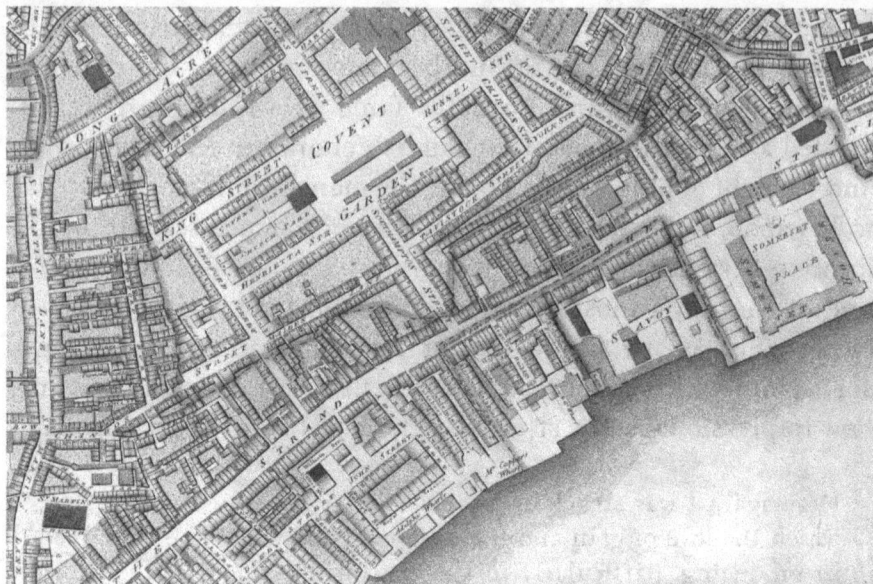

MAP 3. Richard Horwood, *Plan of the Cities of London and Westminster,*
1792–99. Section of one of thirty-two plates in Richard Horwood's monumental *Plan of the Cities of London and Westminster, the Borough of Southwark,
and Parts adjoining Shewing every House,* 1792–99. Seen by the river (right
to left) are Somerset Palace, Savoy Palace and Beaufort Buildings. (RSA,
London)

details the measures taken to respond to the group escorting
Wilkes from Temple Bar to his Princes Court, Westminster
home on 1 July 1771. On the restive Strand, measures were taken
at Beaufort Buildings, the Spread Eagle Tavern on the Strand
(opposite St Mary le Strand) and St Clement Danes.[53]

Following the French Revolution in 1789 and subsequent war
with France, the next quarter century saw growing tensions,
including domestic challenges (with poor harvests and food shortages in some parts), which affected the public mood. The Crown
and Anchor by St Clement's, where the Royal Society Club of
scientists held its annual dinner from 1780, became the stage for
dramatic events. After its expansion in 1790 allowed it to accommodate 2,500 people, it was used for large-scale political meetings.

Reformers and debating societies converged at the tavern in the riotous period that held sway in the early 1790s.

From it came James Gillray's image of the overthrow of the state in *The Hopes of the Party, prior to July 14th* (1791), in which Charles Fox, Whig leader, Member of Parliament for Westminster and a champion of liberty, raises an axe at the neck of George III beneath an image of the tavern.[54] 'From such wicked Crown & Anchor-dreams, good Lord deliver us' wrote Gillray, a loyalist, who viewed Fox's democratic views as traitorous. English loyalist, anti-Jacobin, anti-radical forces mustered in 1792 to form the Association for Preserving Liberty and Property against Republicans and Levellers, also known as the Crown and Anchor Association. 'Long May Old England, Possess Good Cheer and Jollity Liberty, and Property and no Equality', sang members. Touching a nerve, they spread like wildfire with over 2,000 local branches established quickly. They disrupted republicans' meetings, attacked printers of the works of the radical Thomas Paine's and initiated prosecution for sedition, but the movement was short-lived.[55]

The career of Covent Garden-born John Thelwall ran in a counter-revolutionary climate. A republican orator, writer, journalist, political reformer, democrat activist and good friend of Samuel Taylor Coleridge, Thelwall looked into the future. Whereas Jonathan Sisson had necessarily relied on aristocratic patronage, Thelwall forewent any such dependency, being unwilling to pay the price that patronage could extract. By 1793, he was a prominent member of the year-old London Corresponding Society, a federation of republican clubs and debating societies that met at the Crown and Anchor and that argued for parliamentary reform through equal representation obtained by universal suffrage and annual elections.[56] He was charged with high treason following lectures protesting at the arrest of fellow political activists. Tried on 6 December 1794, he was acquitted. Government officials who considered him to be the most dangerous man in Britain placed him under surveillance.

To head off potential disorder, restrictions were tightened on where common people might assemble. In 1795, Prime Minister

William Pitt the Younger's Gagging Acts received Royal Assent (the Treason Act and Seditious Meetings Act). Government spies monitored managers of debating societies and suppressed their activities. Vested interests resisted popular association.

Thelwall took rooms in the Beaufort Buildings at the cost of £130 a year (£19,598 today).[57] He found them small, but they were centrally located and could hold 500 people. He advertised the space as the Political Lecture-Room, where he 'will exercise that expiring privilege of once free and valiant Britons, the liberty of speech, by animadverting'.[58] He spoke on the constitutional right of Britons to annual parliaments, universal suffrage and freedom of popular association. Every Wednesday and Friday evening, the doors opened at 7 and lectures began at 8.15. Between 500 and 700 people paid sixpence each (equivalent to £2 today) to pack into the Beaufort Buildings twice a week to hear Thelwall speak against the inequities resulting from inefficient government, the increasing miseries of the industrial poor and the system of borough-mongering corruption so prevalent at the time.[59] Publishing these in his weekly twenty-four-page periodical *The Tribune*, Thelwall promoted democratic reform, universal suffrage and freedom of speech.

CHAPTER 5

NINETEENTH-CENTURY STRAND

Men, women, children, language, dress, and faces, Lords, Commons, Lackies, Pensioners, and Places, Whigs, Tories, Lawyers, Priests, and men of blood, And even *Radicals* – by all that's good! In a long street, just such as London's Strand is, 'Midst Belles and Beggars, Pickpockets and Dandies

George Cruikshank, 1820[1]

King: Our City we have beautified – we've done it willy-nilly – And all that isn't Belgrave Square is Strand and Piccadilly.
Chorus: We haven't any slummeries in England!

W. S. Gilbert, 1893[2]

Fog on the river obscured the flotilla escorting Lord Nelson's body from Greenwich up the Thames to Whitehall. Author Mary Berry, watching from alongside Whitehall Stairs, saw the coffin arriving and being lifted onto the bier which carried it to the Admiralty, where it spent the night before the funeral. The following day, 9 January 1806, it was placed in a funeral car modelled on HMS *Victory* and taken along the Strand to St Paul's Cathedral. At Charing Cross, she observed the multitude (the largest crowd in London up to that time): hushed, every head uncovered, 'from respect to the object, on which every eye was entirely bent'.[3] Seeing the procession, precocious draughtsman George Cruikshank, thirteen years old, sketched Nelson's funeral car.[4]

Eleven years later a large crowd celebrated the opening of the Strand Bridge of Life. Many among them who were from the Strand had closely watched it being constructed. The first stone for it was laid from the river's south bank. Only three bridges yet crossed the river between the City and Westminster, a long-standing grievance. Under the supervision of engineer John Rennie Senior, the new bridge reached the river's Strand side. Parliament renamed it Waterloo Bridge, to commemorate the decisive victory which ended the long conflict with France. When officially opened on 18 June 1817, George, the Prince Regent, with his brother, Frederick, the Duke of York, and Arthur Wellesley, the Duke of Wellington, in the uniforms of field marshals, led dignitaries across its span from the Surrey to the Middlesex side. Two hundred and twenty guns sounded on their procession, representing the number of cannon taken from the battlefield and heralding the future that peace could bring.

Inspecting the new bridge beforehand, in July 1816, Berry boated up to it and walked along it (being passable by foot though unpaved). A sharp-eyed observer of architecture, she thought its nine arches of 120 feet were beautiful. However, she considered the Tuscan columns placed between every arch were unsuitable: she disliked them because they served little functional purpose.[5] This utilitarian approach became characteristic of the years ahead. Living in Hanoverian and then Victorian England, Berry takes us, with both events, to the closing of an era and the opening of another age. With her we move into the very different worlds of experience occurring from the 1820s onwards when changing demands and advancing technology would mark the Strand and alter its shape and character for the rest of the century.

With the war that had convulsed Europe since the 1790s now over, more extensive and rapid change occurred in the years to the 1840s than had been seen at any time in central London's history since the Great Fire. More sober thought and utilitarianism displaced respect for tradition, veneration for heroes and militarised pomp. 'Reform', once considered synonymous with treason, would become a matter of first principles, with rights and liberties established on a new basis.

The Strand appeared at times to consist of two distinct parts in need of improvement. West Strand would see more building before 1851 than occurred on the street's eastern half, until some of the most substantial construction projects ever seen were completed at east Strand and in its vicinity. Debouching on the Strand between these halves, at Wellington Street, Waterloo Bridge highlighted how pivotal the street's east–west and north–south junction was to traffic seeking to cross London. With its sections of long-time choke points, the much-thronged Strand cried out for improvement, well before the new bridge brought it increasingly heavier traffic. It was an inadequate centre point for the capital of a global-power Britain.

Strand residents saw Waterloo Bridge as emblematic of the future that they anticipated for their street through the Regency of George, Prince of Wales, and his subsequent reign. For, in George IV's architectural ambitions, they saw opportunities to better link the Strand to London's burgeoning West End, and thereby remedy the neighbourhood's labyrinthine navigation, particularly abutting the junction where Charing Cross met Whitehall and Cockspur Street. The northern end of this connection had been poorly maintained for more than a century, since Wren planned the rebuilding of the Royal Mews. Architect John Nash envisioned a grand scheme of metropolitan improvements in an area facing the Royal Mews, taking in where Charing Cross joined Whitehall and Cockspur Street, as part of the management of crown property. Under the immediate auspices of the Prince Regent and under the authority of his government, Nash's design would be the first attempt to extensively renovate a substantial part of central London, on a great scale and to a systematic plan. Parliament approved Nash's design with the Charing Cross Act of 1826. Little objection followed the demolition of buildings for Nash's Charing Cross improvement scheme, to make way for what would be named Trafalgar Square (in about 1835). But reshaping the sloping ground from Charing Cross to Haymarket into a formal square, laid out before the newly established National Gallery, became an ongoing story through the century. Founded in 1824, a building for the Gallery was completed in 1837; improved extensions were finished in 1887 (and more were to follow later).

Strand rate-payers, frustrated at the little progress made by 1830 with supposed Strand improvements, petitioned Parliament

with complaints of how their trade suffered from the disordered
state of their thoroughfare.[6] They wanted it opened up for better
circulation as one of London's key crossroads, besides improvements to their streetscape. Miserable courts and alleys were swept
away from its north-west end, replaced by new streets, named
after the commissioners responsible for crown lands (Duncannon
and Agar Streets) and the monarch and his queen (King William
and Adelaide Streets). This 'quarter' awaited further development without the connection to the West End that Nash intended.
His proposals for street improvements fell victim to economies
enforced by the governments of the late 1820s and 1830s, when
House of Commons select committees investigated and withheld
expenditure on public buildings. The systematic improvement and
building reform called for by Strand-siders were to prove difficult
in the years ahead.

Meanwhile, in 1833, spectators followed Sir Charles Dance's
steam carriage on Wellington Street, which regularly drove past
them as it ran to Brighton at around six miles per hour. By 1836,
Walter Hancock's steam buses included the Automaton, which
could seat twenty-two passengers but that also had an eighteen-seat
trailer; allegedly it could travel at twenty-one miles per hour.[7] That
same year, the first of the London railways began.

London extended and spread out, and by 1841 had grown to a
metropolis of over 2.2 million inhabitants. More traffic travelled
through the Strand and wended through its intricate alleys, lanes
and passages. Gloomy and unsightly, their deficient drainage and
poor air circulation injured the health of those occupying them.
They were tortuous for the traffic passing through them. Heavy
wagons moved at walking pace. Turnings-off, deliveries and
loading deadlocks impeded passage. Repairs or the installation of
gas and water pipes regularly broke up leading streets, subjecting
them to the slow process of relaying the road – bedding, ramming
and recementing its wooden blocks. (Wooden roads, quieter and
less costly than stone, were a feature of Victorian London.)

The Strand was in need of coherent planning. Nothing had
relieved its pinched eastern bottlenecks by St Mary le Strand and

Temple Bar (its plinth lay buried in accumulated mud).[8] Nearby, the carriageway at Fetter Lane was just nine feet wide.[9] Storms made the Strand impassable. It became a canal after a deluge in July 1806, when the sewers could not carry off the water.[10] In 1661, John Evelyn's pamphlet *Fumifugium* had offered remedies for the smoke that polluted London. Steam engines, adopted more widely by the 1820s, polluted even more, with heavier soot and louder noise, and also caused water shortages. The sweep of the Strand's roadway, which was laid with wood paving in 1843, proved abortive when, two years later, the authorities of St Clement Danes advertised for sale as firewood the wood paving laid down between the top of Arundel and Norfolk Streets; the intention was to revert to the noisier stone paving as before.[11]

Despite these problems, west Strand assumed a brighter aspect – suited to its location cornering Whitehall – with the arrival of the Lowther Arcade (1831), Charing Cross Hospital (1831), Exeter Hall (1831) and Hungerford Market (1832–33) and Hungerford Suspension Bridge (1845). The Lowther Arcade – named after William Lowther, 2nd Earl of Lonsdale, the Chief Commissioner of Woods and Forests (1828–30), responsible for the west Strand improvements on crown property – occupied a triangular plot from the Strand's north side at Charing Cross to Adelaide Street by St Martin's churchyard. It brought a fresh, lively note to the street. Diagonally opposite the sombreness of Northumberland House's walled frontage, the Lowther was an architecturally attractive venue that also won London hearts by its democratic display of varied products and experiences. A mall, a bazaar and museum combined in one (resembling what present-day consumers might expect and enjoy in a city landmark), the Lowther would be fondly remembered in song and in stage plays well past Edwardian days.

It catered to an upper- and, increasingly, middle-class clientele who promenaded its elegant walkway, 245 feet long and roofed with glass domes. Under natural light (as well as gas and oil lamps), visitors perused the temptations offered by its twenty-five shops (with six on the Strand), displaying wares from jewellers and silversmiths to merchants of inexpensively priced toys and fancy goods.

Others offering 'minor utilities' made it 'the Bagdad of housekeeping odds and ends' for journalist George Augustus Sala. 'It is noisy ... resonant with the pattering of feet, the humming of voices, the laughter of children, the rustling silk dresses, and buying, selling, bargaining', and from which people leave 'with an armful of toys looking sunny with good humour'.[12]

Punch noted how the wider and loftier Lowther rivalled Piccadilly's Burlington Arcade and drew greater numbers, especially women and children.[13] It became prominent for the 'entertainment' at its north end, where the Royal Adelaide Gallery exhibited objects that instructed and amused. The Gallery was established by the Society for the Illustration and Encouragement of Practical Science, incorporated by Royal Charter in October 1834. It daily displayed over its floors interactive exhibits related to general science and technology. Over time its split-level Long Gallery exhibited upwards of 3,000 models of machinery, steam boats, railroads (including Richard Badnall's eccentric Undulating Railway), as well as sculptures and paintings and an ellipsoidal balloon described as the new aerial machine.

Strand-side experimenters, practical inventors and aspiring industrial entrepreneurs flocked to it, many of them unsung 'foot soldiers' of the engineering profession. Elijah Galloway and Freeman Roe each gained new patents (granted for England in April 1845) for their respective improvements to propel railway carriages and manufacture pipes for conveying water and other fluids (developments that would necessarily preoccupy minds of the day).[14]

This successful meeting place, first known as the National Gallery of Practical Science, was a forerunner of today's Science Museum. The novel and useful objects exhibited attracted 80,375 paying visitors in 1835.[15] For a shilling (close to £8 today), they could see magnetic, optical and chemical instruments and apparatus, such as those manufactured by Irish-born magnetician, optician and scientific instrument-maker Edward M. Clarke, of 11 Lowther Arcade. Demonstrations of instruments such as Clarke's gold-leaf electroscope brought the new electrical science and that of galvanism to those who were outside the scientific elite (or high society), or were dismissive (as was Michael Faraday) of the Royal Society's offer of membership to socially eminent non-scientists.

Working together at the time, Faraday and Charles Wheatstone, close friends and probing thinkers, lived for applied science. From modest backgrounds, eleven years apart in age, both were among the world's greatest 'scientific experimentalists' (though neither received a formal scientific education). Technology developed from their experiments would usher in a revolution that would radically change life and manners. Faraday's laws of electromagnetic induction (1831) – the notion that electricity could act over a distance to induce a current in other, unconnected wires – laid the foundations for the future electrical industry; and his laws of electrolysis (1833) underpinned much future commercial activity (as with electroforming in the production of gramophone records). His appreciation of natural laws (that forces are conveyed by fields) advanced understanding of electricity, magnetism and light.

The challenge of communications inspired Wheatstone. He explored acoustics, optics, synchronic time and electrical generation. He pioneered precise electrical measurements, invented the first stereoscope and the chronoscope in 1840, and made the electric telegraph practicable. This was ironic because, being innately shy, he rarely lectured and relied on Faraday to outline his findings. Their association demonstrated the interdependency of scientific investigation and the technological benefit of its results. Modern telecommunications and understanding of the universe derive from their combined efforts.

While they adopted new approaches to explore concepts which would shape the future, property for sale on the Strand was promoted as offering 'opportunity'. Building materials and three capital houses on its north side, facing Wellington Street, occupied by the Lyceum Tavern, were advertised together in 1833. This promotion appeared with advertisements for literature by Lord Byron and the third volume of *Principles of Geology* by Charles Lyell, FRS, Professor of Geology in King's College London.[16] The College, a Church of England institution, was founded in 1829 upon the bitter contest over conferring degrees that followed the founding of the non-sectarian London University in 1826 (later known as University College London). King's College was soon preoccupied with funding, staffing and erecting from 1831 a building designed by Sir Robert Smirke on the east end of the crown-held land of Somerset House. When finished in 1834, it completed Somerset House's riverside frontage. Wheatstone was Professor of Experimental Philosophy (Physics) at King's College London for forty-one years (1834–75). He conducted experiments on telegraphy in which Charles Lyell, the scion of Scottish gentry, found pleasure.[17]

From 1831 to 1833, Lyell occupied the newly created Chair of Mineralogy and Geology at King's College. Writing to his lifelong friend, fellow geologist and palaeontologist Gideon Mantell, he described his appointment by a group of orthodox prelates, the Bishop of London, the Archbishop of Canterbury and the Bishop of Llandaff:

> They considered some of my doctrines startling enough, but could not find that they were come by otherwise than in a straightforward manner, and (as I appeared to think) logically deducible from the facts, so that whether the facts be true or not, or my conclusions logical or otherwise, there was no reason to infer that I had made my theory from any hostile feeling towards revelation.[18]

Mantell, the dedicated country doctor and cobbler's son who famously identified the existence of dinosaurs, was then lodging in Norfolk Street, and did not live in London on a permanent basis till 1844. Mantell's paper on his discovery of the iguanodon was read at a meeting of the Royal Society in the grand assembly hall of Somerset House in early 1825.[19] This utilitarian Age of Science tested Christianity proper. Lyell's *Principles of Geology* (1833) challenged Bible literalists by demonstrating (as Mantell's dinosaur finds had suggested) that the planet was far older than they had supposed. Lyell (together with approximate contemporary Charles Darwin) presented the evidential backbone for our realistic view of the universe.

Exeter Change, the older arcade of shops that encroached on North Strand between Southampton and Burleigh Streets, was

demolished, clearing passage on the street that it had long ob-
structed. In its place arose Exeter Hall, opened on 29 March 1831.
Erected speculatively and privately financed (like the Lowther), it
was devised for holding public meetings, in step with the mood of
the day. Calls for parliamentary reform grew apace in the shadow
of the hardships of recovery from the Napoleonic wars, harvest
failures, food shortages and an economic slump. The authorities
feared political radicalism and large political gatherings, especially
following the Peterloo Massacre in 1819 (with shocking casualties), and they made outdoor meetings illegal. Exeter Hall met
the growing call for public meetings. Investors in the building
could undoubtedly see it as representing 'polished life' (as did
the Lowther). Bankers Thomas Baring and Henry Drummond
signalled at its opening that Exeter Hall was a non-sectarian auditorium where some of the 336 philanthropic and 50 philosophic
institutions in London could gather.[20] Exeter Hall became the new
place of public assembly, the heart of reforming London, the centre
point for the improving Strand and central to much of Victorian
London (Figure 12).

The main hall, 130 feet long by 76 wide, with a platform to accommodate 500 persons, offered 9,880 square feet to crowds of
3,000 or more.[21] Members of religious, benevolent and reformist
organisations gathered in it: the Bible Society, Christian preacher
Charles Spurgeon, abolitionists, suffragists, the Ragged School
Union, the Temperance Society (though the Hall's cellars were let
to a wine merchant). Within three months of opening, it witnessed
the earliest anti-alcohol protest in London.[22] Friends of the anti-
slavery cause met there in April 1831, and over 3,000 attended the
concluding meeting of the World Anti-Slavery Convention in June
1840. Prince Albert made his first public appearance in England
there, when he addressed abolitionists.

Over seventy general meetings held in the Hall each year contributed to its revenue, as did the musical entertainment provided by
London's Sacred Harmonic Society.[23] It became the home of choral
music. Over 500 sang Haydn's oratorio *The Creation* in January 1847.
Aspiring writer Mary Ann Evans (yet to adopt her pseudonym of

FIGURE 12. *A Meeting at Exeter Hall on the Abolition of the Slave Trade.*
Engraving by H. Melville after T. H. Shepherd, *c.* 1841. The Hall was a
popular public meeting place in Victorian London. (Wellcome Collection)

George Eliot) attended Felix Mendelssohn's conducting of his new
oratorio *Elijah* at the Hall on 28 April 1847. Shortly after, she wrote,
'It is a glorious production and altogether I look upon it as a kind
of sacramental purification of Exeter Hall, and a proclamation of
indulgence for all that is to be perpetrated there during this month
of May'.[24] It was Mendelssohn's tenth visit to London that spring,
and he was given a tumultuous reception. Upon his untimely death
on 4 November that year, members of both the Society and the
orchestra dressed in mourning and marked their association with
Mendelssohn with a performance of Handel's 'Dead March' from
Saul, with the audience standing.

Thomas Joseph Pettigrew, surgeon and antiquarian engaged
in Egyptology, notorious impresario of the staged unwrapping
of mummies, made Exeter Hall the centre for 'platform culture'.

American essayist and transcendentalist R. Waldo Emerson, invited to address the Hall in 1848, entranced his audience, his eloquence such 'as no orator ever succeeded ... [he] became a Titan'.[25] Exhibitions staged there included that in 1862 by Cruikshank, Hogarth's successor as pictorial satirist and moralist. The fledgling Young Men's Christian Association (YMCA) inaugurated a popular series of lectures in 1845 that addressed the growing cultural authority of science (the series ran until 1865). The Hall headquartered the militantly anti-Catholic Protestant Association and later the Society for Irish Church Missions. Religious and philanthropic assemblies, especially by those of Evangelical sympathies, used it and its meeting rooms down to 1907. 'No other place in the world has attracted such crowds of social renovators, moral philosophers, philanthropists, and Christians', wrote Canadian author William McDonnell. He stressed its influence, as in its shout for human rights, by which 'as is always the case, the voice of Exeter Hall is heard over all the earth'.[26]

Beliefs and opinions were contested there, notably scientific findings and theories underpinning the ideology of free-thinkers and positivism, a belief in progress rooted in scientific theory and practice, which in some circles was displacing faith. Critics wishing to be untrammelled by religious dogma reported that Exeter Hall was devoted principally to the use of fanatics and religious madmen – the place where 'the religious hypocrites of the day rant and rave till they are nearly suffocated'.[27] Traditionalists rankled: 'Bigots may bellow, and singers may squall, But Shakespeare is hooted from Exeter Hall'.[28] Pertinently, others observed how 'A traveller along the Strand, about six o'clock on a Sunday evening, would wonder what could be the meaning of a crowd which literally stopped the progress of public vehicles, and sent unhappy pedestrians round the by streets, in utter hopelessness of getting along the wider thoroughfare'.[29] The rush through the Strand to assemble beneath Exeter Hall's roof brought traffic to a standstill, adding to the many city 'nuisances' which vexed Strand-siders. Corinthian columns, three storeys high, grandly flanked its Strand portico to an impractically narrow doorway into the building, inside which circulation was equally awkward; serious concerns were expressed about a crowd crush.

Conditions on the Strand called for practical benevolence, which marked the work of its neighbourhood medical doctor, Benjamin Golding. In 1815, most physicians relied on private practice serving the rich but, prompted by his neighbourhood's overcrowding, Golding opened his home every morning to treat the poverty-stricken population of largely distressed Irish labourers and costermongers inhabiting hovels and tenements in the area around west Strand and St Martin's Church. Demand was such that in 1818 Golding began the West London Infirmary and Dispensary, which grew into a combined hospital and medical school. It relocated soon to 28 Villiers Street, with twelve beds and Pettigrew as its first surgeon. In 1827 it was named the Charing Cross Hospital and began fundraising with royal assistance. Tightly managed and associated with the newly established London University, it could erect its own building with Decimus Burton the architect, its foundation stone laid on 15 September 1831 as a portion of the west Strand improvements. Its new building went up behind St Martin's and the Lowther Arcade, its Grecian-styled façade rounding on the corner of Agar Street at its eastern end just off the Strand. Opening in 1834 with sixty beds, it made Charing Cross a medical hub: it was adjacent to Charing Cross's Ophthalmic Hospital, established in 1816 for relieving the poor of diseases of the eye and which by May 1850 had treated nearly 80,000 persons and restored sight to nearly 2,000.[30]

Notably, in 1850, Charing Cross Hospital treated no fewer than 3,200 accident and emergency cases related to excavating and building alone.[31] In the year ending July 1852, it dealt with 17,995 patients, including 1,200 inpatients. Their injuries speak of the neighbourhood perils encountered daily: 821 people falling from elevated positions; 246 injured by vehicles and steam-powered machinery; 99 hurt in explosions or suffering burns; and 900 having been assaulted or bitten by animals.

John Timbs's *Curiosities of London* (1855) praises Charing Cross Hospital as being among London's 'palaces of humanity'.[32] But it was more than a monument to Christian charity, unlike most of the then voluntary hospitals, which failed to attend to the growing population. They relied on subscriptions, whereby subscribers had the right to 'recommend' patients deemed worthy of 'charity' and therefore fit to be admitted. Golding's charity, however, was distinguished from its start as being intended for public benefit, achieved through combining medical care with a self-supporting medical school. Its receipts partly underwrote the hospital, and both existed to provide medical education and advance medical science.

Among the school's first students (in 1840) was David Livingstone, the explorer and missionary, who paid fees for courses of medical practice, midwifery and botany. He wrote, 'It was with unfeigned delight I became a member of a profession, which with unwearied energy pursues from age to age its endeavours to lessen human woe'.[33] Joining the school in 1842, on a free scholarship, was seventeen-year-old Thomas Henry Huxley, the autodidact who had aspired to be an engineer before his focus turned to the working of anatomy, morphology, physiology. His time there imbued him with his love of science; he would become a brilliant comparative anatomist who profoundly influenced the progress of medicine and ultimately presided over the Royal Society.

Standards of medical training had been very variable and so were tightened in the first half of the nineteenth century. The British Medical Association pushed for regulation and to raise medicine to the status of a profession (resulting in the Medical Health Act 1858). Through the second half of the century leaps were made in the understanding of infectious diseases, in medical learning based on observation, and with the hospital organised (with a university and medical school) to educate and research. At both ends of the Strand advances were made. In addition to the Charing Cross medical school, King's College and its hospital led in this. Medical instruction at King's College took off with Robert Bentley Todd at the helm of its medical school, when appointed to the Chair of Physiology and Morbid Anatomy at the age of twenty-seven, in 1836. Funded by voluntary contributions, its medical staff began offering care from the St Clement Danes workhouse on Portugal

Street, which had been deemed by the Poor Law Commission to be unfit for human habitation. The surrounding area, adjacent to the burial ground of St Clement Danes, was disfigured by poverty; the destitute were 'congregated as thickly as a hive of bees in the miserable dens around Clare Market, Drury Lane and Seven Dials'.[34] The area was in desperate need of the medical care which King's medical staff gave.

King's College Hospital was founded in 1839, shortly after body-snatching scandals shocked people and in the midst of the increasing needs of the neighbourhood's poor. It opened with fifty beds in January 1840 but had grown already to 120 beds by mid-summer. They were made available for teaching purposes, with the hospital dependent on the medical school.

Charing Cross Hospital and King's College Hospital were established when hospitals generally received only cases of temporary and curable illness or injury. Terminally ill patients ('Incurables'), 'hopeless' cases and those with communicable diseases (e.g. consumption) were forbidden hospital care and voluntary charity. Those who were workhouse inmates were in the hands of untrained 'night-watch nurses', such as the gin-swilling, clumsy Sarah Gamp who had little thought for her patients in Charles Dickens's *Martin Chuzzlewit* (1844).

Thomas Huxley described conditions he saw in the courts and alleys he walked through from Charing Cross to the College of Surgeons, Lincoln's Inn Fields (adjacent to King's College Hospital) when pursuing his medical studies:

> Alleys nine or ten feet wide, I suppose, with tall houses full of squalid drunken men and women, and the pavement strewed with still more squalid children. The place of air was taken by a steam of filthy exhalations; and the only relief to the general dull apathy was a roar of words – filthy and brutal beyond imagination – between the closed-packed neighbours, occasionally ending in a general row. All this almost within hearing of the traffic of the Strand, within easy reach of the wealth and plenty of the city.[35]

From his experience working as a doctor's assistant, he knew that drink and disease shortened the lives of the indigent. When he once examined a sick girl in a place where other women (one a deformed sister of his patient) were busy shirt-making, he saw that his patient needed better food than the bread and tea on which they were living:

> I said so as gently as I could, and the sister turned upon me with a kind of choking passion. Pulling out of her pocket a few pence and halfpence and holding them out, 'That is all I get for six and thirty hours' work, and you talk about giving her proper food'.

The 1851 census reported that the Strand district, at 167 acres, was the most densely populated in London, with 11.4 persons to an inhabited house. There were though a diminishing number of houses in the district, some 674 fewer than the census of 1841.[36] This reflected the changing nature of London's central districts (the 'heart of London'). Warehouses, printing businesses, offices as well as railways replaced large numbers of houses tenanted by the working classes and the poor. Rents rose with the shrinking number of properties. Those occupied by the poor were over-crowded. Their miserable nature and unfitness for occupation degraded morals and hastened loss of health and life. The infectious diseases they harboured made them an issue of public health.

The stern facts of social inequities so visible, Louisa Twining directly responded to the Strand she knew so well and to its immediate needs. Among the fifth generation of Twinings on the Strand, she was born in 1820 at 20 Norfolk Street on South Strand, close to St Clement Danes and in its parish, and only some a hundred steps from her family's tea shop.

Characteristically among Strand-side compatriots, the Twinings supported their neighbourhood. Richard Twining III, Louisa's brother, funded the Strand's medical institutions and served on their management committees. He sustained the Public Dispensary on Carey Street and was Honorary Treasurer of King's College Hospital for thirty years.[37] Louisa raised funds when these were needed for its new building, as Secretary of the Ladies' Committee. Her background equipped her for her life's work as a social reformer. Aware of social wants, she spent her life taking

steps to meet them and advocating various reforms. Responding
to issues associated with the introduction of the new Poor Law
in 1851 she sought to improve the medical care of the indigent
poor, and in her advocacy for the destitute she fostered recognition of women's public service. St John's House (established by the
Anglican Church in 1848) in Norfolk Street, Strand, trained nurses,
organised as a lay 'sisterhood', who had to be women over the age of
twenty-eight (and have the requisite level of commitment). Louisa
Twining supported the concept of systematic training for nurses
that Robert Todd started at King's College Hospital with St John's
House, an autonomous women's residential training college of
sorts. Selected applicants who joined St John's House were the
first nurses to be systematically trained in a teaching hospital and,
upon certification, to work as nurses elsewhere. Taking charge of
the wards of King's College Hospital from 1856, St John's House
nurses established the benefit to patients of clinically trained
nursing. Upper-class women (for whom charitable engagement was
a recognised activity) and working-class women (who tradition-
ally provided hospital nursing services) apprenticed to them, took
the same training and worked side by side in the wards. St John's
House was entirely distinct from King's College Hospital, where
it provided nursing for a fixed fee. This innovative model was
inspiring. It generated nursing reforms during the 1860s and 1870s
upon its adoption by eleven other teaching hospitals in London.
St John's House expanded into three properties in Norfolk Street. It
eventually provided nursing for Charing Cross and other hospitals,
as well as private nursing services and the nursing of the sick poor
at their own homes. It was a model for middle-class women to work
in paid occupations. The practice became more readily accepted by
the 1880s.

Louisa was the iron hand in a velvet glove that upbraided the
hard-heartedness of Somerset House's Office of Poor Law Commissioners and England's Board of Guardians with authority
over the Strand Poor Law Union, which included six Strand-side
parishes, from the City to Trafalgar Square. To obviate the injustice
to the indigent, she opened a Fund for Destitute Incurables, from

which workhouses received grants to improve the care they gave. She established the Workhouse Visiting Society, a subscription-raising body to introduce a voluntary system of visiting workhouses by educated middle-class women who could help ameliorate workhouse conditions. As its Honorary Secretary, she mustered support from wives and daughters of Members of Parliament and people of high position and influence who could sway public opinion. She thanked *The Times* and other publications for their support, but always urged attention to what more was needed. Endorsing her sensible methods were *The Lancet* (first published in 1823, by Thomas Wakley, in Norfolk Street); the National Association for the Promotion of Social Science and associated journalist, feminist and social advocate Frances Power Cobbe (who wrote in the neighbourhood of the Strand from the 1860s to 1875); and the Royal College of Surgeons. In 1884, she become one of the first female Poor Law guardians, and held the post until 1890. She continued her advocacy into 1911, seeing the introduction of National Health Insurance that year, before her death in 1912. Twining's empathy for her neighbourhood's community ranks her among the Strand's leading lights, who worked to improve social well-being and handed on the baton for progressive change.

***

'The Great Exhibition: that is the thing. All London, is speculating on its results, and preparing for the onslaught', the press trumpeted in April 1851.[38] The Strangers and Emigrants' Office relocated from the Lowther Arcade to 13 Wellington Street, expanding its offices to register details of lodging houses and private dwellings which would receive visitors.[39] With additional omnibuses and cabs causing havoc on the Strand, and hoteliers making ready, expectations grew of what the Great Exhibition of the World of Industry of All Nations would mean to the Strand.

London now had some 2.5 million inhabitants. If the imminent arrival of crowds excited some, it concerned others. Naysayers cautioned that the Exhibition's Crystal Palace, designed by Joseph Paxton, would be the sole attraction and so rob Strand purveyors of business. 'Like a huge Maelstrom, it will swallow up the time, money, and attention, not only of all strangers, but of the great mass of the inhabitants of the metropolis for months to come'.[40] The hubbub with the Exhibition's opening on 1 May 1851 rang in most ears. Paxton's building, with its vast scale, transparent walls, crystal fountains, peals from organs, marble statues and the works exhibited, drew rapturous reports on first impressions. Notwithstanding the cold, variable and often ungenial weather, and the high prices charged for admission, the numbers who daily thronged the Crystal Palace were counted in thousands. The press reassured readers that the annual 'May Meetings' in Exeter Hall were ongoing:

'The Saints' are in full feather, and among the beards and foreign costumes which make their appearance in the Strand and Regent-street, the raven black and spotless white of the 'serious' frequenters of these meetings, form a conspicuous feature.[41]

All the world seemed to be in London that summer:

The place seems suddenly transformed into the capital of the universe, our own share in the muster being none of the largest.... To detect a real English face, one has to turn to a cabstand, and feelings of sympathy and compatriotism are positively excited by the individual on the box.[42]

Dismissing their usual irritation with the street's cab drivers, spellbound Strand-siders stirred to civic responsibility.

The whole world is in our streets, and it rests with us to show by our behaviour that general good-fellowship and civility are not in-compatible with free institutions, insular independence, and just national pride.[43]

The spectacle of the shuttling crowds on the Strand was re-markable. 'And Such shoals and crowds of human beings – the roofs of vehicles clad, and the interiors filled, with visitants, all crowding westward!' (to Hyde Park).[44] Omnibuses bore large signs: 'Knightsbridge, all the way to the Exhibition'. Every four-wheeled conveyance was put to use behind a pair of horses. Alighting passengers scrambled as best they might for space and safety in the cramped, unventilated conveyances, none lofty nor wide enough for its passengers. 'In the Strand, the stream was visibly great at seven in the morning; while the returning crowd was like that of dispersing theatre audiences, from five in the afternoon till eight or nine at night.'[45] Mrs Keeley declared before the footlights, 'Everything's dear in Exhibition time: why, they charge 4d now for a threepenny 'buss!'[46]

Arresting exhibits in the Crystal Palace were notable *objets de vertu* from Strand-side horologists, silversmiths and jewellers, besides items from its publishers, engineers and inventors. Edward Dent, Charles Bielefeld and the Angell family (in new showrooms at 10 Strand, Charing Cross, from 1849), upheld the reputation that Strand shops enjoyed for variety, artistry and skilled workmanship. Joseph Angell (junior) received a prize medal for his silver-gilt tea and coffee service, embellished with engraved decoration and *champlevé* enamel.[47] Prominent on Paxton's central avenue were Dent's large church clocks: his turret clock, reflecting technological prowess, won him a Council medal. There were also watches from John Jones (338 Strand) and Charles Frodsham (84 Strand), who gained a first-class medal for his exhibits (watches, clocks, chronometers).

An array of guides to the Exhibition from Strand publishers confirmed its position as the centre of newsprint and publishing. After all, it was home to Herbert Ingram's *Illustrated London News*, the world's first illustrated news magazine, which had made its debut on 14 May 1842, and appeared weekly. Peter Cunningham's *Handbook of Ancient and Modern London* responded to a Victorian thirst for information. John Cassell's *The Illustrated Exhibitor* (subtitled *A tribute to the world's industrial jubilee*), issued weekly in thirty issues from 7 June to 27 December 1851, achieved sales of 100,000.

In the spirit of the moment, Algernon Percy, 4th Duke of Northumberland, opened Northumberland House, where for one day (6 June) some 4,606 individuals thronged to its state apartments,

most described as grandees.⁴⁸ On Wednesday 9 July the Queen
visited the City in state by way of the Strand, where spectators crammed to see her processing to the Guildhall for a ball to
celebrate the Great Exhibition. She dispensed with the ceremony of
receiving the keys of the City at Temple Bar.⁴⁹

    Later in 1851 (and springing from Wheatstone's experimenta-
tion), the Electric Telegraph Company's West End office at 448
Strand, Charing Cross, transmitted information instantaneously.
The Company had earlier laid the first ever telegraph cable across
the English Channel to France. The contents of a paper listing the
prices of the funds on the London Exchange were directly com-
municated by telegraph from the English to the French coast.⁵⁰
The Strand's 'time ball' was raised above the Company's office to
visually signal accurate time-keeping. The zinc ball was clearly
visible, about six feet in diameter, painted in bright red, encircled
by a broad white line (suggesting a great globe). Fully raised on
a shaft 129 feet above the level of the Thames, it dropped daily
through a space of ten feet to half-mast shortly before 1 p.m.,
when it rose to its full height.⁵¹ It resembled the time ball which
surmounts the Royal Observatory at Greenwich, which sent electrical signals down the commercial telegraph network to broadcast
signals that indicated Greenwich Mean Time. Both balls dropped
by electric action simultaneously at 1 p.m. to communicate the
standard time of Greenwich and London. Greenwich employed
the instantaneous signals of the electric telegraph to regulate
time throughout Britain and for observatories worldwide; in 1884
the Greenwich meridian was established as the international zero
longitude and so the prime meridian of the world.

    The ever-expanding business of William Henry Smith (Mr W. H.
Smith) enlivened the Strand in the early hours of the morning.
Work to be 'first with the news' began at the head office of the W. H.
Smith company (186 Strand) at 3 a.m. weekdays and at 2 a.m. on the
weekends. To it, horses pulled Smith's scarlet carts, each laden with
loads of 'raw papers' from Fleet Street. Newsprint sheets (the daily
newspapers or the weekend's weekly journals) were hauled into
Smith's packing office to be sorted, folded and bundled into parcels

for their distribution. Each week about 100 miles of twine weighing over 59 tons were estimated to secure them.[52] Smith's employees wheeled the parcels out to the Strand and hauled them back into the carts for deliveries to the railways. 'First on the road' was their maxim.[53] Smith's son, also William Henry, Strand-born in 1825 and with a strict Wesleyan upbringing, followed his news-vendor father in the family business. The Smiths (working together over 1846–57 in the renamed W. H. Smith & Son) took full advantage of the rapid growth of the country's rail system. By mid-century, railway companies founded in or before the 'railway mania' of the 1830s and 1840s had largely linked London and the industrial north-west. The Smiths built connections with these railways to carry the news to the country ahead of competitors and operated news-stands in railway stations from 1848. After his father's retirement in 1857, the younger William Smith met the demand from railway passengers for publications, and the company eventually held exclusive contracts with rail companies for its newspaper wholesale operations, which allowed it to predominate at railway station news-stands.

The company's operations occupied a sizeable part of east Strand. Its Strand office housed the lending department of its circulating library for its news-stands, with upwards of 300,000 volumes in circulation. In offices behind the Strand frontage, entered from Arundel Street, the book department issued a supply of inexpensively priced literature. The company's 'yellowbacked novels' (which sold as fast as they could be printed) were produced with publishers Chapman & Hall on nearby Norfolk Street. Extensive stables, holding between fifty and sixty horses for the service of the scarlet delivery carts, were maintained on nearby Water Street. Workshops there made and maintained the railway bookstalls and frames for railway-station advertisements. The company's printing house, close by in Fetter Lane, prepared and issued the advertisements.

Maps show how, up to the 1860s, the Strand remained insulated from direct rail connection, unlike its neighbouring parts of central London. At its west end, the Hungerford Suspension Bridge, built for foot passengers, under the direction of I. K.

Brunel, opened in mid-1845. Nearly 14,000 persons reportedly used the daily, crossing from the river's South Bank at Lambeth to the Strand's Hungerford Market.[54] At the time, rumours circulated that a rail company had bought the footbridge for almost double what it cost and was negotiating to buy the market to use as its station.[55] Just short of nineteen years later, on 11 January 1864, trains of the South Eastern Railway pulled into their West End terminus on the site of Hungerford Market, at Charing Cross Station, the mainline station nearest to the heart of London. John Hawkshaw's arch – a trussed canopy 164 feet wide that roofed over the tracks nearly 99 feet above the station's six platforms – registered in fittingly spectacular manner the greater measure of scale now called for on the Strand.

The Charing Cross Hotel (by E. M. Barry), with the railway booking office and exit-way from the station, expressed its capitals, balusters, trusses and ornamental elements in terracotta because the polluting effect of increased traffic and industrial activity required new approaches. It was one of London's first buildings to be generally faced with artificial stone. Terracotta better resisted the onslaught of London's polluted atmosphere, which corroded masonry and other architectural elements. Evidence of the atmosphere's destructiveness was plainly visible in the National Gallery's pictures. Strand buildings looked degraded and, far from adding to the city, its soot-blackened buildings induced disgust and melancholy.

Charing Cross Hotel was also notable for its French-made zinc roof and prominent chimneys (with scarcely a room without a fireplace and over 260 flues in the building). With opulent interiors and 239 bedrooms, the hotel prefigured future hospitality. Many parts of the building featured a cross and the letter C, doubled as a monogram. This referred to the Queen Eleanor Memorial Cross which Barry placed in its forecourt; his design was based on details that he researched about the crosses erected by Edward I of England in memory of his first wife. The new building's vivacity made its neighbouring block (with the morosely austere, soot-stained Strand-frontage to Northumberland House) appear incongruous.

More and more, building in London was judged as a desultory piecemeal affair in the columns of the day's foremost architectural journal, *The Builder*. 'Every bad step is followed by a worse' opined its editor, architect George Godwin. He was the third editor of the weekly, which had its publishing office in York Street, a short road between Wellington and Catherine Street, just east of Covent Garden and Burleigh Street. He urged, 'The want of a standing committee or commission for the improvement of the metropolis, to take advantage of such opportunities as occur, to preserve general concord in improvements, and to check injurious proceedings which are now constantly occurring, is greatly needed'.[56]

In 1855 the Metropolis Management Act established the Metropolitan Board of Works, the first metropolitan-wide local authority for London. This new Board of Works, charged with upgrading infrastructure, had considerable powers but limited funds. Its creation brought change to the Strand, in the form of significant construction projects: the Thames Embankment (1864–70), Northumberland Avenue (1876) and the Law Courts (1882). This engineered Strand – in each of its components – reflected the street's pivotal importance to London.

Under consideration for many years, in fact dating from Sir Christopher Wren's plan in the 1660s, the important question of an embankment of the Thames saw different proposals, with a view to improve both communication and public health and recreation. These questions were discussed during many sessions of Parliament from the 1830s. Sir Frederick Trench, aide to George IV, took unwavering interest in city improvements. He imagined a future in which the river was the chief feature of the capital. He revived Wren's embanking scheme to build along the Strand's river shore. Landowners and wharf owners resisted his hopes for parliamentary approval to build a quay and terrace from Blackfriars Bridge to Cecil Street, Strand, with walks and gardens for foot passengers, and carriage roads. With the water closet introduced in the 1830s, effluent flowed into London's waterways. Hydrologist Nathaniel Beardmore laid plans before the Commissions of Sewers in 1840 for the main drainage of the city and the artist John Martin also proposed an embanking scheme. A great obstacle in the way of all propositions to overhaul the area was the value of the riverside property, largely held by a select few of the peerage.

The waves of cholera that hit London from 1830, worsening each time, added urgency to the cleaning up of the river and the building of an embankment. Faraday warned a parliamentary select committee about the state of city sewers. The 'fermenting sewer' he described when on a river steamer in July 1855 so appalled him that he wrote to *The Times* urging a clean-up and warning London it may regret its neglect in hot weather. Alighting at Hungerford Bridge (unable to continue on the river for its unpleasantness), he 'was glad to enter the streets for an atmosphere which, except near the sinkholes, [were] much sweeter than on the river'.[57] *Punch's* cartoon of 21 July 1855, 'Faraday giving his card to Father Thames', pointedly declared that the Thames was more sewer than river (Figure 13). A heatwave struck in 1858: Faraday's warning became London's 'Great Stink'.

Joseph Bazalgette, the chief engineer of the Metropolitan Board of Works, designed and oversaw the formation of an embankment and roadway along the river's shores. This undertaking involved reconstructing for a future city of 4.5 million people a network of underground and street sewers to redirect sewage to distant pumping stations. Thick riverside parapets and landing stages, faced with granite blocks encasing sewer pipes, were constructed. Acres of mud were shifted and reclaimed to build the 100-foot wide embankment with its carriageway, walkways, new public gardens at Charing Cross and expanded Temple Gardens. It extended from the northern end of Blackfriars Bridge to Westminster and included the Metropolitan District Railway between Westminster and Blackfriars. Most of its remarkable achievement was little seen. Under the footway beside the river were meshed together the public railway and subways, the Gas Company's railroad, and gas, water and telegraph pipes. The Embankment reclaimed from the river over thirty-seven acres of land, of which the carriage and footways occupied nineteen acres; eight acres were devoted to garden. It was the biggest achievement in civil engineering seen in London.

FIGURE 13. *Faraday Giving His Card to Father Thames; And we hope the Dirty Fellow will consult the learned Professor.* Photomechanical print, from *Punch, or the London Charivari*, 21 July 1855. The so-called Great Stink in 1858 expedited long-held plans for the shoreline below the Strand, when a new sewerage system was created and the Embankment. Hopes were held that the new Embankment would remove some of the congested traffic on the Strand. (From the Collections of the State Library of New South Wales)

Change was again marching through the Strand. In 1875, the government intended to erect public offices on the Embankment's reclaimed land. William Smith (the son of W. H. Smith), by now popular Conservative Member of Parliament for Westminster (since November 1868), resisted this with a motion in Parliament that the land, which had been reclaimed at the expense of the ratepayers, should be reserved for their advantage as a breathing place and pleasure ground. Smith pursued the matter until the Commissioners of Woods and Forests agreed to redeem the contested ground from being built over; it was given to the Metropolitan Board of Works for a nominal payment of £3,270 (£480,000 today). In May 1875, Smith formally declared open the new public garden built there. It extended from near the Hungerford Viaduct, westward, to the boundary line of the private grounds of Whitehall fronting the Thames, towards Westminster Bridge. Smith thanked those who turned 'what was once a mere receptacle for dirt and filth, and all that was abominable in the outskirts of a great city into a charming garden to please the eye and delight the imagination'.[58] The improvement that the Embankment brought to this part of central London in terms of public amenity was a complete turnaround from the long-degraded riverside.

The creation of Northumberland Avenue, on the site of Northumberland House, connected the Embankment to Trafalgar Square. In 1874, Charles Wheatstone saw Northumberland House come down. It had outlasted Charles Dickens (he died four years earlier), who had been taken, as a treat, to see it from the street as a boy aged around eight years. In his writing, Dickens coloured his views of the ever-changing city he lived in. Some of these changes before and after Dickens sprang from scientific breakthroughs such as Wheatstone's, along with the achievement of Bazalgette's Embankment. Smith's vision for the public enjoyment of the river's foreshore also merits remembrance.

The new Law Courts were erected over five acres of ground on a site bounded on the north by Carey Street, on the south by the Strand and Fleet Street, on the east by Chancery Lane and on the west by Clement's Lane (at St Clement Danes Church). Funds were

Figure 14. *Temple Bar c. 1865.* Photograph by Frank Mason Good. Workmen are repairing the road. Temple Bar became a bottleneck and was dismantled in 1878. It has since been reconstructed in Paternoster Square, by St Paul's Cathedral. (Brian May Archive of Stereoscopy)

allocated to the project in 1865, with George Edward Street eventually appointed architect. It took several years to clear the site for the foundations. Work on the building began in 1874. It took six years to build, having been delayed by labour troubles, bad weather and financial issues. The strain proved too great for Street, who suffered a stroke and died in 1881. The Queen opened the vast block, 514 feet long at its Strand front, and 480 feet deep from north to south, on 4 December 1882.

MAP 4. Ordnance Survey six-inch map of London, 1888–1915, WC1 (2nd edition), showing the cleared site for the future Royal Courts of Justice (top right). (Reproduced with the permission of the National Library of Scotland)

Temple Bar was shored up with timber throughout the excavations for the Royal Courts of Justice. It was then removed when the street was widened in 1878. It was reconstructed and became a gateway for millionaire brewer and politician Sir Henry Bruce Meux, 3rd Baronet, at his Hertfordshire estate, Theobalds Park, where it rested until it was relocated in 2004 to Paternoster Square. Its name lingered on with *Temple Bar: A London Magazine for Town and Country Readers*, a monthly shilling magazine bearing the monument's name. Several other magazines also adopted London place names; one was the contemporaneous publication which William Thackeray edited, the *Cornhill*. Rivalling it, *Temple Bar* first appeared in December 1860; it offered readers a generous 150 pages, edited by G. A. Sala.[59]

These visibly physical changes aside, equations begun by twenty-nine-year-old physicist James Clerk Maxwell at King's College London (1860–65) extended the understanding of previously unknown forces. Maxwell established that electrostatic and magnetic attraction and repulsion, initially thought to be separate forces, were in fact different aspects of just one force, which he called electromagnetism. He determined that light is electromagnetic radiation and predicted other types of radiation beyond visible light (such as radio waves). He also developed the kinetic theory of gases (a foundation of modern physical chemistry). His work on molecular physics would revolutionise conceptions of the nature of matter and illustrate the accelerating rapidity of change. Seeds that he sowed prepared the ground for the leaps to be taken in the future by Alfred Einstein and subsequent quantum theorists.[60]

At this point, electric lighting began to be introduced. Building on Faraday's work, South Foreland Lighthouse, Kent, was the first to shine an electric light in 1858. On 3 September 1860, newly invented mercury arc lamps lit the Hungerford Suspension Bridge.[61] Inventors competed to adjust electrical discharges such that a lamp could be made suitable for general illumination. Until this was achieved, gas lamps lit the Strand. Electric lighting was a novelty. Experimental displays with its glow were a feature of interest at special events such as the opening in 1861 of the new home for the remarkable library of Middle Temple.[62] Originating as a small private library before 1540 and refounded in 1641, it had been a chained library in the eighteenth century, housed in a building on Middle Temple Lane. When it had outgrown its accommodation it was moved to a new building erected for it close to the river in 1861, its bicentennial year. The Prince of Wales's opening of it attracted an estimated 1,000 guests. The library was on the upper floor of a gothic revival building, approached by a narrow winding staircase in an octagonal tower at the side. Two stained-glass windows and smaller side windows of silvered glass (mercury glass) dimly lit the library. Those who reached the ill-lit room through the squeeze on the stairs were thrilled by the sparks and glow of electric light that notable (and Michael Faraday's) instrument-maker William Ladd displayed to them.

Seventeen years later, systems of providing electric lighting were tested on selected London streets, including the Embankment between Westminster and Waterloo Bridges from 16 December 1878. Uncertain of results, gas lamps continued burning while the experimental electric lighting was switched on after dusk on a stretch of roughly 1,200 metres. Illumination from it was found to dispel the Embankment's gloominess. Objects on the river were discernible despite the drizzling rain and murky atmosphere left by the dense fog of the afternoon. Cleopatra's Needle could be seen from certain standpoints.[63]

Amid this experimentation, theatrical entertainment in general remained relatively unremarkable, in part due to government control, which had, since 1737, authorised only theatrical performances at Drury Lane and Covent Garden Theatres. The Theatres Act of 1843 altered these controls; it gave the Lord Chamberlain the role of official censor. Consequently, variety shows and music-hall performances predominated. In 1868, the Strand Musick Hall and adjoining property, extending from the Strand to Exeter Street, and from Catherine to Wellington Streets, exchanged hands. A new theatre was reconstructed on its site. Journalist John Hollingshead (with an ear attuned to change) became its theatrical manager. He first opened the new Gaiety Theatre on 21 December and made it London's most popular theatre.

In the stage-playing business to make money, Hollingshead said, 'my principle was ever to suit my market'.[64] He resisted the restrictions placed on theatres and music halls. He presented farce and musical burlesque (public favourites) in more sophisticated stagings and gradually steered them away from their customary vulgarity. He brought continental operetta (several by Jacques Offenbach) to London, as well as members of the *Comédie-Française*. He distinguished the Gaiety by introducing to London electric light in the theatre's new auditorium in August 1878. Its illuminated façade stood out on the Strand in a large circle of radiant electric light that put the street's gas lamps completely in the shade.[65] Being the first to install electric lighting signalled Hollinghshead's ambition for greater originality in the theatre. In June 1879, he brought Sarah Bernhardt to the Gaiety and in December 1880 he was the first in England to produce an adaptation of a play by Henrik Ibsen. Hollingshead invited composer Arthur Sullivan and librettist William Schwenck Gilbert to collaborate for a Christmas piece. In December 1871, the Gaiety opened *Thespis; or, the Gods Grown Old*, in which the elderly gods, tired of their life in Olympus, swap places with actors and descend to earth. Sixty-three performances followed into 8 March 1872. The satiric spirit that Gilbert and Sullivan celebrated was right for their time, an Age of Transition. In 1875, they followed with *Trial by Jury*, another commissioned work full of comic and musical fun. They looked wryly at their contemporaries and the wealth being made (and lost) by the new industrialist baronets seeking the favour of Edward, Prince of Wales. Further delighting audiences, the creative duo parodied figures who were familiar on the Strand. Audiences applauded the resemblance in *Trial by Jury* of the Counsel for the Plaintiff to leading celebrity solicitor Sir George Lewis, who specialised in handling sensitive cases involving prominent people (including the Prince of Wales).[66] Conservative politician William Smith, from 1877 to 1880 the First Lord of the Admiralty, was satirised as 'ruler of the Queen's navee' in the character of Sir

Joseph Porter when *H.M.S. Pinafore* opened in 1878. Young Oscar Wilde was caricatured as the poet Reginald Bunthorne in *Patience* (1881), which ran for 578 performances.

Population growth in urban constituencies resulted in their redistribution ahead of the 1885 general election.[67] Up to now, the Strand had been the responsibility of several parishes, governed by different vestries. The uncoordinated governing of the many parts of London made it increasingly difficult to respond properly to issues arising with its growth. Partly to redress this and to allow for better electoral representation, the Redistribution Act (Third Reform Act) divided the borough of Westminster into the three separate constituencies of Westminster, the Strand, and St George's, Hanover-square, each to return a Member to Parliament. The Strand division had about 80,000 inhabitants and contained the parishes of: St Martin in the Fields: St Anne, Soho; St Paul, Covent Garden; St Mary le Strand; St Clement Danes; as well as the Liberty of the Rolls and the Precinct of the Savoy. The formation of the London County Council followed in 1889. London gained a municipal government elected directly by London's householders and responsible for building controls, fire safety, drainage, housing and education. A new chapter would begin for the Strand.

CHAPTER 6

EDWARDIAN STRAND

Let's all go down the Strand.
Castling and Murphy, 1909[1]

No one will shed tears of joy in the 'motley Strand', No one will be leisurable any more, or turn over old books at a stall, or talk with friends at the street corner. Noise and evil smells have filled the streets like tunnels in daylight; ... to live in it is to live in the hollow of a clanging bell, to breathe its air is to breathe the foulness of modern progress.
Arthur W. Symons, 1909[2]

Eden Phillpotts stepped from his cab, one of the many hansoms rolling up the entrance court of 80 Strand. The evening of 16 November 1900 was special for him, though it was one like any other at the Hotel Cecil, London's most popular rendezvous. Uniformed attendants helped guests arrive in stately fashion. 'Inside our welcome lifts all gloom', Phillpotts thought when ushered inside. At one of the hotel's banqueting halls, he joined the clerks with whom he had worked at the Holborn headquarters of the insurance company Sun Fire Office. Wishing to write, he had left that company for a part-time editorship at the weekly *Black and White* magazine. By now, with thirteen titles published, he was on the way to the success he would come to enjoy as one of the era's most prolific and prominent authors. To be invited to the Cecil endorsed his sense of achievement, of having 'arrived'. Relishing the hospitality that he found there, he sketched drawings and wrote of his satisfaction,

> The Waiters crowning cups with wine
> Renew its sparkling lease
> And keep the guests in merry vein
> With 'Perrinet et fils'.[3]

To be at the Cecil was to feel included among the celebrities who were seen there. It was one of Edwardian London's most significant destinations. The Royal Literary Fund Banquet had been held there earlier in the year, that charity being one of the large number of august bodies whose associates regularly assembled in the hotel's many banqueting rooms. The year before, the Whitefriars Club had hosted a dinner in the hotel's Victoria Hall for the world-acclaimed American writer Mark Twain.[4]

The Cecil was central London's banqueting centre, besides being Europe's largest hotel; it boasted 1,000 rooms (700 bedrooms and 300 sitting rooms).[5] Its capacity to host regular important events with distinguished guests, in numbers that only regal events might match, mirrored the city at its zenith as the capital of the world's finance and of its largest empire. Fifteen hundred could be seated in its grand banqueting room.[6] Each of its smaller high-end dining halls could variously accommodate between 250 and 500 diners. These were often full on the one same evening, each with its own gathering of celebrities among diners and their guest speakers. One politician noted that where once hotels were of brick, 'now they are of marble – the latest and finest being, perhaps, the Hotel Cecil'.[7] Bernard Darwin, Charles Darwin's grandson (whom he raised) and an acclaimed golfing journalist, regarded it as a self-contained and self-sufficient city.[8] An army of people was engaged in producing the vaunted magic of the Cecil. Some 700 people were employed in the hotel, thirty alone to clean silver. Many others were engaged beyond it, such as at the gardens and conservatories that furnished its palatial rooms with their sumptuous arrangements of flowers and foliage plants.

Aside from the opulence of its Edwardian Baroque interior, it brought a new dimension to the Strand's western end by virtue of size. Developed in several stages, its Strand frontage, crested with domed ends, rose on the street's southern side between 1890 and 1896. The river frontage of its southern block rose thirty feet high from the Embankment before reaching Strand level. Its three wings straddled over two acres, between Salisbury Street on its east and Cecil Street at its western side. This street was the boundary between the parishes of St Clement Danes and St Martin in the Fields. On his arrival, Phillpotts looked on paintings empanelled in the landings of the hotel's marble staircase at its Strand front. They depicted the palace from a former age, of the Cecils, Earls of Salisbury, that once occupied the Salisbury estate on which the hotel now stood.

High living, free-spending personalities stayed, dined and partied at the Cecil, which catered to visitors from abroad, local dignitaries and the socially glamorous. It was the largest of the 'Big Hotels' that rose nearby to receive the growing number of visitors, especially Americans, travelling to Britain in search of the picturesque and historic things they had read about but who also expected modern conveniences.[9] Celebrations to mark the Queen's Diamond Jubilee, periodic Colonial and Imperial Conferences (from 1907) and the coronations in August 1902 and June 1911 brought to them heads of state and their retinues.

The luxurious furnishings and elite clientele of these new palatial hotels gracing the Strand returned some distinction to the begrimed, congested thoroughfare. These new 'Strand palaces' evoked a historical memory of the street's past reputation for golden palaces when home to earlier Tudor and Stuart courtly mansions. The celebrities associated with its latest palaces continually stoked Edwardian impressions of the Strand once again being a 'golden mile'. Of great international fame in this era of duelling divas, Italian coloratura soprano Luisa Tetrazzini dazzled London in 1907. Twenty curtain calls followed her debut at Covent Garden. Back the following year, hailed as 'The voice of the century', the Florentine nightingale brought glory to the street when photographed at the Cecil.[10]

The street's offerings tantalised the pleasure-loving Edwardians. The flood of life that rushed through it magnetised them. Its irresistible pull figured so largely in popular imagination that the lyrics of Harry Castling's well-known music-hall song of 1909 rang:

Let's all go down the Strand
Oh, what a happy land

That's the place for fun and noise
All among the girls and boys
So let's all go down the Strand.

Here was London's playground, across all levels of society. Wednesdays were matinee day at the theatres, and many cheap excursion trains pulled into Charing Cross railway station bringing hordes of 'trippers' to the Strand's shows, lights, sounds and sights. Crowds flocked to it and thronged the street hoping to rub shoulders with its celebrities and 'society' from its Big Hotels.

Eastward along the Strand's south side stood the seven-storey Savoy, with seventy bathrooms. Open since 1889, then extended in 1904, it was one of the world's most luxurious hotels, but only for those with deep pockets. Across on the street's north side, the new Strand Palace Hotel opened in 1909. Engaged to announce its opening, George Sims, long-standing London journalist and *bon vivant*, enthused that it was the last word in richness.[11] Far from the same order as the Cecil or Savoy, this hotel boasted a fixed marble basin with a constant supply of hot and cold water in each of its 470 bedrooms and a telephone installed on every floor. Sims's repartee indicated how in the new century's first decade these hotels represented a new-found prosperity in a nation that was growing progressively richer. Quieter residences on and off the Strand also housed visitors from the worldwide British Dominions and America, foreign in their clothes and speech. These hotels brought the world to the street, making it cosmopolitan.

The shine that they brought to the Strand contrasted with the squalor found in its branching narrow passages, whose occupants lived in cramped, dank rooms, more often than not in misery or vice. They were onlookers of the street's recently adopted lustre, its celebrities and its crowds of foreigners, strangers with clean shaven faces and a nasal drawl.

The street's theatres offered some in the crowd a measure of escape from the realities of a harsher daily life. Theatre-goers bunched up outside the theatres, waiting to get tickets. Most popular was the New Gaiety Theatre facing Waterloo Bridge. Re-opened in late October 1903, and refurbished with an adjoining restaurant and hotel, Londoners loved it as the professed home of gaiety thanks to impresario George Edwardes. He elevated the staging of musical comedy from burlesque and the music hall in his first-class house with its dancing corps of Gaiety Girls. The glamour of the footlights belied the exacting effort called for from the women who, for the weekly wage of £2 (around £300 in today's money) and an eye on something better ahead, were prepared for the beauty contest and stamina that the chorus line demanded.[12]

Gladys Cooper began her career as a Gaiety Girl and went on to become an international star of stage and film, a theatrical manager (of the Playhouse Theatre, at the riverside end of Craven Street and Northumberland Avenue, from 1917 to 1934) and producer, with an acting career that spanned seven decades on stage, in films and on television. She later recalled that, in those early days, the moment the curtain rose 'the air was promise crammed'.[13] The Gaiety Girls made heads whirl among lovelorn stage-door Johnnies who competed for favours from them. Some 'arrived' upon accepting marriage offers from peers. Sylvia Lillian Storey, the daughter of a comedian and scene painter, followed her father onto the stage at the age of six. Twelve years later, she left a production at the Gaiety to marry William Poulett, 7th Earl Poulett. Lambeth-born Olive Mary Meatyard took the stage name of Olive May. She married into the peerage twice; her first husband was Lord Victor Paget, in 1913 and, following a divorce shortly after, her second was Henry Moore, 10th Earl of Drogheda.

A full house of 2,000 theatre-goers crammed into the Strand Theatre in early February 1900 for J. H. Darnley's farcical comedy *Facing the Music*. Laughter rolled up in waves from the audience, who could forget for that moment the icy weather outside. The crowd spilling out of the theatre that night faced swirling snow.[14] The illuminated theatre quickly disappeared in the limited visibility; crossing the street took courage and boarding a moving omnibus called for heroism.

The Strand was a street of stark contrasts: of merriment and misery, of light and dark, where fantasy and reality intermixed. This nature of the street was perhaps most evident during the first

two decades of the new century, when it underwent improvement
and was reinvented. For the time had come to address its shabby
state and to transform it from being a street of sagging purpose
(as Wilfred Whitten, influential editor and popular author of *A
Londoner's London*, saw it).[15] The Strand took centre stage in visions
of a future London as the historic royal ceremonial route, the spine
connecting the crown to the City when the sovereign traversed
from Westminster to Guildhall. It was necessary to make it a
thoroughfare that properly expressed its central location as one of
the world's principal streets in a way that would befit a new London
of the twentieth century.

More than a century of discussion about how to sweep away
inner London's decay and congestion led Parliament to enact laws
to reconstruct London's heart. No longer would it do to let the
Strand, under forty feet wide, stay as congested as it had become.
The urgency of this was apparent when the crowd had their way on
29 October 1900, posing the dangers at large to a city straining at
the seams. That Monday afternoon, the City of London Imperial
Volunteers (CIVs), a corps that took part in the Second Boer War,
which had just returned from South Africa, marched along the
Strand, heading to St Paul's Cathedral.[16] A crowd of over a million,
believed to be a record gathering, surged from the many side
streets which debouched on the Strand and Fleet Street. The police
and military deputed to keep the line of the route were unable to
maintain order. Patriotic frenzy in the crowd pushed the troops
out of their formation into a single file. They struggled to keep
their line. The Lord Mayor, supposed to welcome the CIVs before
the Law Courts, abandoned this plan from fear of the chaos. Two
deaths and over 1,800 casualties were known to have resulted from
the melee. The crowd's enthusiasm spilled over into the evening
and through the night, as they tramped and roared in the streets,
shouted patriotic songs and yelled themselves hoarse over the
return of these citizen soldiers.

The new century, and increasing competition between imperial
nations, called for a thoroughfare worthy of an imperial city.
Parliament gave London County Council the authority to revive

the Strand. The Council embarked on the Strand to Holborn Improvement Scheme: to sweep away and replace the Dickensian rookeries and the mazy laneways and dirty passages of the Strand and its adjoining parts found on the north side of St Clement Danes (Figure 15) with a healthier and more stylish city centre. It was London's most ambitious reconstruction.

FIGURE 15. Old houses in Wych Street, formerly a continuation of Drury Lane, c. 1876. Wych Street in east Strand was one of several ancient streets cleared to make way for Aldwych, which opened in 1905. Its timber buildings recalled the Strand of the seventeenth century. Published by the Society for Photographing Relics of Old London, this looks towards St Clement Danes. (Royal Academy)

The Council promptly tore up the street. Demolishing the Strand's architectural jumble that crowded its narrow sections was key to plans for the anticipated new centre. Buildings were marked out for speedy demolition. Architects felt dismissed by the Council. 'Is new London to be allowed to grow up with as little apparent design as a vegetable – controlled by a thousand influences, some hidden, some vainly directed?', asked William Emerson in his presidential address at the Royal Institute of British Architects in 1900.[17] Plans for the Strand were hotly debated. Of greatest concern was the way it narrowed at its eastern end between its two eighteenth-century churches. The Council cleared away Holywell Street on their immediate north to broaden and remodel the east Strand, create the new Aldwych crescent past St Clement Danes, and link it and the Strand to Holborn by the new artery of Kingsway. All this would create the city's newest commercial precinct.

Sappers also worked further along on the street, at the corner of Norfolk Street, and further west, opposite the Hotel Cecil; this left the street in a chronic state of entrenchment, as it remained through the decade's first four years.[18] This disruption was generally taken as a welcome sign of the times. Removing unsightliness from the heart of London aroused public interest and discussion, and it was thought desirable that new buildings worthy of an imperial capital would rise either side of the street.[19]

Down came buildings with sentimental attachments, interesting and picturesque to artists and antiquarians but which discredited the Strand. The Edinburgh Castle, a historic tavern at 322 Strand, nearly opposite Somerset House, had a frontage of little more than fourteen feet, typical of London's many small buildings.[20] A public house, ninety-nine feet deep, its cellars ran under its entire length and also twenty-seven feet under the roadway immediately in front of St Mary's Church. It was an old-fashioned hostelry with its sanded floor, long narrow entrance and chop house at its rear. Some lamented the tearing down of quaint structures like this, but many welcomed the demolition of such 'old rabbit hutches'. Only a few taps with a hammer seemed to bring them tumbling about the housebreakers' ears, said an observer.[21] Increasing anxieties about public well-being called for modernisation. Rats in condemned Strand buildings migrated to the south side of the river.[22]

Demolition reoriented Strand vistas. Joseph Ashby-Sterry, poet, novelist and journalist, walked the street almost daily. Beloved to readers of the Strand's illustrated weekly, *The Graphic* (writing as 'The bystander' for eighteen years), he quickly spotted that demolition on the street brought it more air and better views of the buildings that remained untouched. An example of this came to him walking eastwards on the Strand's south side, which (with houses having been demolished on the street's north side) gave a clear view of St Clement Danes. Though familiar with the tower, the church's qualities surprised him:

> I am inclined to think I never sufficiently admired the architectural beauties of the church. But now you get a clear view of it you will be able to thoroughly appreciate its exquisite proportions. You will be struck with the dignity and solidity of the structure as well as its grace and lightness. Till the intervening buildings had been cleared away, I had no idea that Sir Christopher Wren appeared to such advantage as he does in the church.[23]

Even to *habitués*, the Strand regularly held surprises.

Congestion remained an issue, nevertheless. In 1904, the Royal Commission on London Traffic found that some 2,582 omnibuses, 1,285 hansom cabs, 790 trade vehicles, 286 four-wheelers (known as 'growlers'), 228 bicycles, 112 carriages and 93 barrows converged over twelve hours daily in the unceasing stream of traffic between Temple Bar and Charing Cross, a distance of some 1,200 yards (a little more than a kilometre).[24] Collisions with fatalities occurred in the confusion of drawn and motorised wheels and human feet. Horses attached to hansoms took fright if startled by the roaring of motorised omnibuses, vans, carts, cabs, carriages, or the noise from church bells, or shouts from hawkers, newspaper boys, cab calls, or shrill whistles.[25] Horses collided with oncoming traffic, upending and smashing vehicles, and (if able to shake free) tore away, sometimes attached to a hansom cab without the driver.[26]

Other hazards jammed traffic. Unreliable electrical wiring could spark fire in the street. Exploding out of the footway before the Gaiety Theatre, flames rose twelve feet high above a manhole; the force blasted glass out from adjacent shop frontages, which shattered and rained down on passers-by.[27] American financier and transportation tycoon Charles Tyson Yerkes could not help thinking what the street's condition would be if omnibuses and cabs were eliminated and replaced with electrified underground railway lines.[28]

Necessarily, improvement and change stalked the Strand. New regulations banned 'crawling' cabs stopping at any moment for passengers.[29] Ranks were provided at every side corner off the street's north side to make the roadway safer for pedestrians. Motorised vehicles, though still largely the pleasure of the rich, signalled the future. In 1908, motor-omnibuses were on the increase. By 1909, the passing of the horsed cab was guaranteed when the London Improved Cab Company substituted motors for their horse-drawn cabs.[30] Even hawkers were gradually removed from the street.[31]

Still, the cries of street vendors and milkmen early in the morning gave little respite at that time. 'If we had a street in New York as noisy as the Strand we should soon take steps to effect an alteration' said Professor Morton Arendt, of New York's Society for the Suppression of Unnecessary Noises, in London when he was studying European cities. 'In New York vendors are not allowed to cry their wares before nine in the morning and they must stop at nine o'clock at night.'[32] Though the County Council made new regulations for London, their enforcement was yet to be fully achieved. Romantic fiction writer Elinor Glyn, when visiting New York in 1907 to write her book *Elizabeth Visits America*, found it comparatively quiet. Nor was the traffic half so great, she thought, compared with what greeted one on the Strand. She found much less traffic and noise in New York:

> No omnibuses shouting their destinations, or strings of people fighting to get into them. No one much in a hurry at night.... There is not that frantic race to get to the supper restaurants because a

ridiculous County Council decrees that everyone must be turned
out to go home to bed at half-past twelve o'clock![33]

Recreation was not the only hallmark of the busy Strand. Fleet
Street to its east was considered by the English press to be the
journal of the whole world. Its journalism – with its close association with politics and power, finance and celebrity – closely
intersected with the Strand's magnetism. Newspaper, magazine
and other publishing offices were headquartered on it and its
adjacent streets. Offices for *The Observer* and *Morning Post, Throne
Newspaper, The Yachtsman* and *Iron and Coal Trade Review* were
among those on the Strand; *Farm, Field, and Fireside* had its office in
Wellington Street, *The Lady's World* and *Freeman's Journal* in Essex
Street, *Country Life* in Tavistock Street.

Established publishing firms, for instance that of the Macmillan
family, consolidated their leadership in the book market by expanding from their long-time Strand office at Henrietta Street, just
off the Strand's north side by Covent Garden, into purpose-built
premises in nearby St Martin's Street. New publishers gravitated to
Henrietta Street, where Gerald Duckworth established himself and
published John Galsworthy's plays. Grant Richards distinguished
himself there with his sharp eye for authors of critical note and the
example he set with the finely designed books he issued through
his peripatetic publishing career. Prominent writers he published
included G. B. Shaw, G. K. Chesterton, John Masefield, Hector
H. Munro (Saki), Eden Phillpotts and Samuel Butler (whose *The
Way of All Flesh* Richards released in 1903). Thomas Fisher Unwin
at Adelphi Terrace from 1905 launched some of the most experimental writers of the period, among them H. G. Wells, Somerset
Maugham, Joseph Conrad, George Moore and Ford Madox Ford.
Taking a different tack when venturing on his own in publishing in 1901, George Godfrey Harrap established his firm George
Harrap & Co. Ltd in 1905 by concentrating on the production of
modern-language and other textbooks. The publication that year of
Heath's Practical French Grammar influenced the teaching of French
in Britain.

The Strand also housed many businesses ancillary to publishing, such as printers, stationers, photographers and their suppliers. Maps for cyclists and guidebooks for tourists, of places around England and their environs, were issued for over thirty years by Bacon & Co., from 127 Strand, where American entrepreneur George Washington Bacon set up business. W. H. Smith and Son, the largest book and newspaper business, occupied the Arundel Street corner with its offices and lending library. To its north, from the office of the National Women's Social and Political Union, at 4 Clement's Inn, near St Clement Danes, came arguments from the Woman's Press for votes for women. The Strand continued to be a hub of information. Legendary journalists working on the Strand added to its allure. Editors, writers, illustrators and increasingly advertising agents maintained the street's mystique. The eponymous *Strand Magazine* furthered the street's fame. Subscribers globally awaited keenly issues of the monthly magazine.

Like so many of the street's occupants, publisher George Newnes seized opportunity when he saw it. The gradual introduction of compulsory elementary education during the twenty-three years up to 1893 had ushered in a mass audience of readers hungry for information and Newnes owed his commercial success to being alert to his readers' interests. They were more inclined to read anecdotes rather than long essays. He gave them the entertaining weekly magazines *Tit-Bits* and *London Opinion*, gave women their first weekly magazine with *Women's Life* and added *Country Life* to his constellation of titles. But he achieved greatest success with *The Strand Magazine*.

Newnes charged the artist and designer George Charles Haité with producing the magazine's cover – a pen and ink illustration that is foreshortened to look eastwards down the Strand towards the two churches, and the neo-Gothic towers of the Law Courts and the church of St Dunstan in the West beyond (Figure 16). The street is busy with wheeled transport and pedestrians cram the pavements. In the foreground, a newspaper boy touts the latest edition on the pavement's edge. The magazine's title overhangs the street from telegraph wires above, resembling the signage at a

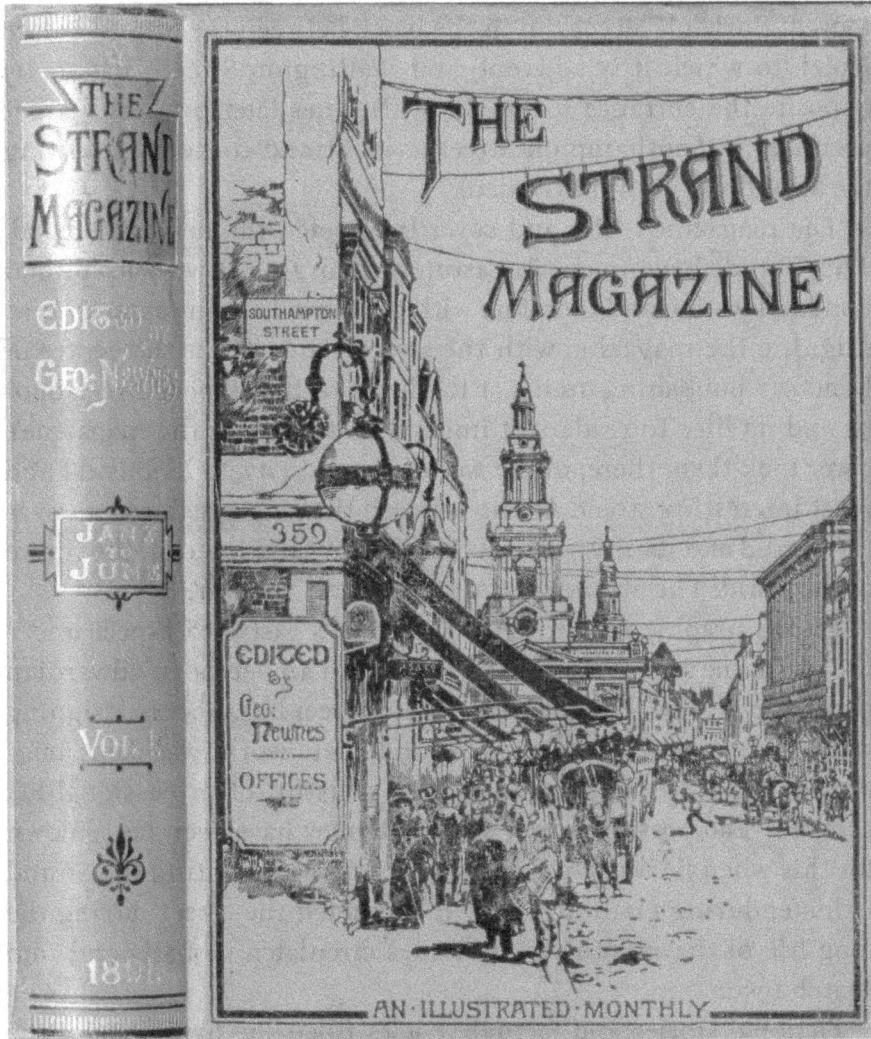

FIGURE 16. *The Strand Magazine: An Illustrated Monthly*, vol. 1 (January to June 1891), published by George Newnes. Shown here as copies were bound for collectors. Monthly issues of *The Strand Magazine* circulated globally for over half a century. Famously, it launched the career of the fictional Sherlock Holmes. (University of Sydney Library Collection)

carnival. The left-hand corner gives the address of its offices, a hand symbol pointing down the side street branching off north-side Strand. The initial cover showed the name of Burleigh Street, home to the magazine's original offices; this was changed when Newnes moved. Burleigh Street ran in the block between the Strand Palace Hotel (to which it is adjacent) and Wellington Street, diagonally opposite the entrance to the Savoy. Newnes later occupied larger premises in Southampton Street at its Strand corner (connecting the Strand with Covent Garden).

The magazine's title and cover trumpeted the neighbourhood. This branded the magazine astutely, twinning it with its pivotal London location and therefore with the Strand's many associations. Aligning the magazine with the street planted it at the centre of London's publishing arena, at the heart of the imperial metropolis and its life. To readers, it implied that opening the magazine's cover took them there, to the world's largest city, to its busiest and most interesting street. At one between the magazine's covers were the Strand and its city, with all their vitality and interest: the centre of the world. The Strand was 'All the world's London'.

Haité's graphic rendering of the street's eastward aspect under the magazine's eponymous title became an archetype of Edwardian times. Haité, a self-taught artist whose career began with designing wallpaper, carpets, leaded glass and metalwork, was kept busy around town by his membership of a fistful of professional art societies (and presiding over some). He may have been best known for this when he was alive, but his picture highlighting the Strand is his enduring claim to fame. It promoted the street during the long life of the monthly – 711 issues circulated globally and into March 1950.

Fictional stories and factual articles filled the first issue of the illustrated monthly in January 1891. Initial sales of nearly 300,000 reflected Newnes's sound business sense. Sales increased to give him a circulation of almost 500,000 copies a month. Those sales took off with Arthur Conan Doyle's Sherlock Holmes stories, beginning with A Scandal in Bohemia in the July 1891 issue and reaching their peak with the serialisation of The Hound of the Baskervilles. Readers lined up outside the magazine's offices, eager to get the next instalment.

Newnes and the magazine's long-running literary editor, H. Greenhough Smith, delivered material that catered to their readers.

They entertained, as did George Edwardes at the Gaiety. These Strand entrepreneurs avoided modernity, which might be unsettling, and bypassed disquieting apprehensions about Britain's waning productivity that were taking hold in the new century's opening decades. Instead, they upheld the certainty of London as the world's financial centre and endorsed the prosperity and high spirits that its primacy brought to their district during the relatively conflict-free 'Edwardian summer'.

But modernity was taking hold. If seemingly removed from its slightly seedy urban surroundings, the Savoy Hotel went with that mood. Richard D'Oyly Carte had lured as the hotel's manager César Ritz (whom the leaders of London society followed wherever he opened a new establishment). Having just opened the Hotel de Provence in Cannes, Ritz was dismayed by reports of London's cramping restrictions over licensing hours. He brought with him two colleagues, his deputy, Louis Echenard, one of the world's supreme judges of wine, as *maître d'hôtel*, and Auguste Escoffier, as chef, making a trinity that established the Savoy legend. Customarily, only men dined publicly, either in their clubs or when taking girls of the chorus or the demi-monde to late-night suppers. They dismissed such customs and refashioned their restaurant, making it attractive to women, whom they welcomed. They softened the lighting, required evening dress to be worn, banned courtesans and encouraged women to host women-only repasts. They both made it fashionable for women to dine publicly and made it acceptable for high society to dine out.

While the Savoy lured the elite, the Strand encouraged the sensational. In the polling week during the 'khaki election' of 1900, two ladders were raised up in front of the office of the *Daily Graphic*, to above the roof of the four-storey building. As the election results came in, a man personifying the incumbent prime minister, Lord Salisbury, climbed up one of these ladders to the rung numbered with the numeral representing the seats to his credit. Another man, representing the opposition Liberal leader, Sir Henry Campbell-Bannerman, mounted the opposite ladder. Throngs out in the road craned upwards following with interest the rise of both hatless 'indicators' as they raced to a majority.[34] Similarly, crowds surged outside newspaper offices eager for the news just wired in of the war in South Africa. From outside the *Daily News* offices on Fleet Street, people belted down the Strand with word of latest developments. A newspaper boy sold many copies by playing to patriotic fervour in crying out news of engagement in the Second Boer War: 'All the winners!'[35]

The pull of the Strand was undeniable. If disorienting when crowded with foreign visitors, the street's enduring hallmarks gave to British expatriates returning home from foreign parts a sense of the continuity that they craved. Those looking for customary certainties took comfort in landmarks such as its twin churches, other known buildings, familiar shops. 'Though the old street is always changing, it is ever the same', wrote an India hand describing the Strand:

> It is the first street of London along which the average foreigner wanders, and the one in which the passer-by may always be sure of meeting some friend from the far ends of the earth whom he has not set eyes upon for many years past ... and it is the first piece of London which the traveller returning from the East sees after years of exile.[36]

The street was one of countless aspects, whatever one's perspective when there, or how it was experienced (Figure 17).

Immediacy continually strode the Strand. As ever, it was where success favoured the daring; where cash went freely; where fortunes might be made and lost, reversed for the better and the worse; where the unpredictable hung in the air. Just by Outer Temple with its lawyer's chambers on the afternoon of Wednesday 29 August 1906, Dr Thomas Leadbeater went into Cogswell & Harrison, gun and ammunition makers, 226 Strand, wanting a pocket revolver. Shortly after, he entered the nearby George Hotel and asked for a whisky. Five minutes later a shot was heard. The forty-nine-year-old surgeon, two weeks in England from Hong Kong, with family worries and deserted by his wife, had discharged one cartridge to his temple from the five-chambered revolver.[37] Conversely, two

FIGURE 17. The Strand c. 1901. Photographic print, stereograph. This view is looking east from outside Lowther's Arcade, opposite Charing Cross Station. (Brian May Archive of Stereoscopy)

newspaper boys near the Gaiety Theatre one April afternoon in 1912 could not believe their luck when a young American tossed them a gold sovereign each (worth up to £650 today).[38] He continued eastward up the street, suspending the traffic by throwing handfuls of sovereigns and silver shillings into the roadway. In the euphoria of having recently inherited a large sum of money, he threw away at least £100 in gold (roughly £13,000 today). Police arrested him for obstructing traffic. Crowds of people continued to hunt for stray coins and the street had to be cleared.

MAP 5. London (1915-Numbered sheets) V.10, 1936, Ordnance Survey, showing the Strand connecting Central London through the creation of the Aldwych Crescent. It was first known as the Strand island site because it was slow to be developed. This map shows the Aldwych Crescent opposite St Mary le Strand and Somerset House, with Kingsway leading from it, north to Holborn; St Clement Danes at its east, the Law Courts behind it, where the Strand adjoins Fleet Street leading east to the City of London. At Aldwych's western end, Waterloo Bridge leads to the Strand off which Covent Garden is found. (Reproduced with the permission of the National Library of Scotland)

Demolishing the old slum area at its east opened the street at that point. The King officially opened the new avenues of Kingsway and Aldwych in October 1905, where more new buildings were planned, particularly along mid-Strand, opposite St Mary's, on the cleared island between St Clement Danes and Aldwych's western end (Map 5). In 1907, the Canadian government proposed building its London offices on this three-acre block.[39] The notable Aberdeen architect A. Marshall Mackenzie, known for the grand gesture (who drew plans for the Waldorf Hotel being built in the new Aldwych), designed a building to span the block and introduce a scale and grandeur to the street that would dwarf Somerset House. Cue for this ambition came from an earlier scheme, proposed in 1902, when an American-led syndicate planned to build a gigantic office block there, to be the largest of its kind in the world, walling the street with a frontage six times longer than that of Somerset House. Those fearing that this mammoth construction would overwhelm the street threw cold water on its proposed addition to the street's medley of architectural disarray. But business heads were at one with *The Times* newspaper, which took a dim view of architectural inertia: 'This country's domestic affairs need a great deal of shaking up, and it is a brotherly thing for the Americans to give them the requisite fillip'.[40] Briefly anticipated, too, on this wasteland, as part of the Strand's longed-for transformation, was a 'French Palace', designed to sell French products in a Parisian theme park, to bring Paris to London. It was not built. Instead, nature reclaimed the empty block with flowers. Their profuse summer blooms opposite St Clement's charmed passers-by, the church providing a picturesque backdrop to their surprising colour.[41] The Vacant Land Cultivation Society hoped the Council would allow it to convert its idle Strand sites into cabbage patches, as was approved on similar sites in Westminster, whereby over 500 cultivators grew crops (turnips, carrots, potatoes) on derelict land awaiting the builder.[42]

Striking, too, was Frederick Pomeroy's gilded bronze sculpture representing 'Progress', perched atop the nearby 'cornstalk' building, Victoria House, that the state of Victoria built in 1909 to promote trading and emigration opportunities.[43] It was the first building to go up on land cleared on the Strand by the London County Council to revive the area. At 120 feet high, it fronted the Strand for twenty-five feet and ran sixty-five feet deep along a new street named Melbourne Place. This led from the Strand to Aldwych and saw the block which the building partly occupied complete the eastern point of the new Aldwych crescent. Its six storeys at 266 Strand towered above condemned buildings nearby.

Onlookers were struck by the incongruity of advance and expansion that Victoria House and its crowning sculpture represented amid the street's surrounding vacant lots and general state of dilapidation. Buildings blocking east Strand at Holywell Street were removed but the London County Council kept the condemned houses in Holywell Street standing until the property to the north of it was bought. With slower responses to its improvement plans than it anticipated, the Council propped them up until development proposals were confirmed. Their crumbling frames, held up by temporary timber struts which the Council installed, presented a dismal view to the street. Towards the west, Somerset House stood soot-blackened, grimy and forlorn for the 1911 coronation. Half-hearted about lighting up for the celebrations, the shuttered Strand looked on its mob of thousands who surged out to rejoice in George V's processional path.[44] Nervous in their attendance were the liveried porters at the Savoy and the Cecil, lined up like a barrier across the entries to their driveway courtyards.

Two and three-storey high hoardings plastered with advertisements went up alongside St Mary's to conceal the ugliness on the Strand. Its 'dead' walls and ugly scaffolding became a street art gallery when they were plastered with advertising on large-scale poster-paintings, such as one that represented John Bull and his family at the seaside to advertise the best-selling *John Bull* weekly magazine.[45] Outdoor publicity like this, with posters that resembled paintings, reflected rapid change and competition in business and the growing revenue to businesses from advertising.

Victoria House waited to become the adjoining south-west corner of a larger building for the Aldwych end of east Strand that was planned by Australia's Commonwealth government. Until built, its entire windowless eastern rear wall became a massive advertising 'canvas', 120 feet high and 65 feet wide, reputedly London's largest billboard. 'Go to Australia', it bellowed.[46] Up went an illuminated signboard at the far east end of the 'Australian' site awaiting builders for the Commonwealth building. The electrified signboard carried changing messages from Australia's government: 'Australia's Daily Message' it read. It announced Australia's scheme of universal military training: 'Australia's share in the defence of the empire for 1912', it trumpeted that August.[47]

On the street, rows of sandwich-men bearing placards imploring people to join the Society for the Prevention of Premature Burial added to messaging pressing for attention.[48] The London Association for the Prevention of Premature Burial, established in 1896, publicised the hazards of hasty internment. Fear of being buried alive was common due to Britain's lax death certification standards and the Association lobbied for burial reform.

The hurly-burly of the street aside, its shops and window displays gave passers-by plenty to attract them, and this explains the scrum often seen on its pavement. Specialist shops displayed necessities, curiosities and innovations. Samuel Smith & Son, of 9 Strand, were watchmakers to the Admiralty, famed for their watches, chronometers and other precision instruments such as their 'Strand' watches and their first 'Perfect Speedometer'.[49] Allan Smith (later Sir Allan Gordon-Smith), a third-generation clock-maker and future manufacturer of motoring instruments and accessories, joined his father in business in 1903. He built on the introduction of the first British-made speedometer in 1904. Rapid business expansion would see the Smiths' firm, English Clocks Ltd, become Europe's biggest clock manufacturer.

Instances of the value of the Strand's prestige abound. A couple of examples reflect the cachet of the Strand brand. Makers of acoustic instruments and hearing aids, F. C. Rein & Son, at 340 Strand, was one of the first companies to manufacture commercially available hearing aids. The firm was so well known from its Strand location that a neighbouring optician, Leslie Victor Kahn, bought Rein's business and changed his name to Kahn-Rein, seemingly for commercial advantage.[50] Another example comes from Villiers Engineering Co., which manufactured small engines for motorcycles and cycle parts in Villiers Street, Wolverhampton, 113 miles from London. It built a motorcycle with a Villiers engine assembled specifically for export to Australia, with which it enjoyed commercial success through its promotion as the Villiers-Strand, which associated it with a vital transport hub for London and a street of premier stature.[51]

Examples abound in literature as well. The villainous Madame Sara in the sought-after novel *The Sorceress of the Strand*, co-authored by L. T. Meade and Robert Eustace and serialised in *The Strand Magazine* from July 1902, reminds us how Strand shops and merchants filled literary imagination. Here, the financially comfortable middle and upper classes of her day were also victims of the misdeeds conducted from her 'beauty shop' on the Strand.

Government agencies followed Victoria's example in opening Strand offices. Their presence, bringing to them visiting statesmen and Dominion representatives, brought additional prestige to the street. Governments of Britain's Dominions opened their offices to the street with window fronts displaying products of their countries, as they competed to encourage Londoners to migrate. The Canadian government ran a shop at Charing Cross. New Zealand's government had offices next to the Adelphi Theatre. Displays of Australian fauna featured in the plate-glass windows of Savoy House, 115–16 Strand, for Western Australia. The shopfronts and emblems of the Dominion states gave the street an aura of imperial significance. Pioneer Welsh aviator and airship builder Ernest Willows endorsed this when he flew above it towards the Houses of Parliament, from Crystal Palace, and back, in 1910. Holding the first of the Royal Aero Club's Airship Pilots Certificate, the young Cardiff aeronaut announced, 'I set out with the intention of encircling the centre of the empire, and I have done it'.[52]

'If any thoroughfare is to rank as the chief street of London it is the Strand', noted Robert Moncrieff, author of *Black's Guide to London*.[53] Tourist guides, and walking and topographical guides for literary rambles, besides those on 'vanishing London', abounded for Edwardian readers worldwide, making 'all the world' familiar with the Strand. Though cut about and having lost many haunts of historic associations, the Strand more than any other street is the epitome of London, wrote Wilfred Whitten. He named it the High Street of the Universe.[54]

Simpson's, at 106 Strand, was an institution that was long connected with the street. It dated back to 1848, when it received its name and expanded from the earlier popular 'home of chess', the Grand Cigar Tavern, that it had been since 1828. Tradition held firm at Simpson's. Roasted meat was offered from silver trolleys so as to not disturb chess players and continued to be served from the trolley in 1903. But, with the street being widened, and the new being welcomed on it, even Simpson's adapted to the times. In 1904, it became another example of how the old and the new blended on the street. Rebadged as Simpson's-in-the-Strand, it offered the novelty of a mixed dining room, enabling men and women to dine together in public, while maintaining its famed service and traditional fare. Arthur Conan Doyle, a frequent diner, used it as a meeting place in many of his tales. Sherlock Holmes proposes dining there in 'The Adventure of the Dying Detective'. He says to Watson, 'When we have finished at the police station, I think that something nutritious at Simpson's would not be out of place'.[55] From its kitchen, found two storeys below ground, with a staff of fifty men, celebrated London cook Thomas Davey, its chef since 1867, famously called 'Davey', reputedly oversaw every plate of food before it was hoisted by dumbwaiter to the dining room. His control made it a place for the elect to eat, where Cabinet ministers and other prominent people were seen on any day. Simpson's was popular with foreigners, and in particular was crowded with Americans during the summer; consequently, New York restaurants vied to lure Davey from his command. The New York Times hailed his loyalty to his post: 'To remove Davey from the Strand would be to take away one of the remaining links between our present hurly-burly and the placid cheer of the days of Dickens and Wilkie Collins'.[56]

Controversy blew up in mid-1908 over the 'Strand Statues'. Jacob Epstein was a young sculptor, twenty-seven years old, when he was commissioned in the spring of 1907 to sculpt a frieze of eighteen nude figures representing the Seven Ages of Man on the new British Medical Association building at the corner of Agar Street. Delighted to have the opportunity to show what he could do on a monumental scale in the heart of his newly adopted city (he had lived there for two years but was born in New York), Epstein threw everything into the commission, including taking up British citizenship. Today, the statues hold our attention as monuments to the futility of prejudice. Within the space of fourteen months the eighteen over-life-size figures were finished. Each was first modelled in clay and then cast in plaster, then carved from stone *in situ* working from the plaster models. Epstein spent a year carving each figure from single Portland stone blocks, working some forty feet above the ground, chiselling on high scaffolding with narrow wooden planks and whatever the weather brought him and two assistants between the summer of 1907 and June 1908.

Completed that June, Epstein's figures representing the human life cycle were inseparable from architect Charles Holden's simplified façade. Jutting from the building's granite front, they balanced the building's vertical emphasis by connecting its upper and lower halves. Block-like in nature, they were of simplified shape, but with pronounced musculature and naturalist detail. Their various poses indicated movement with vitality by fitting snugly within their compressed frame. However, the nudity offended officers of the National Vigilance Association in their offices across the road. They denounced them as 'pagan' and 'obscene' and agitated to have them dismantled. The Strand Statues controversy raged over decency and morality rather than aesthetics. Agitators, significant in neither number nor weight, stirred up a tempest. The *London Evening Standard*, referring to the figures as amazing, headlined a question about the bold sculpture: 'Is it art?' The paper wrote, 'They are a form of statuary which no careful father would wish his daughter and no discriminating young man would wish his fiancée to see'.[57] A policeman sent up the ladder to inspect the statues wrote in his notebook the one word, 'rude'. Agitators argued (as the *Evening Standard* reported) that

> Nude statuary figures in an art gallery are seen, for the most part, by those who know how to appreciate the art they represent; they were *not* for people for whom art galleries are never intended. To have art of the kind indicated, laid bare to the gaze of all classes, young and old, in perhaps the busiest thoroughfare of the Metropolis of the world, and portrayed in the form it is on the new building of the British Medical Association, is another matter.[58]

Confrontation ensued between the prudery of earlier Victorian days and more relaxed prevailing values. The British Medical Association, which had commissioned the statues, refused to take them down. The final salvo came from Sir Charles Holroyd, Director of the National Gallery, who warmly praised the sculpture. Taken in conjunction with the purchase by public subscription of Velasquez's *Venus with the Mirror* (the Rokeby Venus) for the National Gallery in 1906, the question arose as to whether the beautiful and reverent use of the nude in public sculpture should be permitted in London; the statues were a significant marker of more advanced public opinion in England.

Advanced public opinion was also clear for all to see in the mounting call for electoral reform. The closing hours of the suffragists' Mud March from Hyde Park on 9 February 1907 were among the last scenes that Exeter Hall witnessed before its demolition (for the Strand Palace Hotel). The march of 3,000 women was a peaceful demonstration organised by the National Union of Women's Suffrage Societies. Campaigning for the vote increasingly engaged women, many of whom dispensed with their inhibiting hobble skirts and oversized hats with ostrich feathers to distribute suffragist pamphlets and newspapers on the street. Women's fashion suggested a languor that belied the febrile atmosphere of the 1910s.

The new era demanded more equitable conditions. The spirits of Exeter Hall reformists could only have contributed to emboldening activists on the Strand and nearby Essex Hall, where the Fabian Society met. Eviscerating buildings from the Strand's philanthropic and benevolent past might bring to it shiny 'palace hotels'. These might be thought to better suit the gay living of Edwardian days, freed from the imperial wars of the Victorian era. Yet shiny Edwardian 'palaces' could not quell the Strand's ongoing affinity with the everyman.

Reckoning with the new age was in the air. Charlotte Despard, first President of the Women's Freedom League, writing from its headquarters in 18 Buckingham Street, responded to a notice from the Inland Revenue Office that she needed to pay income tax. The sister of the Inspector-General of the Army, Sir John French, Despard lived for what she thought was the common good and allied herself with the Adult Suffrage Society, which refused to accept any franchise extension that did not establish full citizenship. She notified the Office that, 'As taxation without representation is acknowledged in England to be a form of tyranny, I, being Unrepresented, decline to pay this tax'.[59] Passive resistance, which she advocated, called for more than chalking suffragette slogans on pavements and walls by night. Aged sixty-three, she instituted the Women's Tax Resistance League, which adopted as its maxim 'No Vote, No Tax'.

News of civil disobedience like hers, and increasing industrial unrest in Britain, was relayed from wireless stations installed above the Strand, on the roof of the Royal Society of the Arts and at Marconi House. Guglielmo Marconi, Italo-Irish inventor of wireless transmission, looking to earlier Strand inventor Benjamin Franklin, took over 336 Strand (the Gaiety Restaurant and Hotel complex) and turned it into the headquarters of the Marconi Company. The wireless station on the roof of Marconi's building housed the night office of the *New York Times* and also served as an adjunct to the school inside the building that Marconi ran to train wireless operators in the latest methods of telegraphy.[60] When many in Britain worried that the country was complacent about losing its competitive advantage, Marconi was intent on demonstrating further leadership in the one technological development where Britain led. Ever experimental, he and his team worked on microwaves, which would take them on the path to developing

FIGURE 18. Stranded: Charing Cross, *c.* 1912–13. Lantern slide. A motor bus on route 1 is caught in the snow outside the Eleanor Cross, Charing Cross Station. (Brian May Archive of Stereoscopy)

radar. His rooftop wireless station established communication with vessels proceeding up and down the Channel. From the Strand in 1912, contact could be made across distances of up to 600 miles (exceeding that the equipment on ocean liners could achieve under normal conditions).[61]

Below, on the street, in late June 1914, a show of cosmopolitan character and striking pageantry was displayed at the Salvation Army Congress, to which came some 12,000 delegates from around the globe and soldiers of the Army's London corps. They, with some 3,000 band players, and decorated floats, processed to Hyde

Park, where General William Booth could address them all. A hall for this Congress of Nations was temporarily erected on the still vacant middle Strand between St Mary's and Aldwych. Grandly called the Great Salvation Hall, it formed the nucleus of the Congress, where an enthusiastic audience assembled.[62] Delegates from fifty-eight countries met there, among them Zulu, Japanese, Laplander, American Indian, Arctic and Alpine salvationists, displaying on their approach great diversity of colour and costume. They sweltered in the heat of the corrugated iron pavilion, straining to hear speeches over the roaring traffic outside.

With the outbreak of war in 1914, the Strand became more cosmopolitan than ever. Headlines from French and Belgian newspapers were cried on it, and one evening journal was issued in Flemish.[63] Offices were set up on east Strand to support Belgian refugees, and a Prisoners of War Information Bureau opened on Wellington Street. Almost every European language was heard on the pavements. With more men needed in the forces, single men who had yet to enrol were given until 30 November 1915 to present themselves to recruiting stations. The Royal Naval Division Recruiting Station on the Strand had a board reading 'The photograph of the man we want' above a mirror.[64]

When German Zeppelins threatened the city from above, the Strand dimmed its night-time brilliance. The throngs hurried along in murky darkness. Vehicles steered by the aid of red and green hurricane oil lamps. A sober mood prevailed in the street. Detachments of allied troops filled it: Serbian troops in their great coats marched from Charing Cross, omnibuses behind them.[65] 'It is far better to face the bullets than to be killed at home by a bomb; Join the army at once & help to stop an air raid', read posters showing a feared dirigible in the night sky over London.[66]

Officials were concerned about overseas troops on furlough in London. The YMCAs from Australia, New Zealand, Canada, England and the United States formed the Strand-based International Hospitality League. Social services were given to Allied troops as they returned from France. Temporary hutments spread out at Aldwych, with sleeping, café and entertainment accommodations, where the wearied men could rest, freshen and relax. The Strand became a haven for them.

The American YMCA installed Eagle Hut, which took in Americans and any of the Allied Forces in uniform. The Law Courts became a Red Cross barracks and canteen for American sailors. Servicemen played baseball in the street, amid fog that burned in their throats.[67] The Canadians opened Beaver Hut in late October 1918, which served 2,500 meals daily.[68] A hut for Jewish soldiers opened in January 1919. Japanese sailors docked into London and 600 took tea on the Strand. News made it to Australia that a bootblack who gave his address as the Beaver Hut, Strand, told the magistrate at the Marylebone Police Court that he was employed at the hut, making £2 a day (£130 in today's money) and sometimes more.[69] Just under 1.2 million men enjoyed the huts and their social rooms.

Authorities were concerned about the welfare of servicemen who were preyed upon by young women, who were often thieving, or worse. A voluntary body of women patrols kept their eye on the night-time Strand; their visibility on the street until sunrise helped keep order. The Women's Police Volunteers (later the Women's Police Service) were largely of independent means and wore the police uniform which they devised. Many had been militant suffragettes, so they possessed a thorough knowledge of the district, with its many alleyways and courts tucked away from view. They deflected assaults and brawls, prevented thieving, and gave help and advice to servicemen, refugees and 'those of bad character', men and women alike. The police objected to their efforts, but the military authorities were glad for their presence; soldiers and members of the International Hospitality League Patrol gave their assistance. From January 1918 to April 1921, their street patrols dealt with over 800,000 men.[70]

As servicemen anticipated their discharge in England and embarkation home, they bid their farewell to the Strand. On 26 April 1919, in fine springtime sunshine, over 5,000 soldiers processed down the Mall towards the City. Their march was among the Victory Parades held in London during the spring and early

summer that year. Huge crowds watched the troops turn into
the now orderly, well-mannered Strand. Flags were festooned
across almost every building. Two mounted Australian regiments
processed down the street. The Australian artillery was represented by an eighteen-pounder battery. The infantry were in
fighting order, bayonets fixed, haversacks and greatcoats slung
on the back.[71] At the head of the parade were Indian veterans who
had fought with the Australians at Gallipoli. At Australia House,
the Prince of Wales took the salute. The Australian Flying Corps
performed intricate displays at low altitudes above the parade.
They rivetted spectators with surprising diversions overhead.
Two Handley Page planes rose high above; a dozen smaller Snipes
darted beneath them. They dove down close over the chimney pots
of the precinct, before swooping above the procession, looping
back to thrill the packed street with their turns. The Strand always
welcomed a spectacle.

CHAPTER 7

INTERWAR STRAND

The sight of all the wrecked beauty was enough to break the hardest heart.
Reverend W. Pennington-Bickford, 1941[1]

The Strand erupted into loud cheers, whistles and yells as word spread of the announcement made by the King from Buckingham Palace that peace had been signed at Versailles. It was shortly after 6 p.m. on Saturday 28 June 1919. Tens of thousands jammed the street and rejoiced at the news, linked arms and danced, relieved that the war was over.[2] When night fell, searchlights illuminating the sky above added to the victory jubilations. The war had personally involved so many in the crowd, thought actress Nancy Price, aged thirty-nine. She could not forget her lucky escape on the night when Zeppelins came over central London and left behind a deadly trail. She had taken shelter in a restaurant doorway in the Strand. Others under cover nearby had been killed. Narrow escapes had taken their toll, she thought. 'We had worked, known privation, suffered very considerably – and we were tired.'[3]

The Strand had not escaped aerial bombardment but had been spared from major damage. The immediate aftermath of the war found the street in a seemingly more settled state than it had been throughout its prewar years, when sappers and rubble regularly invaded it for its rebuilding. Though the war had dimmed the brilliance of its star attractions, it was anticipated that its places of entertainment would quickly revive.

Yet there was no escaping its dreary, deserted appearance. Stark timber hoardings every few hundred yards offended the eye; they concealed whatever rebuilding was being undertaken in the uneasy course of reconstruction. For three years, the Hotel Cecil had been occupied by the government to serve as headquarters of the Air Ministry. There was no serious damage to its exterior and its reopening was much hoped for, but it was left in a shabby state when officially demobilised in mid-1919, and it needed repairing and general refitting internally before it could welcome guests. It managed to reopen on the last night of 1919. By then, relatively few servicemen remained on the Strand. Overtaking them on the street were British provincials, visitors from Britain's overseas possessions and a larger number than usual of Chinese and Japanese visitors.

At its eastern end where Aldwych swung past St Clement Danes, the grandeur of newly built Australia House compelled attention. London's first purposely designed chancery was built by the second most geographically distant of the four self-governing Dominions of Britain's Empire. King George V opened the building on 3 August 1918 to the wearying world that was then still at war. Its French-mannered façade, with paired columns seried under a bronze mansard and a sumptuous entrance and exhibition hall of Australian marble of different colours, suggested that the civilised order of prewar days would be restored to public life. It immediately became an emblem of future possibilities. Its scale, and bronze, marble and stucco furnishings, were a striking contrast to the YMCA hut and similar utilitarian sheds around it that marred Aldwych.

No significant structure yet stood on the Strand's midpoint, where temporary shelters blanketed its Aldwych eyesore. Demountables that served troops were ugly to behold and were peppered over open spaces that could be found in central London, many edging the Strand. Hopes were held that the Strand's longed-for development could stem from the agencies of the Empire's Dominions or their provinces and those of associated bodies whose offices dotted the thoroughfare. Some with prominent shopfronts displayed their products: sheaves of New Zealand wheat, taxidermied Australian marsupials, and other curiosities. Among their ensemble were the Canadian Pacific Railway (62–65 Charing Cross), New Zealand Government Offices (413–416 Strand), the

British South African Company (138 Strand), the Overseas Club (a stone's throw from the church of St Clement Danes) and the Royal Colonial Institute (the forerunner of today's Royal Commonwealth Society, on Northumberland Avenue, two minutes from Charing Cross Underground Station). They signalled that the Strand had indeed become London's – and the Empire's – imperial centre and political capital, as imperialist circles had advocated. They were among the buildings that made the Strand one of London's show streets. 'It *is* London to the ordinary inquisitive traveller', wrote E. V. Lucas in A *Wanderer in London*. 'Almost everything that English provincials, Americans and other foreigners come to London to see is there.'[4] It became the epicentre of London's postwar reconstruction. Events that occurred there and innovations made on it confirmed the central position it held in London. For good reason, it continued to be regarded as the centre of the world.

Anticipation of a brighter future for the street was bolstered when construction sprang up on Aldwych, west of Australia House. American transportation magnate Irving T. Bush swung into action soon after hostilities ended. Bush brought his New York architect Harvey Wiley Corbett to London to erect a lofty new complex of three buildings to front the Strand and also face up Kingsway. Corbett was a futurist who aimed to build for the 'metropolis of tomorrow'. He had built for Bush one of New York's earliest skyscrapers, the neo-gothic 30-storey Bush Tower on Manhattan's 42nd Street. Effectively a world trade centre, Bush intended to build something similar in London. Work began on the sizeable complex of three buildings, a central block and two wings, that came to be known as Bush House. By August 1929, the east and west wings of the Bush House complex, fronting on Aldwych, had been completed and plans were underway to extend its central block with a front on the Strand.

New buildings such as Bush House revealed the pragmatism of the day. They met postwar needs for better circulation, lighting and ventilation. Changes in building techniques and materials, with steel and reinforced concrete, allowed faster construction, more open floors and office space, and rounded and moulded sections.

The preference grew to have more open offices, bright floors, larger windows. A more tempered classicism dressed buildings, without the ornamentation that typified those of prewar days. By the late 1920s, neo-classicism pared down architectural design.

Concern mounted about how the metropolis could cater for its mushrooming population, which grew between 1911 and 1939 from 7.25 to 8.73 million. This question dampened ongoing debate about losing traditions. The London Society was among those calling for redress of London's slovenliness. It urged the necessity for stimulating a wider concern for the beauty of the capital city, for the preservation of its old charms and the careful consideration of its new developments. Discussion about building for a London in fifty years' time triggered talk about building skywards.

Eventually, compromise was reached. Artistic sensibility (let alone architectural etiquette) dictated respect for central Strand's existing buildings, particularly Somerset House and its two late seventeenth-century and early eighteenth-century churches. Charmed by the intimacy of London's Georgian scale, Corbett curbed desires to push skywards and, in keeping with London's height-level restrictions, he removed an intended sky tower from plans for Bush House's central block. When completed in 1935, it therefore met the existing (if contested) regulations on building height. And while of a size that modern purpose called for, Bush House's simplified appearance was sympathetic to its neighbouring earlier landmarks. This nod to the street's architectural expression, together with the new complex's scale, added dimension to the Strand and gave it a new dignity and quality.

The Strand's pre-eminence in radio transmission and its leadership in improving and elaborating communication in the wireless age also boosted its importance. On 11 May 1922, a radio broadcast was first transmitted from the London station 2LO on the top of Marconi House. Jack Dempsey, heavy-weight champion of the world, resplendent in tuxedo, and credited with earning £20,000 a year (over £2.4 million in today's money) for refereeing fights, brought to the world his ringside view of the contest at Olympia between the betting favourite, French boxer Georges Carpentier, and the sentimental favourite, England's Ted 'Kid' Lewis.[5] Radio magic transfixed listeners who heard Dempsey describe the fight, a first-round knockout win by Carpentier. Shortly after, the station was transferred to the newly created British Broadcasting Company. It set up broadcasting studios in nearby Savoy Hill House, where it would expand to nine studios and in 1927 change its status to Corporation (the BBC).

Arthur Burrows, journalist and avid wireless enthusiast who predicted many developments in wireless telegraphy and telephony, had been responsible for experimental transmissions from Marconi House. The small number of people (no more than 30,000) holding wireless licences heard him inaugurate British broadcasting officially upon reading the first broadcast news bulletin transmitted by the BBC, on 14 November 1922. 'It was the day of the declaration of polls in connection with the General Election, and the news for that evening consisted in the main of election results' he recalled in his 1924 book, *The Story of Broadcasting*.[6] Appointed Director of Programmes, he had a considerable part in the framing of the programme policy of the BBC in its first years.

Burrows championed the possibilities of broadcasting as a means for developing a closer understanding between peoples. Australia's High Commission also seized on this potential. Some 2,000 guests invited to a reception at Australia House listened in to the All Australian concert arranged by the BBC to mark Australia Day on 26 January 1923. As a feature of the concert, diva Dame Nellie Melba spoke from the building's library into a broadcasting machine, and her voice was transmitted by wireless to the different parts of the building and then throughout the world. Fifteen months later, the King would take to broadcasting to open the British Empire Exhibition, as he believed that it could bridge the Empire.

With the ending of wartime restrictions, many on the Strand wasted no chance to make the most of extended opening hours. On the reopening of the Aldwych Theatre on 3 November 1919, after its long closure, it was anticipated that there would be more places of entertainment open than had been the case for a long time past.

In addition to the opera at Covent Garden, more than ten theatres and music halls and picture theatres stood in the Strand and its district. It was already noticeable, however, that this number would be insufficient to meet demand. Theatre-goers waited for hours in long pit and gallery queues outside, often soaked with the rain, splashed with mud from passing motorcars, wet-footed and uncertain whether, at the end of their wait, they would get a seat or whether they would be told there was standing room only. Call for entertainment was a feature of the day, as it offered escape from its political uncertainties and economic hardships. Like architecture, entertainment would improve immensely in imagination, originality and technical skill.

Entertainment impresario Charles B. Cochran played a large hand in these improvements from his agency offices at 60 Strand. In the business of anticipating trends, he brought to London Florence Mills and the Blackbirds Company and Orchestra. The pre-eminent female jazz dancer of the Harlem Renaissance mesmerised audiences with her signature song 'I'm a Little Blackbird Looking for a Bluebird'. She visited in 1923 and again in 1926, and established the authenticity of black song and dance beyond portrayals by blackface performers.

The year 1926 was that of the Charleston, the hyperactive, wild-stepping dance that many dance floors prohibited, for fear of casualties. Mills, with her supple limbs and birdlike grace, showed how to spring with the Charleston and kick away restrictions.

Women's bobbed hair and bare arms most visibly reflected changes. Skirts were at their shortest, reaching the knee, in shift-like dresses. Hairstyles, too, shortened, cut in shingle style, worn with cloche hats fitted closely to the head.

The American invasion was another register of unstoppable change. In August 1926, Anita Loos arrived in London, aged thirty-eight, fresh from Hollywood and on the heels of her Jazz Age classic 1925 comic novel, *Gentlemen Prefer Blondes*. Its heroine, a blonde vamp named Lorelei Lee, was a practical young woman who equated culture with cold cash (for whom 'a diamond bracelet lasts forever'). Loos's whip-smart quips touched on many preoccupations of the Jazz Age, and endeared her, like Mills, to London's Bright Young People.

Slick American farces were being shown on the London musical stage in 1929 as the talkies began, with *The Jazz Singer*, the first feature-length talking film. That autumn, Noël Coward's *Bitter Sweet* (initially a Cochran production) opened in New York with Evelyn Laye as leading lady (where she made the hit of her career). Like Mills's performances, *Bitter Sweet* was without equal. Coward, with his innate timing and swift and sure instinct for the right thing in theatre, depicted the flashy superficiality of the Cocktail Age, and satirised the decadent and effete.

Oppressed minorities clamoured to be heard as well. Mills was a staunch and outspoken supporter of equal rights for African Americans, her hit song being a heartfelt plea for racial equality. By April 1927, 'Blackbirds' had reached its two hundred and fiftieth performance, every one of which Mills delivered personally, and without an understudy. In keeping with the craze for black culture that was prevalent among bohemian types in Paris, some in London among what the Victorians called the 'highest ranks of society' adopted Mills and invited her to their homes and parties.[7] She anonymously redistributed the many tokens of appreciation they showered on her, their gifts of flowers, fruits and other delicacies. 'Let's bring a little happiness into the City of "Despair"', she would tell her driver, having him give them to the down-and-out people along the Embankment, as well as money to any especially needy looking patrons of its roadside coffee stalls.[8]

While the upper set partied at the Savoy, the Cecil succumbed to liquidation. In August 1930, some 200 workers began its demolition.[9] In 1931, a landmark arose on its site in a sweeping scheme of rebuilding. Shell-Mex House was a new touchstone for the Strand and for London. With a frontage to the river of 200 feet and some 300 feet deep, it became the most pronounced feature of the Embankment and the largest single office building in London.[10] Its width and height still dominate the riverfront. Its south front, fifteen floors high, features a prominent central clocktower with a giant clock high above, exceeding Big Ben's dimensions. Popularly dubbed Big Benzene, it consists simply of the plain Portland stone face of the tower, upon which the clock's gigantic dials, twenty-five feet square, visible to the north and south, indicate the hours. Knowing heads at the time read it as the register of the new industries of motors and electrical machinery which were replacing those that were stalling, such as coal and shipping.

Reconstruction continued apace along the Strand in the 1930s. India House, London's second purpose-built High Commission building, built to the design of imperialist architect Sir Herbert Baker, along the convex curve of Aldwych, opened in mid-1930. New offices for the High Commissioner for the Unions of South Africa involved the reconditioning of the entire block between Trafalgar Square, the Strand and Duncannon Street. Here, Baker wrestled with the awkward corner site to construct an 'Empire product', that is, another imposing Dominion house, to the street. Following the model set by Australia House, many of the materials for this new building came directly from South Africa. The Agent-General for Ontario built similarly, using Ontario materials when the province's government building, Ontario House (at 163 Strand), was reconditioned.

Unseen, beneath the street, the Kingsway tramways subway was reconfigured to allow for large double-deck Pullman cars to run through it. In less than eleven months, the old subway was enlarged, deepened and improved. Its Aldwych branch was a little-used branch line that had opened as the Strand Station in 1907. It was to have been the terminus for the Great Northern and Strand Railway, which linked the river to King's Cross and Finsbury Park; the intention to make a river crossing to Waterloo never happened. It became effectively a dead-end, one-station branch of the Piccadilly line at Holborn.

Noise and bustle were synonymous with the Strand, and its increasing traffic was another marker of changing times. More omnibuses careered along it than any other street out of the City. By 1925, they had been doing so for twenty-eight years. The London General Omnibus Company warned they would vanish from the street, in the same way that earlier steam versions had become

FIGURE 19. Strand, looking west, toward Trafalgar Square, 1927. Photograph. The congested Strand with the Hotel Cecil (left) and Nelson's Column seen in the distance. (Collections of the State Library of New South Wales)

obsolete.[11] Covered-top buses, 'Generals', replaced them and were running on the road for the first time that year.

Gyratory systems of traffic control that merged different streams of vehicles in a one-way direction were another innovation. One-way traffic was trialled on each side of the churches of St Clement Danes and St Mary le Strand in 1929. Most drivers proceeded in the desired, westerly manner down the Strand, but some drove against the general flow, being either unaware or un-accustomed to the trial. That April, an officer of the Royal Air Force entered the Strand from Essex Street and drove without stopping against the one-way traffic; he narrowly missed one omnibus and damaged vehicles when swiping against another. He was judged to have driven dangerously (reportedly driving at an estimated speed of twenty to twenty-five miles per hour), but it is notable that this incident was reported more as an example of how bodies such as the police were yet to be fully authorised to enforce evolving traffic regulations.[12] Other incidents reported to cause traffic chaos were flooding from burst water mains, sheep being herded to market, improperly packed produce cascading from lorries onto the street, parades and student rags.

In September, one-way and roundabout traffic schemes were established. Traffic flowed one way on either side of the two churches, around the island on which the Gladstone Statue stood and Melbourne Place to Aldwych (from north to south). Traffic direction signs went up and white lines were laid down on these routes. By 1931, one-way traffic was extended so that Aldwych became a one-way street (from west to east), as did the Strand between St Clement Danes and Wellington Street (from east to west). Arundel Street and Melbourne Place ran from south to north and Surrey Street from north to south.

Dangers posed by the corner of St Clement Danes and the courts at its north were often reported. The church's rector protested against the speed of motorbuses hastening towards Ludgate Hill.[13] He pleaded that a speed limit be applied to prevent the fatalities and injuries that occurred at this point. In 1934, readers of the *Daily Express* voted for Transport Minister Leslie Hore-Belisha as the paper's 'Outstanding Political Figure of the Year'. Especially favoured was his introduction of road crossings for pedestrians marked at each end by what became known as a Belisha beacon, a yellow globe on a black and white post. As well, the public favoured his bringing in speed limits of thirty miles an hour in built-up areas and his prohibition of cars hooting at night.

Loud on the street were the ever-present thuds resembling the dull ring of a mallet on wood blocks. This forceful sound that vehicular traffic characteristically made reverberated beyond the clattering of vehicles' engines or the honking horns. The clang and clatter of it all was stopped only on 11 November, when the maroons sounded for the Two Minutes' Silence. In 1925, the roar of the traffic on the street was heard until, at the eleventh hour, all was still. The Silence was followed by Paul Robeson, the bass baritone and future freedom activist, heard from 2LO. He gave a talk on the origin and significance of black African song. That broadcast was followed shortly after by another on 2LO, when he gave a recital of these songs.[14] A lawyer and athlete (who had been approached to take on Jack Dempsey), as well as actor and singer of remarkable versatility, Robeson gained a prominent place in theatre and films, as concert singer and popular recording artist. In 1928, his singing, especially of 'Ol' Man River' in Jerome Kern's *Show Boat*, profoundly moved audiences. He packed the Theatre Royal Drury Lane, renovated in 1922 as a four-tiered theatre. Charles Cochran respected Robeson's songs as an artistic achievement of great expressiveness, poignancy and profound religious sentiment.[15] As actress and critic Marie Seton observed, Robeson's song expressed something felt most deeply, where real experience is transmuted into art:

... Tote that barge and lift that bale,
You get a little drunk,
And you lands in jail.
I gets weary and sick of tryin',
I'm scared of livin' and feared of dyin'.[16]

Robeson performed in Shakespeare's *Othello* which opened at the Savoy Theatre on 19 May 1930 (Figure 20). No black African actor

FIGURE 20. Paul Robeson as Othello with Peggy Ashcroft as Desdemona, in the London stage production of *Othello*, Savoy Theatre, 1930. (James Weldon Johnson Collection, Beinecke Rare Book and Manuscript Library)

had played Othello in England since the 1860s and Robeson's performance was acclaimed.[17] At the end of the first performance he received twenty curtain calls. Robeson was the most sought-after artist in London.[18]

Meanwhile, the thorny problem of Waterloo Bridge highlighted the Strand's key riverside location, a crucial juncture for traffic intersecting London. John Rennie's bridge of 1817 was regarded as the finest masonry bridge in London and among the most beautiful in Europe. In December 1923, its centre piers had subsided (by almost eight inches in one spot) and a definite curve appeared in its roadway. A steady increase in the volume of goods carted to Covent Garden was thought to be among the factors contributing to the deterioration of the bridge. Merchants Geo. Monro Ltd was a family-run affair, whose business outgrew the seven separate premises it occupied at Covent Garden (it also had branches in Manchester, Berlin and Paris). It constructed its own sizeable building that straddled Tavistock and Essex Streets, as well as a post-order department in Exeter Street. Its fleet of thirty-five heavy Leyland trucks delivered produce to Covent Garden that came from Australia and New Zealand, South Africa and the Canaries, North America and Europe. Its high-class fruit business and floral selling and distribution was conducted on an industrial scale.[19]

London County Council called in experts to inspect the bridge. The cracks convinced engineers that a new one was needed. The Council invited proposals for developing it and cross-river traffic and issued requirements for any scheme. As land on the Strand had become so valuable, the Council had built its new County Hall on the south side of the river (opened in 1922, completed in 1939). This required an embankment to be constructed on that Surrey side from the new County Hall to Waterloo Bridge. As well, the Council stipulated that proposed schemes encourage northward traffic over the new road bridge to keep Trafalgar Square clear, with any inter-section of Strand and bridge traffic to be not less than 200 yards from Trafalgar Square. Proposals should offer the best possible aesthetic amenities with opportunity for harmonious architectural treatment and suitable vistas from all principal points.

The problem of designing for London's complex traffic en-tanglements occupied the minds and pens of the day's foremost architects and urban-thinkers. Among them were Professor S. D. Adshead (a proponent of the new profession of town planning), artist T. Raffles Davison (who respected London's historic features) and the prominent London architects Sir Reginald Blomfield, H. V. Lanchester and Paul Waterhouse. Twenty-five alternative schemes from them and others were proposed to replace the bridge and resolve the issues that the Council had identified.[20] (Even the 1857 scheme drawn by Sir Charles Barry was considered.) One plan envisaged moving Charing Cross Station and Hotel to the south side of the river, and building a new bridge over the Strand to the west of Waterloo Bridge. This scheme involved demolition of the existing bridge and its replacement by a double-decked steel overpass over the Strand, about eighteen feet above and behind St Martin in the Fields, the lower deck carrying six railway tracks, the lower one a roadway sixty feet wide (for traffic), with two pavements each of fifteen feet (for pedestrians). This vision appeared like it might have come more from the pages of futurist drawing boards devised by Harvey Corbett (and his New York colleague Hugh Ferris) than anything seen in London. It was never built, though it was favoured by the 1926 Royal Commission on London Cross-River Traffic.

By the 1930s, striking features punctuated the Strand's western end. Art Deco/Moderne style was in vogue, especially with cinemas, which promoted the Hollywood aesthetic. In 1929, the Savoy Theatre was completely remodelled. Modernist architects Easton and Robertson sharpened the Savoy Court elevation. Glazed doors framed in stylised drapes were installed within a polished stainless-steel canopy supporting the theatre's name in oversized steel sans-serif letters. Frank A. Tugwell with Basil Ionides decorated the theatre's foyer and two-tier auditorium in silver-leafed rectangles, which created an inspired and eye-catching Art Deco/Moderne interior. Walking into the entrance foyer of the Strand Palace Hotel, one could feel star-struck, transported to the gleaming glamour of Hollywood. Oliver P. Bernard's orchestration of chromed steel with translucent moulded glass, internally lit and geometrically shaped, dazzled in its geometry and brilliance.

Nearby, Ernest Schaufelberg rebuilt the Adelphi Theatre at 409–412 Strand (an image can be seen on the cover of this book). Renamed the Royal Adelphi, the theatre's latest iteration was very much of its age. Its foyer was lined in black marble under a stepped angular ceiling. Polished wood, marble and chromium added glittering glamour to its straight-sided, angular auditorium with two concrete-framed cantilevered balconies. From 1937, showman Charles Cochran staged long-running plays and revues on its revolving stage. Even business houses favoured internally lit glazed features, such as were seen in the new London headquarters of the Halifax Building Society (51–55 Strand) in 1934, and with the tiered glass columns down the length of Charing Cross's Grand Arcade.

Still, some traditions held – and charmed, as they did, even for futurist Harvey Corbett. In celebration of the *Pickwick* centenary, members of the worldwide Dickens Fellowship celebrated the first meeting of the Pickwick Club. Dressed in their nineteenth-century costumes, they boarded the Commodore Stage Coach from the Strand's Golden Cross Hotel (opposite Charing Cross), as Mr Pickwick, Tracy Tupman and Mr Snodgrass did on 13 May 1827, and journeyed for Rochester in accordance with the past custom of horses being changed every twelve miles.[21]

Providing havens from entertainment's razzle-dazzle ablaze on the Strand were the two churches at its ends. St Martin in the Fields at its west end and St Clement Danes at its east (a road-island gem, the traffic swirling around it, at the busy part of the Strand by the Law Courts) were among London's most prominent churches. Under the guardianship of their ministers, they served useful purposes, provided care and reflected their community and the street's soul.

William Bickford's connection with St Clement Danes began with assisting the then widely known and loved rector of the church, Reverend J. J. H. Septimus Pennington, with its musical services, both at its seventeenth-century organ and in the choir. It became a matter of course that Bickford, of a similar steadfast nature and lofty vision to Pennington, should continue caring for the building that he admired as one of Wren's masterpieces, and its community. He married Louie Pennington, ten years his senior, the daughter of the rector whom he succeeded. Under her care, the church served the Covent Garden flower girls and became known as their church. He added her surname to his out of respect for the Penningtons' tireless work to revive the church and ensure its contribution to central London's life. Reverend Pennington-Bickford, minister of St Clement Danes from 1910, lived by the rhythm of the church, with its regular services, marriages, funerals and annual commemorations of thanksgiving or remembrance. He was steeped in the building's fabric and historical associations, and those of its surroundings, and was dedicated to their preservation and contribution to its parish.

The bells of St Clement's were famed. The church's Sanctus bell, its oldest, dated back to 1588. In 1913, they became silent when a new frame was needed to support their weight. After rehanging the ten bells, and ringing in the peace in July 1919, Pennington-Bickford introduced in 1920 a special children's service held annually at the end of March on what is known as Oranges and Lemons Day. In a twist of the old being made new, when reinstalling the bells he added to the carillon the tune of the famous nursery rhyme (which first appeared in print in 1744) and had the carillon's peal of the tune broadcast on Radio 2LO.[22] As the church's Sanctus bell struck 5 p.m. the bells played 'Oranges and Lemons' for the first time while about 500 children were presented with one of each as they left the church door, two by two.

In September 1931, London turned on 10,000 floodlights to make it into the world's brightest flood-lit city.[23] The purpose was to honour Michael Faraday, who a century earlier had discovered the electromagnetism which nearly all modern applications of electricity were based on. Each evening, half a million people flocked to London's central area and, in the greatest revel since Armistice night, crowds packed the streets to see the sights of London illuminated. Bus routes and police control stalled, unable to continue, but all kept shuffling along cheerfully.

By this time, entertainment and labour unrest went hand in hand. Elegance and want were seen cheek by jowl. Sharp divisions could not be ignored. Murmuring discontent and deepening shadows grew as government bungling tattered the economy and industrial action spread across the country. Dangers feared from the General Strike of 1926 had been averted on the Strand. The main rallying point for the May Day demonstrations was the Thames Embankment near the Temple Station, from which the procession was marshalled for the march to Hyde Park. Demonstrators sang marching songs and called out Labour war cries with shouts to 'Help the Miners'. Demonstrations that day spared the street from violent outbreaks that were seen elsewhere. The May Day revels organised by the Labour Party were held that afternoon at the Strand Theatre on Aldwych.

Paul Robeson lived eleven minutes' walk away from Aldwych, at 19 Buckingham Street. His experience there left a deep imprint on him and influenced his outlook on world affairs, from which he took the path of his life, to take his voice wherever 'there are those who want to hear the melody of freedom or the words that might inspire hope and courage in the face of despair and fear'.[24] Robeson was the most admired and respected American in London; he mixed easily with polite society and the intelligentsia.[25] He moved in a wide range of circles: Welsh miners, Indian seamen, African students, Labour activists. On 17 November 1928, a small group of Labour MPs invited Robeson to lunch at the House of Commons, probably the first actor to be so honoured. He sat beside Ramsay MacDonald, the former prime minister, who talked to him about the future of the British colonies. Robeson later wrote that it was in London, as the centre of the British Empire, where he 'discovered' Africa.[26] With his success, he grew in confidence about his own identity as an African.

He was becoming a champion of the dispossessed. A picture of how this developed comes from his encounter with a group of un-employed Welsh miners in the closing days of 1929. As he crossed the Strand near his home, he came upon them singing on the curb side. Mostly thinly clad, having tramped through bitter weather to London, they were singing for money to sustain themselves. One of their signs said they had walked all the way from South Wales, the area worst hit by unemployment, to petition the government for help. Hearing the harmony of their singing, Robeson joined them, humming along, and was impressed by their spirit and their suffering. When he sang 'Ol'Man River' and spirituals to his new friends, translating their hopes into song, it was a transforming experience.[27] He provided them with their passage home, and gave supplies of food and clothing for the miners of the Rhondda Valley and their families. He contributed the proceeds of one of his concerts to the Welsh miners' relief fund and visited the Rhondda Valley in person to sing for its mining communities and talk with their people. A lifetime of ardent friendship grew between Robeson and the people of South Wales.

The poor have always been part of London, but the Great Depression increased their number. By 1932, there were 2¾ million people unemployed in Britain. In late October, the National Unemployed Workers' Movement aimed to present a petition against a proposed means test to the House of Commons. The Hunger Marchers who converged on London numbered 100,000. As the hungry 1930s wore on, protests against poverty became louder and more violent.

St Martin in the Fields was the parish church of the monarchs of England (it is the only parish church in London to hold a royal pew) but was also the soldiers' church and a haven for homeless people. St Martin is the patron saint of beggars, soldiers and conscientious objectors; consequently, the care for the poor and a willingness to take seriously the responsibilities of those in authority, while at the same time being willing to challenge them, has been characteristic of the church. St Martin is also the patron saint of innkeepers and drunkards (which explains the phrase 'Martin drunk'). Hence St Martin's became famed as the parish church of all the world. With a long tradition of service lying behind its ever-open doors, Reverend 'Dick' Sheppard, vicar of St Martin's from 1914 to 1927, was behind many of its modern developments. A great populist, he directed the church to practical welfare work; this included opening its crypt to the destitute and homeless. Millions listened to his monthly radio broadcasts from the pulpit and knew him from 1924 as the Bishop of Broadcasting. A padre in France during the war, he held deep concerns over the disillusionment that he saw about him, especially the timidity of the Labour government of Ramsay MacDonald and the failure of the Labour Party to address the desperate plight of the unemployed. Unemployment soared – not least after 1929 – and with it came dreadful hardship. As domestic and global tensions rose, and aware how much mending needed doing, Britain's best-loved padre appealed in his broadcasts for shelter for those left damaged by the war who were yet to see anything of the promises made to them, such as having decent living conditions in 'a land fit for heroes to live in'. He noted, 'Fourteen years after the Armistice and we are still being pleaded with to give a sufficiency of comfort to those for whom, while the War lasted, we could not do enough'.[28]

St Martin's Day falls on 11 November; it was a striking co-incidence that this should also be Armistice Day. To Sheppard, observance of 11 November was aptly named Armistice Day, for it remained uncertain whether peace had been made permanently at all. A new arms race threatened, one worse than that which made the catastrophe of 1914 inevitable. He asked, was every Armistice Day only a pause, and what could be done to make it more abiding? Tirelessly championing pacifism, Sheppard rallied a Peace Army, as a non-violent means of protest, among those who believed they should volunteer to place themselves unarmed between combat-ants. The Peace Army would be called upon to operate only in the event of the League of Nations failing in its object of stopping war. Some 900 individuals joined the movement.[29] Lasting peace had to be found. Sheppard prayed that a Christian solution could resolve the struggle between the old idea of nationalism that pitched against the new concept of cooperation through the League of Nations. He resisted war: 'But because war is met with such courage and endurance, we are no more justified in permitting it than we should be in Mr. Winston Churchill allowing disease, torture and unemployment to continue because its victims bear their suffering so bravely'.[30] He held to his faith in a Christian solution and in co-operation: 'I believe in the ultimate decency of things, aye and if I awoke in hell would still believe it'.[31]

Amid mounting concerns about threats from abroad, the City of Westminster Council planned for civil defence. In 1935, it took action to provide shelters and to organise Air Raid Precautions (ARP) Committees. It cautioned the public to take precautions against the threat of invasion and poison gas attack, and to prepare for home defence and evacuation. These steps were largely ignored to begin with, although it was only twenty years since London had come under aerial attack. Massive subterranean shelters neared completion under what is now the Strand Aldwych quarter. At St Martin's the crypt was cleared and turned into an air raid shelter.

By 26 September 1938, active work on air raid precautions had begun in earnest. Sandbags were unloaded on the pavement outside office buildings. Trenches were dug in parks. The dead-end branch of the Kingsway tramways subway was organised to become a bomb shelter. The disused subways and platforms at Holborn and Aldwych Stations, and the disused tunnel between them, were prepared for the storage in emergency of articles from the British Museum and the Registry Office. Plans were set in train to evacuate children from London. Bills pasted up on walls listed places where forty million gas masks were being distributed free to civilians.

By the close of the 1930s, there was no escape from provocations elsewhere. The rise of fascism impinged on one of the mainstay communities of the Strand. Events in Italy tested loyalties within the Italian community, the largest and best-organised foreign community in Britain. Some 17,000 strong in London alone, and normally mutually supportive, with leading Italian industrialists, caterers, restaurant proprietors, doctors and business people among them, many of its professional and benevolent associations were centred at the Italian Cultural Club (4–6 Charing Cross Road, a few steps north of St Martin's). In April 1927, Marconi had become head of the British branch of the Italian Fascist Party, which made its headquarters at the Club. It provoked unease with its installation of portraits of Mussolini and its posting of black-shirted guards at the Club's entrance. At the time of Marconi's death in Rome in 1937, he and the 1,500 members of the British branch of the party were being closely watched by MI5.

Those known for holding anti-British views were rounded up by the police immediately when, on 10 June 1940, Mussolini declared war on Britain and France. In Italian quarters many heard of their country's entry into the war for the first time from police officers who had taken them into custody. The Custodian of Enemy Property seized the Italian Cultural Club's building and on 9 August 1940 Mrs Winston Churchill opened it as a social club for the New Zealand forces. At the start of that year, the Gatti family had enrolled with the Westminster City Council's Civil Defence Services to turn their theatre-restaurant and ballroom at

436 Strand into a dormitory and canteen.[32] Gatti's (once a favourite rendezvous for men about town, diners-out and celebrities) became a stopping-off place for the night for His Majesty's fighting forces.[33]

With the Strand having survived the Zeppelin raids of the Great War largely intact, some might have believed that it would survive further aerial assault. The Vaudeville Theatre was reconfigured from horseshoe to rectangular shape when remodelled by architect Robert Atkinson for brothers John and Rocco Gatti in 1925–26. It was an intimate theatre, with just 266 seats in the stalls and 166 in the balcony. There, theatrical all-rounder Archie de Bear produced a 'pocket revue' called *Moonshine* that picked up on the term's meaning as a colourful way to say 'nonsense'. It began with Beethoven's *Moonlight Sonata*, revived memories of the Strand when it was a street down which everybody was proud to go and ended with the defiant chorus from Harry Castling's song 'Don't sing a song about the war'.[34] Entertainment like this gave audiences some sense of continuity and relieved civilians when they were soon to endure the air raids of the next war. Black-out orders darkened the Strand, making it again a street of 'dreadful night', lit only by the inferno brought to it by waves of Luftwaffe bombers. New Zealand soldier Walter Bell found himself at the forces' club. 'One of our duties was bomb watch and we spent many hours up on the roof with our bucket of sand, and actually put four incendiary bombs out that fell on the roof.'[35]

From September 1940, London became the chief, almost the exclusive, target of a relentless series of raids by German bombers. On average 160 bombers attacked nightly, dropping high-explosive bombs and innumerable incendiaries over London. Such was the conflagration that the attacks became known as the Second Great Fire of London. The docks were a prime target but bombs hit buildings such as the Tower of London. Those lucky enough had Anderson shelters built in their gardens or Morrison shelters inside the house. Far more went down into the Underground stations. By late September 1940, some 177,000 people were sleeping in the Underground system. That October, singers (sometimes with accompanists) entertained those sheltering in rest centres and air raid shelters, with programmes to suit the audience – sea shanties, folk songs and choruses in which the audience would join.[36]

At the Strand Theatre, actor Donald Wolfit staged the 'Shakespeare Lunch Hour', at which actors performed abridged versions of some of the finest scenes that Shakespeare wrote. Wolfit delivered a memorable performance as Falstaff while air raid sirens sounded. The removal of the BBC to its new headquarters of Broadcasting House in Portland Place in the first weeks of 1932 had suspended its nearly nine-year association with the Strand and Savoy Hill, but in 1940 the BBC transferred its European Services to Bush House after Broadcasting House was bombed. It thereby resumed its tie with the Strand (which ultimately became the home of the BBC World Service), where it remained for another seventy-one years.

St Clement Danes and its surrounds sustained several hits from German bombs between September 1940 and July 1944. The church was severely damaged when it was hit in November 1940. Its famous old bells withstood this onslaught. To safeguard them, they were lowered and buried in sand at the bottom of the tower for safety. On three other occasions the church received the blast of bombs falling near it and on another night a fire bomb fell on the roof but was put out. Regarded as probably the most bombed church in London, St Clement Danes had seemingly defied the Blitz. Then, on the night of 10 May 1941, an incendiary bomb hit the church and left it a smouldering shell (Figure 21). But for the excellence of Wren's building, it might have collapsed entirely and been totally obliterated, the Reverend Pennington-Bickford believed. Nonetheless, it was left a charred shell of walls, its interior razed to the ground, and roofless, but its spire still rose to the sky. 'The sight of all the wrecked beauty was enough to break the hardest heart', Pennington-Bickford lamented.[37]

Denmark's Constitution Day was marked in solidarity on the following 5 June. Danes representing the Danish resistance movements marked the anniversary of Denmark's constitution at a service held within the bomb-damaged shell of the church. The rector could not be there when two Danish soldiers serving in the British Army presented the church with a Danish flag to

FIGURE 21. St Clement Danes ablaze on 10 May 1941, during the Blitz. (City of Westminster Archives)

replace the one destroyed when fire gutted the building. Reverend Pennington-Bickford could not bear the damage done to the church. His death was announced on 12 June 1941, at the age of sixty-six. The burning of his church was believed to have hastened his death: *The Times* reported that the blow may well have proved fatal to him, although he was planning its restoration after the war.[38] The congregation reflected on his service to the community during his thirty-six years in the parish. His was a rare record, one of only three known in the London Diocese to have served one particular church for so long.

A memorial service for him was held on 23 June in the ruins of the church. The stark reality of the damage to it was striking in the bright light of that day. Wren's steeple survived and the outside walls were standing, but all else was obliterated. Gone were its windows, woodwork, galleries, highly ornate pillars and ceiling. Yellow ragwort that sprang up where the charred wreckage had been removed gave the impression the ruin was of long-standing, transplanted from some country valley or hillside into the middle of the traffic-ridden Strand. The presiding bishop remarked, 'Yet this had been one of the most typical of the older London churches, of a particularly opulent kind of classical architecture.... So much for the temples of man's building, all of which are fated to come only to one end'.[39]

Three months after the death of her husband, Louie Pennington-Bickford, similarly grief-stricken at the loss of the historic church, was found dead on the garden path of her country home in Sussex. An inquest into her death stated that she had jumped from an attic window and died from a broken neck. A verdict of suicide while temporarily mentally unbalanced was returned. She left a legacy to repair the bombed church, an early part of the international effort that it took to restore it. It was reconsecrated in 1958 as a perpetual shrine of remembrance to those who died in the service of the Royal Air Force.

CHAPTER 8

TO THE TWENTY-FIRST CENTURY

The first time I saw the Strand, and it instantly went to my head and to my heart, and I have never loved another street in quite the same way. My Strand is gone for ever; some of it is a wild rock-garden of purple flowers, some of it is imposing new buildings; but one way or another, the spirit is wholly departed.

Arthur Machen, 1922[1]

The 1950s began unprepossessingly for a drab and war-damaged Strand. Bombs and high explosives had clustered around the Aldwych and Savoy during the Blitz, between 1940 and 1941, and dotted the length of the thoroughfare near Charing Cross, the result of opportunistic German bombers following the line of the river while targeting London's docks and Square Mile (Figure 22). Atrocities like the lunchtime V1 'doodle-bug' raid on 30 June 1944 at the eastern end of Aldwych were designed to undermine civilian morale through their indiscriminate randomness: the raid killed forty-six, destroyed two London double-decker buses and damaged Australia House, Aldwych Theatre, Bush House and the headquarters of the Air Ministry. The blast tore off the arm of one of the two figures on the sculpture located at the north entrance of Bush House. The product of Rodin's pupil, Malvina Hoffman, and depicting the friendship between the English-speaking peoples of the United States and the British Empire, it was reattached only in time for the Queen's Silver Jubilee in 1977. Shrapnel from the explosion pockmarked previously handsome stone frontages; scars remain visible even seventy years later.[2]

FIGURE 22. The plume of smoke from the explosion of a V1 doodlebug flying bomb at Aldwych, June 1944. This view is looking west from Fleet Street. (City of Westminster Archives)

Adjacent to India House – the High Commission following the country's independence in 1947 – lay the skeleton of the Gaiety Theatre, with its characteristic Renaissance-style cupula topped by its trademark statue, a gilded teak angel blowing a trumpet, facing westwards down the length of the Strand. It had closed in 1939 for the road-widening scheme associated with the new Waterloo Bridge, before German bombers sealed its fate. It remained cloaked in darkness until demolition in 1957, despite the best efforts – and life savings – of 'Lambeth Walk' comic actor and stage manager Lupino Lane, who bought the wreck in 1946, hoping in vain to introduce the venue to new audiences. Its 'Spirit of Gaiety' statue was, however, carefully lowered to the ground. Recently restored, it now resides in the Victoria and Albert Museum.[3]

Nearby, the burnt-out ruins of St Clement Danes remained undisturbed for seventeen years, a home for roosting birds and colonies of wildflowers such as verbena and rosebay willow. It was a principal subject of the most famous painting by the artist Richard Mathews, commissioned by the War Artists' Advisory Committee to memorialise bomb sites throughout the capital. Nearby, ninety feet below ground was the platform of Aldwych tube station. During the war, it provided safe storage to many of the British Museum's finest treasures. Not least of these were sections of the Parthenon Marbles, the surviving frieze and other sculptures brought to London from Athens by Lord Elgin and later purchased by the British government. Directly above their wartime nest had been the Earl of Arundel's Carolean classical sculpture garden. Fifty years after the war ended, the papers of the British Committee for the Reunification of the Parthenon Marbles, an organisation founded in 1982 to lobby for the return of the monument to Greece, were deposited in the archives of neighbouring King's College London. Also stored in Aldwych was a recent acquisition – the Anglo-Saxon grave goods of King Raedwald of East Anglia unearthed at Sutton Hoo in Suffolk only months prior to the outbreak of war, perhaps the finest British archaeological discovery of the twentieth century – and now swiftly reinterred below London's pavements. Among its many precious gold and silver artefacts were the remains of a small ship, a helmet, sword, shield, buckles and drinking horns. The wartime curators of these treasures in Aldwych would have been unaware at the time that this underground vault lay beneath the heart of Anglo-Saxon London, Lundenwic, where ships such as the one buried with the King were pulled ashore some thirteen centuries before.[4]

These scenes stood as a backdrop to the streetscape of patient snaking queues of shoppers even after rationing of groceries such as bread, meat and eggs fully ended in 1954. The Great Smog of December 1952 turned the Strand monochrome. The worst example of otherwise familiar pea-soupers made more deadly by the burning of coal and high-pressure weather systems during a series of especially cold winters, it killed between 4,000 and 10,000 people compromised by asthma, tuberculosis and influenza; it blanketed the Strand and slowed its traffic to a virtual standstill amid zero visibility. Patterns of traffic and the appearance of commuting in central London also changed fundamentally around this time with the withdrawal of the capital's last remaining trams in 1952 and the closure of the Kingsway tram tunnel below the Strand on 5 July.[5]

Yet, amid this landscape momentous changes stirred that would eventually overturn familiar patterns of life, and they centred on the Strand in the 1950s. This was, perhaps, a 'hinge of fate', a term used by Winston Churchill as the title of the fourth book in his 'The Second World War' history series, a volume published in 1950 which described the events in 1942 and 1943 that be believed had transformed the course of the recent war decisively to the Allies' advantage. Churchill himself returned to office at the head of a Conservative government in October 1951 with a slim majority after a snap general election called by the Prime Minister, Clement Attlee.

Change came also in the arts and sciences. At the time of that election, on the South Bank of the river, opposite the Strand, stood the now empty buildings of the Festival of Britain, which had opened in May 1951 to huge fanfare but also political and jour- nalistic scepticism. Eight years in the planning, the Festival was a celebration of the scientific, technological and artistic achievements of Britain; it marked a century since Victoria and Albert's Great Exhibition. It had been dedicated by the King and Queen, who, accompanied by Princess Margaret, rode in an open-top carriage from Buckingham Palace to St Paul's down a Strand lined with cheering crowds. More than eight million visitors were drawn to its many attractions and events; thousands flocked to the Strand to attend the flower festival opened by Herbert Morrison at Covent Garden on 12 June, where he was accompanied by pearly kings and queens, and officiated over basket races and drinking competitions. Meanwhile, the promise of the sights and sounds of the Southbank were clearly visible and audible from across the river on the Embankment. The London centrepiece of the nationwide events – among pavilions celebrating science and the arts – included the futuristic Dome of Discovery, the 300 feet-high Skylon sculpture and the Royal Festival Hall. The best examples of modern British ingenuity were showcased, including the Festival Pattern Group's designs of carpets, curtains and upholstery, which drew inspiration from new scientific insights into molecular structures derived from crystallographic analysis.[6]

The mood, then, was one of celebration and optimism at the beginning of a new era of peace and prosperity, a flourishing of contemporary British triumphs in health, housing and industry. The Festival was, in part, an antidote to austerity at a time of great economic challenge: the United Kingdom's national debt peaked at 200 per cent of gross domestic product (GDP) at the end of the war and the country borrowed heavily from the United States to stay afloat through loans negotiated by the economist John Maynard Keynes. The global political situation was perhaps even more challenging when, just months later, in February 1952, Elizabeth was proclaimed Queen Elizabeth II. Churchill had delivered his famous 'Iron Curtain' speech in Fulton, Missouri, in March 1946, warning of a new era of ideological, economic and military deadlock with the Soviet Union. The term 'Cold War' was coined in 1947, but the explosion of the first Soviet atom bomb in 1949 and the outbreak of the Korean War in 1950 brought matters to a head. Britain in turn detonated its first atomic bomb in autumn 1952, on islands off Western Australia. A new, more terrifyingly destructive era in human affairs had commenced.

It was during this tumult that a new academic department began to flourish at King's College London, tucked away in the basement of a carpark visible between the railings of an unassuming brick archway adjacent to government offices in Somerset House. There, molecular knowledge, the new science of crystallography, engineering excellence and an enterprising team of scientists converged, under the shadow of nuclear death, to investigate the origins of life. Their work was pivotal in unravelling the intrinsic structure of the secret genetic code – deoxyribonucleic acid or DNA – and ushered in a new, ongoing era of medical discovery, the consequences of which we have yet to fully comprehend. Its architect was John Randall, a plain-speaking Lancastrian physicist, impatient with hidebound bureaucratic traditions in universities and keen to try new approaches to solving scientific problems. Randall had been pivotal in co-developing the cavity magnetron during the war at the University of Birmingham, a no-nonsense innovation that improved the performance of radar used to track enemy aircraft. He was recruited by King's in 1946 to establish a new type of inter-disciplinary department – a biophysics unit – that would unite physicists, chemists, biologists, mathematicians and engineers – to solve scientific riddles. Foremost of these was the structure of DNA, already identified by chemists, physicists and biologists in the United States and Britain as the likely source of genetic information in cells.[7]

Postwar King's – and Britain – though exhausted by wartime endeavours, remained a place of impoverished ambition yet remarkable inventiveness. King's students included the author Arthur C. Clarke, who recognised the potential of geo-stationery satellites, and Peter Higgs, who one day would be awarded the Nobel Prize for the theoretical particle called the Higgs boson. During the 1950s, the College rooftops below which these scientists beavered comprised an elaborate cat's cradle of wires, part of an apparatus designed to detect Soviet atomic tests. This was progressively threaded across the campus by members of the cricket team, who attached the wires to cricket balls and bowled them between the adjacent buildings. Into this place, bombed and blackened by war and time, came Randall. He lost no time in recruiting a New Zealander, Maurice Wilkins, a veteran of the Manhattan Project that had developed the nuclear bombs that had destroyed Hiroshima and Nagasaki in Japan in 1945.

Wilkins was horrified by his role in the nuclear invention, and what he saw as the misappropriation of physics for destructive purposes, and he would go on to establish the Campaign for Nuclear Disarmament. He turned to biology and the trending science of crystallography – the use of X-rays to reveal the microscopic structure of organic crystals – to peer into the molecular mysteries of cells.[8] The team that Randall and Wilkins assembled notably included: the mathematician Alex Stokes; the co-discoverer of the 'sliding filament' mechanism of muscle fibre, Jean Hanson; a young graduate student, Raymond Gosling; and a recruit from Paris who joined in January 1951, the gifted crystallographer Rosalind Franklin. Together, they approached scientific problems from different directions: theoretically at the blackboard, experimentally at the lab bench and practically through model making. King's basement, meanwhile, was occupied by a team of skilled tool-makers, including Ted Benfield and Len Pitches, veterans of high-precision engineering made to order in wartime aviation, now employed to design new types of scientific equipment.

The Biophysics Department thus merged complex personalities and diverse skills; 'Randall's circus', as it was described disparagingly by more conventional academic colleagues, worked and played hard, building *esprit de corps* through sport and common-room parties. This was make-do-and-mend science: Gosling even repurposed plasticene and paperclips from the Strand's Woolworth to mount rehydrated DNA in special cameras while leaks of hydrogen from the cameras were plugged using a condom. So it was that a prophylactic and a paperclip revealed life's secret structure, DNA's double helix.[9]

Each experiment could take up to 100 hours of directing X-rays at samples of DNA with great precision, with personal risk from fire or accidental radiation exposure. In May 1952, a breakthrough was achieved by Gosling and Franklin, who isolated the B form of DNA to take Photograph 51 – a vivid X-shaped formation of dots suggestive of DNA's helical structure, and arguably one of the most important photographs ever captured. Wilkins shared it with James Watson and his colleague Francis Crick, in Cambridge. The pair immediately recognised its significance and quickly built a model of a double helix; its elegant and simple beauty was able to explain the transmission of genetic information when cells divide. The results of the findings of the King's and Cambridge scientists were soon published in three papers in the journal *Nature*, in 1953, before Watson, Crick and Wilkins were awarded the Nobel Prize for Physiology or Medicine in 1962.

Franklin could not be considered for a Nobel Prize as these are never awarded posthumously and she had died, aged only thirty-seven, in 1958, from ovarian cancer, possibly the result of long-term radiation exposure. Since then, her biography has become the subject of many books, films, television series and a successful West End stage play starring Hollywood actress Nicole Kidman as Franklin, who rehearsed scenes from the play in the very laboratory where the most important experiments were conducted. It is suggested that sexism and Wilkins's rivalry conspired to cut Franklin out of the story of one of the most important ever scientific discoveries. Randall was keen to promote women scientists, though, and he employed an unusually high proportion for universities at the time: eight out of thirty-one staff in 1951, including several in senior roles. There was, nevertheless, inevitable friction between the key personalities, partly owing to fundamental disagreement over the communication of Franklin's research to third parties – Watson and Crick – without her permission. This arose from Wilkins's understanding of scientific discovery as a team game. As he saw it, progress emerged more from collective endeavour, a process of sharing data and ideas, debate, and free exchange of thoughts. Credit in all this is also due to Gosling: modest and generous, he chose to step aside from the controversies that have dogged the discovery, and while he was then a PhD student, he was but a few years younger than Franklin and arguably deserves equal billing alongside her.[10]

In any event, arguably it was perhaps the unique alchemy of the Strand at that time – poverty fuelling creative application and problem-solving in a tight-knit locus – that made this scientific breakthrough possible. King's was part of a thriving hub at the east end of the Strand, close to the still-beating heart of Britain's newspaper industry, to which many of the best talents of the world were drawn.

The European Service of BBC overseas radio broadcasting – which began in 1938 – relocated to Bush House in 1941, where it was joined by other services and remained until 2012. At the outbreak of the Second World War, the BBC was tasked with monitoring the output of enemy broadcasts and by October 1941, 500 staff were put to work reviewing some 250 bulletins in thirty languages. By 1942, the BBC was broadcasting from the Strand in forty-five languages from a world trade centre that had now been transformed into a world communications centre. The BBC at Bush House drew upon an extraordinary pool of talent in war and peace. One of its tasks was to sabotage enemy morale, and so it broadcast to Germans the adventures of the satirical Frau Wernicke, a character played by the exiled German cabaret artist Annemarie Hase. Its broadcasts to South Asia sought to neutralise enemy propaganda about British imperialism. Zulfikar Ali Bukhari, a director of the Delhi Broadcasting Station, was recruited to set up the Indian Section of the BBC's Eastern Service and in 1941 he in turn recruited the writer George Orwell – who cultivated a network of Indian friends and acquaintances – as a talks producer. Bukhari was a programme organiser and translated Orwell's words into Hindustani, but his responsibilities were very diverse; he assembled a team of freelance contributors and even accompanied Richard Dimbleby to France in 1940 to report on Indian soldiers stationed with the British Expeditionary Force. After Partition in 1947, Bukhari was appointed Controller of Broadcasting at Radio Pakistan in Karachi. Meanwhile, Bush House – a warren of offices, common rooms and grand imperial suites – inspired Orwell to dream up

Room 101, the fictional torture chamber in his dystopian novel 1984.[11]

The postwar BBC at Bush House – it was rechristened BBC World Service only in 1965 – was home to a vast diaspora of exiled journalists, refugee translators, writers, dissidents, engineers and technicians – including the art historian Ernst Gombrich and the publisher, George Weidenfeld – such that it has been compared to a 'giant ocean liner cruising through the dark, lights blazing'. The building was a labyrinth of small offices and studios occupied by people of different nationalities, who together broke bread in the staff canteen and shared dormitories during long night shifts. The place forged numerous careers, friendships and marriages. A multiplicity of languages and cultures were represented there: Swahili, Pashtun, Urdu, Russian, Hungarian, Bulgarian – to name but a few. There was also a wide variety of programming: news, features, documentaries, plays, poetry and music. The BBC adapted to the geopolitics of the Cold War, as seen notably in its reports on crises such as the Hungarian Uprising in 1956, the Soviet invasion of Czechoslovakia in the Prague Spring of 1968, the rise of the Solidarity movement in Poland in 1980, as well as the fall of the Soviet Union in 1991. A job at the BBC was not without risks – witnessed by the assassination in September 1978 of the Bulgarian dissident journalist and broadcaster Georgi Markov, who was killed by a poisoned umbrella tipped with deadly ricin while waiting for a bus at Waterloo to take him to the Strand.[12]

Opposite Bush House, King's College had long provided a welcome for overseas students and refugees, notably Belgian refugees in the First World War and arrivals from Hungary following the Soviet invasion in 1956. Decolonisation from the 1960s added to the cosmopolitan flavour of this end of the Strand. Black and white students also left South Africa to study in England once apartheid restrictions began to tighten. These included the later Archbishop of Cape Town Winston Ndungane, the Bishop of Cape Town Christopher Gregorowski and Bishop Godfrey Ashby. Perhaps its most famous alumnus was Desmond Tutu, who studied there between 1962 and 1966. He went on to become the first black General-Secretary of the South African Council of Churches and was awarded the Nobel Peace Prize in 1984. During the 1960s through to the 1990s, the international movement against apartheid – whose demands included a boycott of both arms sales and sporting links with South Africa, the imposition of sanctions against the country and the release of Nelson Mandela from captivity – was centred on the South African embassy in Trafalgar Square, which at one time attracted a twenty-four-hour vigil, and the Rhodesian High Commission in the Strand, following its Unilateral Declaration of Independence (UDI) in 1965 (Figure 23). Among the most notable events were the march organised by the Anti-Apartheid Movement on 2 November 1985, fronted by its President, Trevor Huddleston, Oliver Tambo, President of the African National Congress, and US civil rights activist Jesse

Figure 23. Demonstration at Rhodesia House on the Strand, 3 March 1968. This was one of many demonstrations against white majority rule in Rhodesia. (Keystone Press/Alamy Stock Photo)

Jackson, and the state visit of Nelson Mandela in July 1996, when he greeted crowds from the balcony of the South African embassy.[13]

Among many distinguished South Africans to study, visit or write about the Strand was the journalist and broadcaster Noni Jabavu (Figure 24). The granddaughter of the first editor of a black newspaper in South Africa, *Black Opinion*, she moved to England in the early 1930s to complete her education; a decade later and Jabavu had forged a successful career as a journalist. In 1949, she began to appear as a freelance contributor on BBC Radio, where she remained for fifteen years, writing scripts for schools, participating in book reviews alongside authors such as J. G. Ballard and appearing regularly on *Woman's Hour*. The subjects of her talks were often eclectic and sometimes controversial: women jazz musicians, African music, first impressions of London, the European idea of romantic love, the African idea of old age, contrasts between African and English culture, the challenges of mixed-race marriages such as her own, and racial attitudes among black people.[14] During this time, her career blossomed and she earned critical acclaim in 1960 with the publication of her breakthrough memoir *Drawn in Colour*. This described her experiences, as a black woman, of colonialism and prejudice in southern and eastern Africa. In 1961, Jabavu was then appointed the editor of a new literary monthly called *New Strand*. A revival of *The Strand Magazine*, which had finally ceased publication in 1950, this mix of short fiction and feature articles – it included contributions from, among others, Dennis Wheatley and Robert Graves – was the brainchild of the proprietors, Ernest Kay, and the successful crime novelist Ray Creasy. Although this was Jabavu's editorial debut, Kay was confident she was the right person for the job. He declared that 'Miss Jabavu has led such a varied life that she will bring a completely fresh outlook to the magazine. She certainly couldn't be conventional if she tried'. Her appointment caught the eye of the wider black community, too; a headline in *Ebony* announced: 'South African woman to revive Britain's most popular magazine'. Jabavu's tenure was brief, however – she resigned from the magazine in March 1962 – and the periodical ceased publication. Nevertheless, she acknowledged the

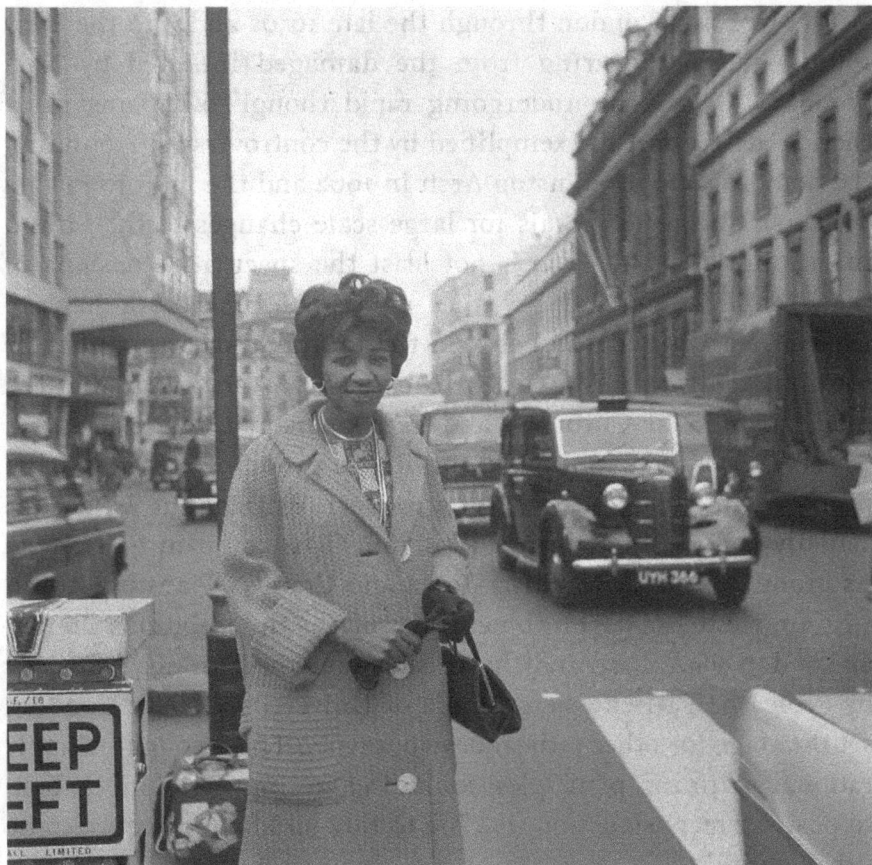

FIGURE 24. The South African journalist Noni Jabavu pictured standing on the Strand in London, 1961. Jabavu was editor of the *New Strand Magazine*. (Rolls Press / Popperfoto via Getty Images)

wider significance of her promotion as one of the first black women appointed to a senior editorial position in London:

Getting this job was a surprise to me. It's delightful that people are beginning to accept that jobs of this sort can be done by black people, or brown people, or yellow people. This sort of progress is bound to come. People see them washing up in cafes and think: 'That's what coloured people are good for'. They accept them as cricketers or athletes or entertainers, but somehow, they can't consider what counts.[15]

The fabric of London through the late 1950s and into the early 1960s – still recovering from the damaged inflicted by Nazi bombers – was now undergoing rapid though often unsympathetic redevelopment, exemplified by the controversy surrounding the demolition of the Euston Arch in 1962 and the fight to save St Pancras Station. Proposals for large-scale changes to the Strand in fact pre-dated the war – not least the speculative designs of the architect Maxwell Fry that envisaged the comprehensive demolition of buildings between the Strand and river and their replacement by a forest of tower blocks. These were inspired by the modernism of Le Corbusier and were sponsored by the so-called Glass Age Town Planning Committee, a group of architects that proposed futuristic designs for a modern Britain, but which was actually underwritten by the Pilkington Glass company to promote its product. The far-reaching Town and Country Planning Act in 1947, previewed in part by blueprints such as the ambitious County of London Plan (1943) and the Greater London Plan (1944) devised by Professor Patrick Abercrombie of University College London, set the stage for other radical developments. These sought to apply rational planning principles, including zoning and a green belt, to postwar reconstruction in a bid to tidy up London's unwelcome urban clutter.

Developers and planners now turned their attention to the Strand. Despite the Blitz, the Covent Garden fruit and vegetable market to its north had retained a vital national economic role – in 1962/63 it still processed in excess of a million tons of fruit and veg annually, among which was one-third of the UK's imports. It supported some 1,700 permanent workers, while its streets were clogged with a typical 7,300 vehicles a day; the market and its neighbourhood were now beginning to look run down and congested. In 1961, a Covent Garden Market Authority was formed, which effectively nationalised it, in advance of relocation to a purpose-built facility in Nine Elms in south London. The year 1968 saw the publication of the Covent Garden Scheme, promoted by the new Greater London Council in partnership with local authorities and private contractors. This ignited a war of ideas waged on the streets and in the media that pitched the local community of traders and residents against the planners. The Scheme envisaged the disappearance of the market and the demolition of a huge swathe of the city as far north as High Holborn and as far south as the Strand and its replacement by new office blocks, a sports centre, hotels, an international conference centre, a public square, residential flats and a system of roads feeding a monster carpark capable of accommodating thousands of vehicles. A new cut-and-cover super-highway was planned to replace Maiden Lane, to take eastbound traffic, while westbound traffic, it was envisaged, would be directed along a Strand dual carriageway. Elevated pedestrian walkways similar to those in other urban projects such as the Barbican would have lined the road that connected it with Trafalgar Square and Leicester Square. The scheme – put simply – would have transformed the Strand into Slough, erasing its unique historical character and that of the neighbourhood to its north, including Drury Lane and Seven Dials, and replacing it with a ninety-six-acre car-congested modernist carbuncle. A hint of this alternative future is provided by Arundel Great Court, the brutalist hulk actually constructed at 180 Strand on the site of the old Arundel House between 1971 and 1976.[16]

The Covent Garden Scheme provoked a huge public outcry and spurred the mobilisation of local residents and businesses threatened with compulsory purchase. Together they formed the Covent Garden Community Association in 1971 to lobby the press and galvanise public opinion during the lengthy public inquiry into the plans, to organise sit-ins and demonstrations, to give television interviews and to host candle-lit vigils led by its figurehead, the redoubtable vicar of St Martin in the Fields Austen Williams and the activist architect Jim Monaghan. These efforts were part of a growing countermovement, represented by conservation organisations (e.g. the Victorian Society, founded in 1957) and campaigners (e.g. that Society's originator, the Poet Laureate Sir John Betjeman, and its later chair, Nikolaus Pevsner) who sought to protect London's older buildings, sightlines and public spaces, including those in the Strand endangered by such schemes. Betjeman was one voice lending his opposition to the Covent Garden project; he declared, for example, that Rules restaurant in Maiden Lane, threatened with demolition in the plans, was 'unique and irreplaceable, and part of literary and theatrical London'. Thankfully, the plans – although passed by the inspector and supported by the Heath government – were upon consideration eventually replaced with more modest proposals, with the renovation of most of the existing historic buildings, which duly reopened to the public as an upmarket shopping experience in June 1980. Covent Garden – and the Strand – lived to fight another day. A victorious Betjeman then switched his attention to supporting the decaying St Mary's Church, with its declining fabric and diminishing congregations, and its fundraising campaign in the Jubilee year of 1977. He dedicated to it one of his last ever poems, penned in 1981: 'There's nothing quite so grand/As the baroque of your Chapel/Of St Mary in the Strand'. The campaign was evidently at least partially successful as, soon after, it was deemed to be in sufficiently good repair to be made the official church of the Women's Royal Naval Service, the Wrens.[17]

The Strand continued to hold a place in popular culture and society, though this frayed from the 1960s onwards. It featured as the backdrop to the ill-fated launch of the Strand Cigarettes brand in 1959, a name perhaps redolent of the glamour of the Strand's heyday. Its television advertising in the style of a film noire movie depicted an apparently lonely male character in a deserted street lighting up a cigarette. The film declared, 'You're never alone with a Strand', but sales flopped, presumably because the advert associated the product with negative connotations such as social isolation and depression, and the cigarettes were quickly rebranded Embassy. The advert is even today used in marketing classes as an example of what not to do. Similarly invoking old-fashioned glamour was Roxy Music's popular 1973 track 'Do the Strand', which imagined a dance of that name – it remains one of the band's most popular songs.[18]

The India Club restaurant and bar was opened in 1951, following Indian independence, and relocated in 1964 to 143 Strand, where it remained until it closed in 2023 to make way for a luxury hotel, and despite a petition calling for a stay of execution that gathered more than 26,000 signatures. Resolutely resisting modernisation, it offered cheap food and nostalgia and became a home from home to members of the South Asian community, staff at India House, visiting dignitaries and West End theatre-goers in search of an early evening meal. At the other end of the scale, the Savoy Hotel continued to offer glamour and luxury. Princess Elizabeth and Prince Philip hosted their wedding reception there in 1946; the ball thrown to celebrate her coronation in 1953 had 1,400 guests. Beefeaters lined the river entrance, and the hotel and restaurant were adorned with Tudor-themed decorations that took twenty people thirty-six hours to assemble. The evening's cabaret featured Laurence Olivier, Bing Crosby and Noël Coward. The hotel remained resolutely traditional in some respects, attracting political leaders such as Winston Churchill and silver screen stars such as Cary Grant, Judy Garland, Ava Gardner, Marlon Brando and Charlie Chaplin, who stayed there annually from 1952 until 1977. But increasingly it also attracted the 'in-crowd', particularly for theatre or film opening nights, award ceremonies and residencies; these included the Beatles, Sophia Loren, Marilyn Monroe, Muhammad Ali, Dionne Warwick and Petula Clark.[19]

The Strand began a downward spiral as early as 1951, when it was described by the historian H. V. Morton as a 'slightly shabby street' that had 'lost its gaiety and also its air of richness'.[20] It largely missed out on the Swinging Sixties that gripped Carnaby Street and Chelsea's King's Road, with the exception of the glitterati who continued to frequent the Savoy. Britain then experienced a lengthy economic downturn in the 1970s and early 1980s, characterised by a cost-of-living crisis, widespread strikes, mass unemployment and civic unrest exemplified by events such as the Three-Day Week in 1973–74 and the Brixton riots in 1981. The Strand, too, suffered the effects of this prolonged austerity. These impacts were arguably deepened by the ripple effect on the local economy of the decision by News International to move the printing of its newspapers, titles that included *The Times* and *Sun*, to Wapping in 1986. This triggered a chain reaction that eventually saw all of Fleet Street's national newspapers quitting the area, taking their business with them; the last two journalists finally left in 2016. During the 1980s, a decade when recorded crime rose 47 per cent, so-called 'down and outs' or homeless rough-sleepers began to appear in the doorways of the Strand; at one time they numbered more than fifty. In June 1990, neighbourhood police initiated Project Burlington, which cleared 80 per cent of these rough-sleepers off the street, while the accountancy firm Arthur Andersen at 180 Strand spent some £80,000 removing forty permanent encampments located in its air conditioning system. Local businesses, led by the Savoy, also did their bit to clean up the area, by reinstating the old Strand Association and introducing new French-made sanitation vehicles to keep pavements clear. This evidently was not the whole answer, as in May 1994 the *Evening Standard* complained again about the Strand's 'down-at-heel, litter-laden and dosser-ridden image'.[21]

Throughout this time, familiar landmarks began to disappear, and even John Nash's 'pepper pot' buildings in west Strand – a feature since 1832 – came under renewed threat of demolition, until they acquired listed status in 1975. The Tivoli cinema disappeared – once London's largest American-style picture house. The famous Lyons Corner House at Charing Cross also shut down, one of the largest and most popular branches of the familiar chain that supplied inexpensive and wholesome food served by 'nippy' waitresses in elegant and comfortable surroundings. This closed its doors around 1974, although it was briefly revived in 1982. Similarly closing its doors around 1955 was the café run by the ABC – the Aerated Bread Company – near the Gaiety. This was one of a chain of self-service eating houses that had a national reach rivalling that of Lyons, though offering cheaper fare; it had once appealed to lone women – especially office workers – who wished to eat undisturbed. Gatti's restaurant – the founding family had once owned a considerable portion of the Strand, including the Adelphi and Vaudeville Theatres – closed in 1981 after a century of trading. The local branch of Oxford Street's Peter Robinson department store at 65 Strand – designed by the renowned architect, Sir Denys Lasdun, and the first postwar building in England to be clad in bronze – was demolished in the 1990s. The Strand branch of Yates's Wine Lodge at 417, Mooney's at 395 with its pink marble bar and the branch of Henekey's (now the Lyceum Tavern) with its old-world wooden panelling, all closed around 1980. Civil Service Stores at 425 Strand on the corner of Bedford Street was the retail branch of the Civil Service Supply Association, a cooperative of civil servants; it ceased trading in 1982 after a serious fire. The postwar years had not been kind to the Strand.

Such closures were not the whole story, however. The Strand was widened in 1959 to eighty feet near Charing Cross to accommodate the traffic; in 1962, the London County Council revealed that it was now London's noisiest thoroughfare. In May 1972, the Queen opened a splendid New South Wales House at 66 Strand; 'ultra-modern and laid out on open plan lines', it featured white birch veneer on its walls and a new restaurant called the Great Australian Bite. The new headquarters of Coutts Bank – reopened in 1978 – was the first fully fledged atrium office building in the capital. The world-famous stamp dealers, Stanley Gibbons, which had occupied premises at 391 Strand for a century, also moved to a new head-quarters, at 399 Strand. The London branch of Joe Allen's New York restaurant, which began serving food in 1977, soon attracted the theatre and film star crowd, and in 1979 the Heaven nightclub flung open its doors to London's gay – and straight – communities in the arches below Charing Cross.[22]

Change slowly came about from the mid-1980s, the point at which London's population, which had fallen to its lowest point in a century, began to recover quickly. By 2001, it had risen to 7.2 million, an increase of 360,000 in a decade. A resurgence in the finance industry accompanied the easing of exchange and credit controls and in the aftermath of the deregulation in 1986 of banking and financial practices in the Square Mile, dubbed the Big Bang. New developments and high-rise towers – not least Canary Wharf in Docklands in the early 1990s – put the spring back in the step of the property market in the Strand, too. An improvement scheme added new York stone paving to the street in 1995. Some older customs and ways of life disappeared in the

1990s: not least familiar *Evening Standard* sellers with their characteristic cries of '*Standaaard*', and local Italian sandwich shops, driven out by high rents and the rise of chains of convenience shops. In 1994, Aldwych Tube Station closed for the last time. New businesses arrived: British Aerospace moved into the Civil Service Stores redevelopment, along with Xerox in Bedford Street, while Dixons opened a swanky new store to take advantage of the new fad in mass-produced electrical goods. The fresh broom left room for new tenants, notably the luxury One Aldwych hotel located in the converted former *Morning Post* building opposite the approach to Waterloo Bridge, which opened in 1998. In 2000, the *Evening Standard* declared the Strand 'The new new thing'.[23]

These gradual improvements mirrored a transformation over two or three decades in the numbers of international visitors, which began to rise steadily from the 1960s, when the London Tourist Board was set up and then when Swinging London was in full swing. The number of hotel rooms in central London climbed from 44,000 in 1966 to 150,000 in 1977, then ballooned again as cheaper air transport became available in the form of new budget services from carriers such as Ryanair in 1984 and EasyJet in 1995, and when direct Eurostar train services to Paris commenced in 1994. Longer-term visitors to London came to work and study, not least after the accession of new countries including Poland to the European Union in 2004, which profoundly changed the ethnic mix of employees in the Strand, particularly in the hospitality sector. Shorter-term visitors to London came for retail therapy, to visit family and friends or to enjoy its many heritage or cultural attractions. Such cultural tourism was boosted by substantial income from the National Lottery, which started in 1994, which enabled numerous museums and galleries such as the Great Court and Round Reading Room of the British Museum to undergo refurbishment. The excitement grew with the Millennium celebrations and with the Olympics in 2012, when London welcomed a remarkable 27.6 million visitors. The Strand was on the route of the triumphant procession that welcomed its medal-winning athletes – a sea of Union Flags, cheering crowds and open-top buses.

In the Strand, the closure of Covent Garden Market in 1974 had begun to transform the look and feel of the area, part of a trend in which blue-collar workers gradually disappeared from inner London. This phenomenon was accelerated by the relocation of the Port of London and the progressive gentrification of parts of the capital. While it remained true that the Strand district was largely dependent for its employment on offices, retail and hospitality activities, notably connected to its theatres, cultural tourism became increasingly important. Examples of this included the growth of the neighbouring Covent Garden piazza and refurbished Royal Opera House, which reopened after a major expansion in the late 1990s. In 1989, the Courtauld Gallery of French Impressionist and Post-Impressionist art moved to its new home, one previously occupied by the Royal Academy, overlooking the Strand. Then, in 1997, the Somerset House Trust was established to manage the restoration of William Chambers' buildings. This took place in several stages, completed after the Inland Revenue fully vacated the site in 2011. Its drab carpark, meanwhile, was transformed into a fine public square – the Edmond J. Safra Fountain Court – that has since hosted seasons of outdoor films and a winter ice rink. The Strand, after decades of decline, had rediscovered its roots as a place of art and high culture.[24]

In 2013, the new Northbank Business Improvement District was established to oversee urban renewal and attract new business to the Strand and its neighbourhood. Improvement to the quality of the environment was one of its major concerns. With this in mind, and in collaboration with Westminster Council, proposals were published in 2017 to pedestrianise the southern portion of Aldwych to create a new public plaza. Strand Aldwych, as it is called, was inspired by the successful transformation of the north side of Trafalgar Square in 2003 by Sir Norman Foster and Partners; it sought to 'improve the public realm' by creating a more welcoming experience for pedestrians and cyclists in the area, improving its air quality and placing a new cultural quarter on Westminster's perimeter. Taking centre stage in this space are the three local universities, King's, the Courtauld Institute of Art, the London School of Economics, Somerset House, the nearby exhibitions venue 180 Studios (occupying the former Arthur Andersen building) and at its heart the refurbished St Mary's Church, no longer islanded amid the fumes of buses and taxis. Work commenced in January 2021 and the scheme officially opened on 6 December 2022, despite delays owing to the COVID-19 pandemic.

The Strand had fallen silent in that seemingly unbroken sunshine during the first lockdown in response to the pandemic in the spring and summer of 2020. This began with an announcement on 23 March by the Prime Minister, Boris Johnson, of legal restrictions on the movement of people. The country had already slowed to a standstill as schools were closed, families reunited in anticipation of being quarantined, shops and businesses were wound down, cinemas darkened, and restaurants and pubs served last orders. A public health event of comparable seriousness had not occurred in living memory, with the great flu pandemic after the First World War. New routines were quickly learned, of exercise, play and social distancing. Working from home became the norm for millions of people, who were ordered to 'Protect the NHS' and 'Save lives', but exemptions to the lockdown restrictions were made for key workers, a widely drawn category that eventually extended to curators such as this author with valuable collections in their care. Stepping out of the workplace, normally roaring with traffic, was to be confronted by an earie stillness, the roadway and pavements entirely empty, much as streets used to be early on Sunday mornings. In the entrances to the Strand's several theatres, in its shop windows and doorways along its length, hastily scribbled notes apologised for premature closure and promised business as usual in a week, a fortnight, a month – who knew when? For many – not least in hospitality and retail – government support proved insufficient, and their customers – often tourists – never returned. Even a year after the crisis had abated, several of these smaller shops in the Strand remained disused. Such desertion was perhaps not unprecedented – at the height of the Blitz, given warning, people had sought shelter, but the air then was still filled with the ominous drone of engines, the wail of air raid sirens and the thud of bombs.

In previous, much more serious, pandemics such as the Black Death, the equivalent today, in proportional terms, of five million Londoners perished – but in the absence of a social safety net, life for survivors had to continue and the city bustled on. But this silence was different perhaps, one into which nature had begun to flow again and was an evocation of older times, or a premonition of times still to come. During the spring following the opening of Aldwych's piazza, it was apparent that its new trees, attractive planting and generous seating had swiftly improved the quality of life in this part of the Strand. Traffic had again fallen silent and the air grew noticeably clearer. Under the delphinium-blue skies and alongside the fulsome white and pink of magnolia blossom, birdsong could be heard properly for perhaps the first time in a thousand years.[25]

CONCLUSION

The Strand has offered up multiple perspectives to those who have lived and worked there. To British Prime Minister Benjamin Disraeli, its very grandeur, celebrated in buildings of monumental stone and brick, was a reminder of the vast sweep of history: 'perhaps the finest street in Europe, blending the architecture of many periods'. Contrastingly, the novelist Virginia Woolf, describing the humdrum experience of homeward-bound commuters streaming down the Strand, captured the genius that resides in the domestic and familiar. To her contemporary, the theatre critic and mystic Arthur Machen, it instead offered – in its highways and byways – a window on a past that was fast disappearing, and one that was romantic, mysterious and deeply spiritual.[1]

If the Strand is anything, it is the sum of its geography, both real and imagined, and the celebration of the innumerable lives that have passed through it from far and wide. At its inception a road laid down by the Romans on land deposited by melting glaciers, it later accommodated a thriving port that became a market for many nations. A thousand years ago and since, it witnessed the unfolding of England's history, and connected the country's powerbrokers, the clergy and crown at Westminster to the merchant class represented by the City. Along its length, in a great chain of churches, the faithful gathered in prayerful congregation. Yet, this district remained extramural and suburban, its otherness harbouring proponents of heterodoxy or novelty, adherents to the Roman Catholic faith in the midst of a Protestant nation, devisers of new ideas on the shaping of knowledge and the condition of human society such as Bacon, Hobbes and Locke, impresarios, political reformers and suffragettes.

At one time a mile-long art gallery and museum, the Strand was put on the world stage to make treaties in a new age of exploration and amid broken religious promises. Then in the shadow of the restored court, it attracted all the fashions and raw commercial energy that war and money made, when it became the principal thoroughfare of what was then the world's largest and most vibrant city. Down its length flowed the *elan vital* of creativity that explored the boundaries of science and reflected the preoccupations of the modern world – it was a place of publishing, entertainment, music and dance, consumerism, reforming zeal, progressive optimism and imperial pomp. Beneath darkling skies and newly dressed in stone and glass, it repelled the bombs of its wartime enemies and cast a net of radio around the world that reached the homes of hundreds of millions of people.

This was not a single hub with an identifiable centre but rather a promenade divided by cardinal districts, each with subtle cadences and rhythms – to the north it bordered first fields and then the new elegance of Covent Garden, to the south it overlooked the broad vistas of the river, then new bridges and monumental public works, to the east it gazed at the City and the symbol of St Paul's and to the west it exhaled its overcrowded masses to make a new town: the West End. Thus, Charing Cross was distinct from mid-Strand, despite being separated by only a few hundred yards, while the industry of the busy riverfront wharves, warehouses and factories that pre-dated the Embankment were distinct from the nearby roadway's warrens, passageways and courtyards of artisans, shop-keepers, taverns and brothels.

Behind impressive gateways of stone for 400 years sat grand houses and their complexes of chapels, breweries, barns, quads and gardens, discrete communities that were filled with households of servants, clerks and clergy. In the east, the legal quarter surrounding Temple Bar rubbed shoulders with a thriving community of printers and publishers. The nearby slums of Clare Market, the blood of its butcheries running down its alleys, abutted the Tudor crinkle-crankle of Wych Street and the 'Straits of St Clements', barely wide enough to admit a single cart. This essentially medieval

Strand was a timber gully: noisy, rude and narrow, dark with smoke and stir, and enclosed by overhanging jetties resembling the Shambles in York today or surviving parts of old Shrewsbury. Later, this was swept away as the road was widened and metalled by speculators and town planners who constructed connecting avenues and attractive new estates girdled by the Embankment and its railway, and bookended by Trafalgar Square and the Aldwych and Holborn developments. It became an imperial thoroughfare that attracted the world to its smart new hotels, shops and theatres. Now the Strand awaits its next chapter.

What, then, for the future of the Strand? Given its 2,000-year history, and its various evolutions and incarnations, it is likely that the Strand will prevail. Its continued vigour, though, arguably depends on deepening its relationships with neighbouring districts, the West End and the City of London, cultivating new friendships with the important contacts on its doorstep – embassies and high commissions, including those of Canada, South Africa, Uganda and India – and attracting the attention and investment of London's businesspeople. Casting its eyes to the east implies a closer working partnership once again with Fleet Street, denuded as it has been of its publishing industry and its self-confidence, and this could be one based upon a common appreciation of the heritage afforded by the English language, news and broadcasting.

Since the pandemic, the downsides of home working have become all too apparent – boredom, loneliness, distractions from the task in hand and separation from colleagues and friends. Offices in cities are thus unlikely to disappear entirely, but a considerable reduction of their number in the Strand is feasible, which would lead to it becoming almost exclusively a boulevard of leisure. Such a scenario might include the conversion of the Shell-Mex Building – on the footprint of the old Hotel Cecil and presently offices – into a grand new residence, mimicking the palaces which once lined the riverbank. Theatregoing will probably continue to boom – despite the high costs associated with staging performances and consequently high ticket prices – which will give need to accommodate more visitors and locals. To do this, the theatres in the Strand will require substantial investment to improve the quality and comfort of the visitor experience, including air conditioning and elevators. A new Gaiety Theatre could arise to wow audiences, perhaps to incorporate immersive and mixed-reality experiences, a stone's throw away from where Charles Wheatstone perfected stereoscopy during the nineteenth century. The decline of general retailing is likely to accelerate as purchasing moves ever further online, leading to the conversion of shops into housing for socially diverse communities. The Strand could thus begin again to resemble the street it once was before the twentieth century *sans* the slums and brothels, a place where people lived, worked and played.

Further improvement to the physical environment of the Strand, such as the partial pedestrianisation of its western end and limiting vehicular access to taxis and buses, is perhaps now more likely, given the provisional success of the Strand Aldwych quarter – and could provide the means to attract more bespoke and artisanal businesses. A pedestrian area – and accompanying street market – might then connect the Strand seamlessly with Trafalgar Square to fully realise the vision of architect John Nash and also lead to the overdue refurbishment of Charing Cross Station. Such new businesses might include a mix of arts and crafts, luxury goods, fine foods (including bakeries, charcuteries and breweries) or even micromanufacturing workshops using new technologies like 3D printing, thus reviving a 300-year tradition of craftworking. The street's educational jewels, among them the Royal Society of Arts, Courtauld and King's, would ideally work more cooperatively, perhaps with a focus on supporting the crafts with a revival of the local traditional excellence in applied arts and design.

It is to be hoped that the Strand's landmarks will be preserved, notably the Savoy Hotel, Simpsons, Somerset House and the churches. While the Strand continues to be used occasionally for processional purposes – relatively recent examples include the celebration of the marriage of Charles and Diana in 1981 and the Olympics parade in 2012 – this could be made more regular, perhaps by routing the annual Lord Mayor's Show back down the Strand for the first time in 650 years. A symbolic re-erecting of a maypole could be part of this reimagining. A permanent authority to better represent its interests could be created, but arguably this would itself be out of character, since the Strand has always been more a chorus of conversations than a singular voice of a controlling authority.

The much longer-term prospects for the Strand are hazy and halting. The author Samuel Butler, who lived in Clements Inn, near Temple Bar, described at length in his fantastical novel *Erewhon* (1872) the consequences of the rise of thinking machines, which he predicted might evolve at frightening speed. Butler warned that 'The machines are gaining ground upon us; day by day we are becoming subservient to them; more men are daily bound as slaves to tend them'. Today, Butler is recalled as a father of artificial intelligence (AI). In a far-flung future, machines resembling humans may occupy the Strand, unaware or dismissive of their fleshy ancestors, fiercely intelligent but unsympathetic and unyielding. Made in the image of their proud creators, though, they may slowly acquire the capacity and consciousness to love and be loved.[2]

Global warming represents a similar existential threat, with the prospect of vast movements of populations from the south to the north seeking safety, making a refugee camp of the Strand, or else, with the melting of the icecaps and a consequent catastrophic rise in sea levels, be subject to a return exodus. Such an inundation – so the geological record tells us – has happened before, to which the Strand has been witness. The global loss of the icecaps and glaciers – an improbable scenario and one that would take thousands of years to reach fruition – would drown London under 200 feet of water. In this view, the Strand's many landmarks such as St Mary's and Somerset House would be transformed into mere underwater ruins, a submerged Easter Island of drowned monuments.[3]

A new and more terrifying pandemic remains a third possibility, perhaps one combining the virulence of diseases such as Ebola with the transmissibility of the common cold, leaving a pathetic rump of the population to eke out a living in exiled lands. This Dark Age Strand is deserted, progressively overgrown by weeds, then reclaimed by the forest, its prehistory revisited.

But the future is mysterious. Perhaps none of these things will happen. Instead, during the century ahead, the Strand may step out with a bold stride and refresh its story at the heart of a regenerated and confident London and in the midst of a technological and humanist renewal. New characters and new generations will add their stories to the Strand's long history.

Along its length, on summer daybreaks, its buildings and byways will be illuminated still by the glow of the rising sun in the east.

ABOUT THE AUTHORS

Geoff Browell

Geoff currently manages special projects at King's College London's Libraries & Collections, to unlock the potential of its valuable books and archives. Prior to this, he was Head of Archives at King's for over a decade. He is chair of AIM25, a charitable consortium of the archives of 150 cultural organisations in London, and is an editor of Strandlines, a blog that explores life on the Strand. He has developed numerous public engagement and technology projects over more than thirty years, including digitisation initiatives, theatre productions and apps. Current projects include exploring new ways of reimagining history and improving lives using virtual and augmented reality, and Archives Africa, which seeks to develop a single archive catalogue for the continent. He is a Fellow of the Society of Antiquaries of London.

Eileen Chanin

Eileen's interest in history is wide-ranging. Her career has seen her work with cultural collections and present exhibitions, for which she has written histories. Her books encompass architectural, art and cultural history, biography and military history. Awards her work has won include the Australia History Prize and the Royal Marines Historical Society Literary Award. She has long had an interest in the history of London. A Senior Visiting Fellow of King's College London, she wrote of the Strand's reconstruction with the creation of Aldwych-Kingsway in her previous book, *Capital Designs, Australia House and Visions of an Imperial London*. She is presently a Research Associate of the Australian National University.

ACKNOWLEDGEMENTS

To begin, we must thank the Strand itself, which we have both walked countless times, always reflecting on its remarkably long history, over years working at King's College London and long before we began working on this book.

We are particularly grateful to Clare Brant, eminent historian, Professor of Eighteenth-Century Literature and Culture at King's College London, and Director of Strandlines, the digital community and history project about the street, that she was instrumental in setting up. Since 2011, she has contributed tirelessly to revealing its history through life writing. She led to our meeting on a walking tour of the Strand, where exchanging stories set us on sharing further our mutual interest in its history.

A King's College London Australia Partnership Seed Fund in 2019 further encouraged us to begin working jointly. Support for this came from associates who shared their interest in Strand life: Frank Bongiorno, Professor of History, Australian National University (and lecturer at King's College London from 2007 to 2011), and Simon Sleight, Reader in Urban History, Historical Youth Cultures and Australian History at King's College London. Both previously took part in relaying aspects of stories from the Strand in their association with the Menzies Centre for Australian Studies (today's Menzies Australia Institute), which has operated from King's College London since 1999. The support of King's Libraries and Collections Department has been important throughout the research for and writing of this book.

As well, we are grateful to the many individuals with whom we have shared thoughts about the Strand and discussed its story. Our special thanks go to the members of the Strandlines community and the wider research and editorial community. Taking great interest in this history, several individuals especially encouraged us. Among them were Susan A. Snell, Archivist and Records Manager, the Library and Museum of Freemasonry; Michael Trapp, Professor of Greek Literature and Thought at King's College London; Barbara Cornford, reader; Dr Christine Kenyon Jones, historian of King's College London; Tam McDonald, CEO of Cradle of English; fellow colleagues presenting papers at the King's Symposium 'Convivial Spaces? Encounters in Twentieth Century' in 2019 coordinated by Dr Anna Maguire, Lecturer in Public History, University College London; Peter Babington, Priest-in-Charge of St Mary le Strand; Peter Maplestone, Church Warden, St Mary le Strand; Tess Cash, editor; and historians and literary scholars, including Jonathan Clarke, Andrew Cormack, Richard Edgcumbe, Gabriel Egan, Elizabeth Eger, Gillian Greenwood, Michael Mainelli, Giles Milton, Gregory O'Malley, Andrew Saint and Richard Tames. A very special thanks goes to Valerie Soar, archivist of modern poetry, for her great help and support. And to Charlie Viney for his interest. In memory of the late Dr Andrea Tanner, Archivist of Fortnum & Mason, for her kindness, support and friendship.

Archivists and librarians have been vital to researching this book. Of great help were the staff of the City of Westminster Archives Centre; London Metropolitan Archives; King's College London Archives; Royal Academy of Arts Archive; Institute of Historical Research; British Library; State Library of New South Wales; University of Sydney; and Australian National University.

Our thanks to the team at Manchester University Press. Working with its commissioning editor Kim Walker and with its editor Alun Richards and the Press's team (including freelance copy-editor Ralph Footring) has been a delight.

Last, but not least, are our families and so many of our friends who have unbegrudgingly allowed us the time spent away from them, and so patiently asked about progress being made and kindly looked after our well-being, while we worked on this book.

FIGURES AND MAPS

Figures

Maps

ABBREVIATIONS

BBC   British Broadcasting Corporation

BHO   British History Online – https://www.british-history.ac.uk (accessed 22 September 2024)

ODNB   *Oxford Dictionary of National Biography* – online edition at https://www.oxforddnb.com (accessed 22 September 2024)

YMCA   Young Men's Christian Association

NOTES

Introduction

1 Nancy Price, *Into an Hour Glass* (London: Museum Press, 1953), p. 156.

2 E. Beresford Chancellor, *The Annals of the Strand: Topographical and Historical* (London: Chapman & Hall, 1912).

3 Alan Brooke, *Fleet Street: The Story of a Street* (Stroud: Amberley, 2010); Midge Gillies, *Piccadilly: The Circus at the Heart of London* (London: Hachette, 2022).

4 Fernand Braudel, *The Mediterranean in the Ancient World* (London: Penguin, 2002); Peter Frankopan, *The Earth Transformed* (London: Bloomsbury, 2023).

5 Manolo Guerci, *London's 'Golden Mile': The Great Houses of the Strand, 1550–1650* (New Haven, CT: Yale University Press, 2021).

6 Carl T. Odhner (ed.), *Annals of the New Church, 1688–1850* (Bryn Athyn, PA: Academy of the New Church, 1976), p. 316; Peter Ackroyd, *Blake* (London: Random House, 1995), pp. 35–8, and ch. 26.

7 Peter Jackson (ed.), *John Tallis's London Street Views, 1838–40* (London: London Topographical Society, 1969); Thresher & Glenny collection consulted in the City of Westminster Archives.

8 Byron quotation thanks to Dr Christine Kenyon-Jones.

9 Congreve observation with thanks to Dr Stephen Miller.

10 Rosemary Ashton, *142 Strand: A Radical Address in Victorian London* (London: Random House, 2008).

11 Charles Booth's London, https://booth.lse.ac.uk (accessed 5 January 2024).

12 Neil McKenna, *Fanny & Stella: The Young Men Who Shocked Victorian England* (London: Faber & Faber, 2013).

13 Rudyard Kipling, *Something of Myself* (Ware: Wordsworth Editions, 2008), pp. 43–6.

14 Jimena Canales, *The Physicist and the Philosopher: Einstein, Bergson, and the Debate That Changed Our Understanding of Time* (Princeton, NJ: Princeton University Press, 2015).

15 Havelock Ellis, 'Mescal: a study of a divine plant', *Popular Science Monthly*, vol. 61 (May 1902).

16 Potter reference courtesy of Mr David Pepper.

17 Vincent van Gogh: The Letters, https://vangoghletters.org/vg/letters/let307/letter.html (accessed 2 April 2024).

18 On Monet's room numbers see https://www.strandlines.london/2019/09/09/the-savoy-monets-pied-a-terre (accessed 15 November 2024).

Chapter 1. Beginnings

1 Rudyard Kipling, *The River's Tale*, https://www.kiplingsociety.co.uk/poem/poems_riverstale.htm (accessed 22 September 2024).

2 Robb Dinnis and Chris Stringer, *Britain: One Million Years of the Human Story* (London: Natural History Museum, 2013), pp. 7–13.

3 *Ibid.*, ch. 2.

4 London Geodiversity Partnership, https://londongeopartnership.org.uk/wp/wp-content/uploads/2018/08/GLA47.pdf (accessed 20 February 2024); Jürgen Ehlers, Philip D. Hughes and Philip Leonard Gibbard, *The Ice Age* (Chichester: Wiley-Blackwell, 2016); P. L. Gibbard, 'The history of the great northwest European rivers during the past three million years', *Philosophical Transactions of the Royal Society of London, Series B: Biological Sciences*, vol. 318, no. 1191 (1988), pp. 559–602; D. R. Bridgland (ed.), *The quaternary of the Thames* (London: Springer, 1994); R. A. Ellison, M. A. Woods, *et al.*, *Geology of London: Special Memoir for 1:50000 Geological Sheets 256 (North London), 257 (Romford), 270 (South London), and 271 (Dartford) (England and Wales)* (London: British Geological Survey, 2004).

5 Nicholas Barton, *The Lost Rivers of London: A Study of Their Effects Upon London and Londoners, and the Effects of London and Londoners Upon Them* (London: Phoenix House, 1962).

6 Bjorn Kurten, *Pleistocene Mammals of Europe* (London: Routledge, 2017).

7 D. Overend, J. Lorimer and D. Schreve, 'The bones beneath the streets: drifting through London's Quaternary', *Cultural Geographies*, vol. 27, no. 3 (2020), pp. 453–75; J. W. Franks, 'Interglacial deposits at Trafalgar Square, London', *New Phytologist*, vol. 59, no. 2 (1960), pp. 145–52; Linda Phillips, 'Vegetational history of the Ipswichian/Eemian interglacial in Britain and continental Europe', *New Phytologist*, vol. 73, no. 3 (1974), pp. 589–604; A. J. Stuart, 'The history of the mammal fauna during the Ipswichian/last interglacial in England', *Philosophical Transactions of the Royal Society of London, Series B: Biological Sciences*, vol. 276, no. 945 (1976), pp. 221–50.

8 Paul Slack and Ryk Ward (eds), *The Peopling of Britain: The Shaping of a Human Landscape* (Oxford: Oxford University Press, 2002); Rebecca Sykes, *Kindred: Neanderthal Life, Love, Death and Art* (London: Bloomsbury, 2020); K. Scott, 'Late Middle Pleistocene mammoths and elephants of the Thames Valley, Oxfordshire', in G. Cavarretta, P. Giola, M. Mussi and M. R. Palombo (eds), *La Terra degli Elefanti/The World of Elephants: Proceedings of the First International Congress* (Rome: Consiglio Nazionale delle Ricerche, 2001), pp. 247–54; Katharine Scott and Christine Buckingham, *Mammoths and Neanderthals in the Thames Valley* (Oxford: Archaeopress, 2021).

9 British Museum collection online, https://www.britishmuseum.org/collection/object/H_SLAntiq-246 (accessed 10 January 2024).

10 Chantel Conneller, *The Mesolithic in Britain: Landscape and Society in Times of Change* (London: Routledge, 2021).

11 Andrew Powell, Matt Leivers, Catherine Barnett, Stephanie Knight and Chris J. Stevens, 'Mesolithic, Neolithic and Bronze Age activity on an eyot at Addington Street, Lambeth', *London and Middlesex Archaeological Society Transactions*, vol. 63 (2013), pp. 10–32; Clive Waddington and Karen Wicks, 'Resilience or wipe out? Evaluating the convergent impacts of the 8.2 ka

event and Storegga tsunami on the Mesolithic of northeast Britain', *Journal of Archaeological Science: Reports*, vol. 14 (2017), pp. 692–714.

12 Duncan Garrow and Neil Wilkin, *The World of Stonehenge* (London: British Museum Press, 2022).

13 Catherine Ross and John Clark, *London: The Illustrated History* (London: Allen Lane, 2008), pp. 20–5.

14 I. M. Stead, 'Celtic dragons from the River Thames', *Antiquaries Journal*, vol. 64, no. 2 (1984), pp. 269–79; on farmsteads at St Martin's: Dominic Perring, *London in the Roman World* (Oxford: Oxford University Press, 2022), pp. 42–3; on the origins of London: Peter Ackroyd, *London: The Concise Biography* (London: Random House, 2012), p. 10; on the Thames as a name: R. Coates, 'A new explanation of the name of London', *Transactions of the Philological Society*, vol. 96, no. 2 (1998), pp. 203–29; on the Celtic river: Rainer Pudill and Clive Eyre, *The Tribes and Coins of Celtic Britain* (Ipswich: Greenlight, 2005).

15 For a recent summary of the debate surrounding the Roman crossing of the Thames, see Perring, *London*, pp. 60–2; Montagu Sharpe, *Middlesex in British, Roman, and Saxon Times* (London: Bell, 1919), pp. 33–49; Nicholas Farrant, 'A Romano-British settlement at Putney', *London Archaeologist*, vol. 1, no. 16 (1972), pp. 368–71; Julius Caesar, *The Gallic War*, trans. H. J. Edwards (Cambridge, MA: Harvard University Press, 2006), p. 79. On elephants: quotation from Polyaenus in Sharpe, *Middlesex*, p. 46; Michael Charles and Michael Singleton, 'Claudius, elephants and Britain: making sense of Cassius Dio 60.21.2', *Britannia*, vol. 53 (2022), pp. 173–84; David Woods, 'Claudius and the elephants for Britain (Cassius Dio 60.21.2)', *Britannia*, vol. 54 (2023), pp. 321–5.

16 Ivan Margary, *Roman Roads in Britain* (London: Phoenix, 1955), vol. I, pp. 13–16; Robert Cowie and Lyn Blackmore, *Lundenwic: Excavations in Middle Saxon London 1987–2000* (London: Museum of London, 2013), p. 105; Perring, *London*, pp. 176–7.

17 'Archaeology: the Romano-British period', in J. S. Cockburn, H. P. F. King and K. G. T. McDonnell (eds), *A History of the County of Middlesex, Vol. I: Physique, Archaeology, Domesday, Ecclesiastical Organization, the Jews, Religious Houses, Education of Working Classes to 1870, Private Education From Sixteenth Century* (London, 1969), pp. 64–74, at BHO, http://www.british-history.ac.uk/vch/middx/vol1/pp64–74 (accessed 27 January 2024); Margary, *Roman Roads*, vol. I, p. 48; B. McCann and C. Orton, 'The Fleet Valley Project', *London Archaeologist*, vol. 6, no. 4 (1989), pp. 102–7. On Roman Westminster: Robert Shepherd, *Westminster: A Biography. From Earliest Times to the Present* (London: Bloomsbury Academic, 2012), p. 6; 'Introduction: London after A.D. 60', in *An Inventory of the Historical Monuments in London, Vol. III: Roman London* (London, 1928), pp. 33–56, at BHO, https://www.british-history.ac.uk/rchme/london/vol3/pp33–56 (accessed 27 January 2024).

18 Examples are listed in evaluations and reports published by Museum of London Archaeology and on the Archaeology Data Service website, https://archaeologydataservice.ac.uk (accessed 22 September 2024).

19 Richard Hingley, *Londinium: A Biography* (London: Bloomsbury, 2018), pp. 35, 51–6, 76–9; see also David Mattingly, *An Imperial Possession: Britain in the Roman Empire, 54 BC – AD 409* (London: Allen Lane, 2006), ch. 10; material on and from Tacitus in this and the preceding paragraph are from his *Annals*, translated in Peter Marsden, *Roman London* (London: Thames & Hudson,

1980), p. 31. On the amphitheatre and bone analysis: Perring, *London*, pp. 117–20, 348–9.

20 Museum of London Archaeology blog, https://www.mola.org.uk/discoveries/ news/excavations-holborn-viaduct-reveal-complete-roman-funerary-bed (accessed 13 February 2024); D. Sankey, (2021), *Norman House: The Strand London WC2R, An Archaeological Watching Brief*, at Archaeology Data Service, https:// doi.org/10.5284/1091858 (accessed 10 February 2024); Alistair Douglas, Murray Andrews, Karen Deighton, *et al.*, 'Roman quarries and burials, medieval and later development: excavations at Alderman's House, 117, 119, 121 Bishopsgate and 4–37 Liverpool Street, City of London, EC2', *Transactions of the London and Middlesex Archaeological Society*, vol. 72 (2021), pp. 49–112.

21 Stephen Laker, 'Changing views about Anglo-Saxons and Britons', in H. Aertsen and B. Veldhoen (eds), *Six Papers from the 28th Symposium on Medieval Studies Held at the Vrije Universiteit Amsterdam on 15 December 2006* (Leiden: Leiden University Department of English, 2008), pp. 1–38; Gildas, *On the Ruin of Britain* (trans. J. A. Giles), e-book, at https://www.gutenberg.org/cache/ epub/1949/pg1949-images.html (accessed 22 September 2024).

22 Angélica Varandas, 'From Ambrosius Aurelianus to Arthur: the creation of a national hero in Historia Brittonum', in Carlos Viana Ferreira, Adelaide Meira Serras, et al. (eds), *A Scholar for all Seasons: Homenagem a João de Almeida Flor* (Lisbon: CEAUL, 2013), pp. 177–88.

Chapter 2. Medieval Strand

1 R. A. B. Mynors and Bertram Colgrave (eds), *Bede's Ecclesiastical History of the English People* (Oxford: Clarendon Press, 1992), p. 143.

2 Martin Biddle, 'The road to Lundenwic', in Jonathan Cotton *et al.*, *Hidden Histories and Records of Antiquity: Essays on Saxon London for John Clark, Curator Emeritus, Museum of London* (London: London and Middlesex Archaeological Society, 2014), pp. 13–16.

3 Rory Naismith, *Citadel of the Saxons: The Rise of Early London* (London: Bloomsbury, 2018), ch. 2. On exemptions from tolls, see P. H. Sawyer, *Anglo-Saxon Charters: An Annotated List and Bibliography* (London: Royal Historical Society, 1968), pp. 93–4, 98. On the first references to Lundenwic and subsequent analysis of the archaeology of the settlement, see Robert Cowie and Lyn Blackmore (eds), *Lundenwic: Excavations in Middle Saxon London 1987–2000* (London: Museum of London, 2013), p. 10.

4 Roy Leslie, *Three Old English Elegies* (Liverpool: Liverpool University Press, 1988); Richard Hamer (ed.), *A Choice of Anglo-Saxon Verse* (London: Faber & Faber, 1970), p. 27.

5 Margaret Gelling, *The Early Charters of the Thames Valley* (Leicester: Leicester University Press, 1979), p. 148.

6 Derek Keene, Arthur Burns and Andrew Saint (eds), *St Paul's: The Cathedral Church of London 604-2004* (New Haven, CT: Yale University Press, 2004), ch. 2; Malcolm Gordon, David Bowsher and Robert Cowie, *Middle Saxon London: Excavations at the Royal Opera House 1989–99* (London: Museum of London, 2003), p. 18; Gustav Milne, *The Port of Medieval London* (Reading: Tempus, 2003), ch. 3.

7 Adrian Miles and Virgil Yendell, 'The eastern boundary of Lundenwic? A

watching brief at the London School of Economics, Sheffield Street, WC2',
London Archaeologist, vol. 14, no. 4 (2015), pp. 98–9; Milne, *The Port*, p. 39.

8 Bede's account of the pestilence is quoted in John Maddicott, 'Plague in
seventh-century England', *Past & Present*, vol. 156 (1997), pp. 7–54.

9 The Anglo-Saxon Chronicle reproduced in Dorothy Whitelock (ed.), *English
Historical Documents, 500–1042* (Oxford: Oxford University Press, 1979), vol. I,
pp. 180–1, 187; Alcuin in same volume, pp. 842–4.

10 Account of the Viking landings in the Anglo-Saxon Chronicle in Whitelock
(ed.), *English Historical Documents*, vol. I, pp. 180, 187, 842–4; Thomas Williams,
Viking Britain: A History (London: Harper Collins, 2017), pp. 92, 200–9.

11 Robert Cowie, 'Lundenburgh: the archaeology of late Saxon London', in
Hidden Histories and Records of Antiquity, pp. 17–21.

12 The contemporary charter in which Akeman Street is described is repro-
duced in Margaret Gelling, 'The boundaries of the Westminster charters',
Transactions of the London and Middlesex Archaeological Society, vol. 11 (1953),
pp. 101–4; Tim Tatton-Brown, 'The medieval and early Tudor topography of
Westminster', in Warwick Rodwell and Tim Tatton-Brown (eds), *Westminster
Part I: The Art, Architecture and Archaeology of the Royal Abbey* (London:
Routledge, 2020), pp. 1–22; Marjory Honeybourne, 'Charing Cross riverside',
London Topographical Record, vol. 21 (1958), pp. 44–78; English Place Name
Society, *The Place-Names of Middlesex* (Cambridge: Cambridge University
Press, 1942), p. 167. On 'knight's bridge', first mentioned in the reign of
Edward the Confessor, see Alan Vince, *Saxon London: An Archaeological
Investigation* (London: B. A. Seaby, 1990), pp. 121–2. Akemann Street should
not be confused with the east–west road of the same name near St Albans.

13 On Domesday: Gervase Rosser, *Medieval Westminster: 1200–1540* (Oxford:
Clarendon Press, 1989), p. 17; Samuel Pegge (ed.), *FitzStephen's Description of
London* (London, 1772), pp. 26–7. On 'waste place': Peter Mapplestone, *St Mary
le Strand* (London: CreateSpace, 2019), p. 3. On 'Stronde': Gillian Bebbington,
London Street Names (London: Batsford, 1972), p. 312. On City privileges:
Christopher Brooke, *London 800–1216: The Shaping of a City* (Berkeley, CA:
University of California Press, 1975), p. 126.

14 Rosser, *Medieval Westminster*, pp. 36–7.

15 *Ibid.*, ch. 1 and pp. 76, 167, 215–16.

16 Patricia Croot, Alan Thacker and Elizabeth Williamson (eds), *A History of the
County of Middlesex, Volume XIII: City of Westminster Part 1* (London: Victoria
History of the Counties of England, 2009), pp. 3, 148–51, 162–4, 185–6, 194;
Mapplestone, *St Mary*, pp. 4–13.

17 'Additions to the Chronicles: assize of buildings (Richard I)', in H. T. Riley
(ed.), *Chronicles of the Mayors and Sheriffs of London 1188–1274* (London, 1863), pp.
179–87, at BHO, https://www.british-history.ac.uk/no-series/london-mayors-
sheriffs/1188-1274/pp179-187 (accessed 10 January 2024); John Stow, 'Bridges of
this Citie', in C. L. Kingsford (ed.), *A Survey of London. Reprinted from the Text
of 1603* (Oxford, 1908), pp. 21–7, at BHO, https://www.british-history.ac.uk/
no-series/survey-of-london-stow/1603/pp21-27 (accessed 10 January 2024).

18 Richard Vaughan (ed.), *Chronicles of Matthew Paris: Monastic Life in the Thirteenth
Century* (London: Sutton, 1984), pp. 118–19; David Carpenter, *Henry III,
1207–1258: The Rise to Power and Personal Rule* (New Haven, CT: Yale University
Press, 2020), pp. 474–8.

19 Henry Lucas, 'The great European famine of 1315, 1316, and 1317', *Speculum*, vol. 5, no. 4 (1930), pp. 343–77; Ian Kershaw, 'The Great Famine and agrarian crisis in England 1315–1322', *Past & Present*, vol. 59 (1973), pp. 3–50; Bruce Campbell, 'The European mortality crises of 1346–52 and advent of the Little Ice Age', in Dominik Collet and Maximilian Schuh (eds), *Famines During the 'Little Ice Age' (1300–1800): Socionatural Entanglements in Premodern Societies* (Cham, Springer International, 2018), pp. 19–41; Barnie Sloane, *The Black Death in London* (Cheltenham: History Press, 2011), pp. 14, 55, 84–92, 108, 122.

20 Honeybourne, 'Charing Cross riverside', pp. 44–78; Henry Thomas Riley (ed.), *Memorials of London and London Life, in the XIIIth, XIVth, and XVth Centuries: Being a Series of Extracts, Local, Social, and Political, from the Early Archives of the City of London. AD 1276–1419* (London: Longmans, Green & Co., 1868), vol. I, p. 368; A. Moreley Davies, 'London's first conduit system: a topographical study', *Transactions of the London and Middlesex Archaeological Society*, vol. 8 (1913), p. 42; Caroline Barron, *London in the Later Middle Ages* (Oxford: Oxford University Press, 2004), pp. 256–7; Martha Carlin and Joel Rosenthal (eds), *Medieval London: Collected Papers of Caroline M Barron* (Kalamazoo: Medieval Institute Publications, Western Michigan University, 2017), pp. 116–17. On the ordinance, see Manolo Guerci, *London's 'Golden Mile': The Great Houses of the Strand, 1550–1650* (New Haven, CT: Yale University Press, 2021), p. 79, and the condition of the road, Walter Thornbury, 'The Strand: introduction', in *Old and New London: Volume 3* (London, 1878), vol. III, pp. 59–63, at BHO, https://www.british-history.ac.uk/old-new-london/vol3/pp59-63 (accessed 20 March 2023).

21 Sir George Henry Gater, Frederick R. Hiorns and Walter H. Godfrey, *Survey of London: Trafalgar Square and Neighbourhood (the Parish of St. Martin-in-the-Fields)* (London: London County Council, 1940), pp. 7–9.

22 L. W. Cowie, 'The Savoy – palace and hospital', *History Today*, vol. 24, no. 3 (1974); Guerci, *London's 'Golden Mile*, p. 79; David Preest and James G. Clark (eds), *The Chronica Maiora of Thomas Walsingham (1376–1422)* (Martlesham: Boydell & Brewer, 2005), p. 123.

23 'The chapel and hospital of St. Mary Rounceval', in G. H. Gater and E. P. Wheeler (eds), *Survey of London: Volume 18, St Martin-in-The-Fields II: The Strand* (London: London County Council, 1937), pp. 1–9, at BHO, https://www.british-history.ac.uk/survey-london/vol18/pt2/pp1-9 (accessed 24 January 2024); David Maxfield, 'St. Mary Rouncivale, Charing Cross: the hospital of Chaucer's pardoner', *Chaucer Review*, vol. 28, no. 2 (1993), pp. 148–63; Samuel Moore, 'Chaucer's Pardoner of Rouncival', *Modern Philology*, vol. 25, no. 1 (1927), pp. 59–66.

24 John Williamson, *The History of the Temple, London: From the Institution of the Order of the Knights of the Temple to the Close of the Stuart Period* (London: John Murray, 1925), pp. 12–40.

25 'Hospitals: Domus conversorum', in William Page (ed.), *A History of the County of London: Volume 1, London Within the Bars, Westminster and Southwark* (London, 1909), pp. 551–4, at BHO, https://www.british-history.ac.uk/vch/london/vol1/pp551-554 (accessed 25 January 2024); 'Domus Conversorum', in *Jewish Encyclopaedia*, at https://jewishencyclopedia.com/ (accessed 22 September 2024); Carpenter, *Henry III*, pp. 299–305.

26 Stephen Mayson, 'The regulation of barristers: past, present and future' (2008),

at https://www.lincolnsinn.org.uk/news/the-regulation-of-barristers-past-present-and-future-stephen-mayson (accessed 10 January 2024); Christopher Hibbert and Ben Weinreb (eds), *The London Encyclopaedia* (London: Pan Macmillan, 2008), pp. 419–20.

27 Simon Thurley, *Somerset House: The Palace of England's Queens 1551–1692* (London: London Topographical Society, 2009), ch. 2; Guerci, *London's 'Golden Mile'*, pp. 9–13.

28 Carlin and Rosenthal, *Medieval London*, ch. 15, 'Centres of conspicuous consumption: the aristocratic townhouse in London, 1200–1550'; Guerci, *London's 'Golden Mile'*, p. 127; William Campbell (ed.), *Materials for a History of the Reign of Henry VII* (London: Longman & Co., 1873), vol. I, p. 481, vol. II, p. 430.

Chapter 3. Early modern Strand

1 'Letter from Albert Way, Esq. Director S.A., to Sir Henry Ellis, Secretary, accompanying copy of an indenture of lease from the Earl of Bedford to Sir William Cecil, of a portion of pasture in Covent Garden', *Archaeologia*, vol. 30 (1844), p. 497.

2 Gillian Tindall, *The Man Who Drew London* (London: Random House, 2013); Richard Pennington, *A Descriptive Catalogue of the Etched Work of Wenceslaus Hollar 1607–1677* (Cambridge: Cambridge University Press, 2002).

3 On watermen: Norman Brett-James, *The Growth of Stuart London* (London: George Allen & Unwin, 1935), p. 30; On Agas's map: 'The map of early modern London', at https://mapoflondon.uvic.ca/index.htm (accessed 10 January 2024).

4 Henry Robert Plomer, *A Dictionary of the Booksellers and Printers Who Were at Work in England, Scotland and Ireland from 1641 to 1667* (London: Bibliographical Society/Blades, East & Blades, 1907).

5 Graham Parry, *The Trophies of Time: English Antiquarians of the Seventeenth Century* (Oxford: Oxford University Press, 1996), ch. 1; Kevin Sharpe, *Sir Robert Cotton, 1586–1631: History and Politics in Early Modern England* (Oxford: Oxford University Press, 1979).

6 Giles Milton, *Big Chief Elizabeth: How England's Adventurers Gambled and Won the New World* (London: Hodder & Stoughton, 2000), pp. 64–73.

7 Vanessa Harding, 'The population of London, 1550–1700: a review of the published evidence', *London Journal*, vol. 15, no. 2 (1990), pp. 111–28.

8 'Appendix: The grant of the hospital of St. Mary Rounceval to Sir Thomas Cawarden', in G. H. Gater and E. P. Wheeler (eds), *Survey of London: Volume 18, St Martin-in-The-Fields II: The Strand* (London: London County Council, 1937), p. 130, at BHO, https://www.british-history.ac.uk/survey-london/vol18/pt2/p130 (accessed 10 January 2024).

9 Barrett L. Beer (ed.), *The Life and Raigne of King Edward the Sixth by John Hayward* (Kent, OH: Kent State University Press, 1993), p. 100.

10 Walter Thornbury, 'Somerset House and King's College', in Walter Thornbury (ed.), *Old and New London: Volume 3*, pp. 89–95, at BHO, https://www.british-history.ac.uk/old-new-london/vol3/pp89-95 (accessed 10 January 2024).

11 Beer (ed.), *The Life and Raigne of King Edward*, pp. 100–1; W. K. Jordan (ed.), *The Chronicle and Political Papers of King Edward VI* (London: Allen & Unwin, 1966), p. 18; Sir Henry Spelman, *The History and Fate of Sacrilege ... wrote in the year 1632* (London, 1698), p. xiv.

12 'Diary: 1554 (Jan–June)', in J. G. Nichols (ed.), *The Diary of Henry Machyn, Citizen and Merchant-Taylor of London, 1550–1563* (London: Camden Society, 1848), pp. 50–66, at BHO, https://www.british-history.ac.uk/camden-record-soc/vol42/pp50-66 (accessed 13 February 2024).

13 John Baker, 'The third university of England', in *Collected Papers on English Legal History* (Cambridge: Cambridge University Press, 2013), pp. 143–67.

14 'Silver-streaming Thames': Edmund Spenser, *Prothalmion*; Anthony Wells-Cole, 'Some design sources for the Earl of Leicester's tapestries and other contemporary pieces', *Burlington Magazine*, vol. 125, no. 962 (1983), pp. 284–1.

15 Elizabeth Goldring, *Robert Dudley, Earl of Leicester, and the World of Elizabethan Art* (New Haven, CT: Yale University Press, 2014); Glyn Parry, 'John Dee and the Elizabethan British Empire in its European context', *Historical Journal*, vol. 49, no. 3 (2006), pp. 643–75.

16 Thomas Birch, *Memoirs of the Reign of Queen Elizabeth* (London: A. Millar, 1754), vol. II, pp. 462–80; A. F. Kinney, 'The Essex rebellion: a new account', *Papers of the Bibliographical Society of America*, vol. 66, no. 296 (1972), p. 2.

17 Burghley House is also the name given to William Cecil's large country house in Stamford as well as, confusingly, for a short time, his Strand residence. Stephen Alford, *Burghley: William Cecil at the Court of Elizabeth I* (New Haven, CT: Yale University Press, 2008), ch. 10; Manolo Guerci, *London's 'Golden Mile': The Great Houses of the Strand, 1550–1650* (New Haven, CT: Yale University Press, 2021), ch. 5; Jill Husselby and Paula Henderson, 'Location, location, location! Cecil House in the Strand', *Architectural History*, vol. 45 (2002), pp. 159–93.

18 Rebecca Brackmann, *The Elizabethan Invention of Anglo-Saxon England: Laurence Nowell, William Lambarde, and the Study of Old English* (London: D. S. Brewer, 2012).

19 Pauline Croft, *Patronage, Culture and Power: The Early Cecils* (New Haven, CT: Yale University Press, 2002); Lynn Hulse, 'The musical patronage of Robert Cecil', *Journal of the Royal Musical Association*, vol. 116, no. 1 (1991), pp. 24–40. Parrot quotation: Jennifer Potter, *Strange Blooms: The Curious Lives and Adventures of the John Tradescants* (London: Atlantic Books, 2014).

20 Charles Lethbridge Kingsford, 'XII. Bath Inn or Arundel House', *Archaeologia*, vol. 72 (1922), pp. 243–77.

21 Mary Frederica Sophia Hervey, *The Life, Correspondence and Collections of Thomas Howard* (Cambridge: Cambridge University Press, 1921), pp. 255–6, 284; David Jaffé, 'The Earl and Countess of Arundel: Renaissance collectors', *Apollo: The International Magazine of Arts*, vol. 414 (1996), pp. 3–8.

22 Evelyn quoted in Kingsford, 'Bath Inn'; Sandrart: Hervey, *Life, correspondence*, pp. 255–6.

23 *A catalogue of seeds, plants, &c. sold by Edward Fuller at the Three Crowns and Naked Boy at Strand-Bridge*, at https://www.proquest.com/books/catalogue-seeds-plants-c-sold-edward-fuller-at/docview/2240869681/se-2 (accessed 20 January 2024).

24 Husselby and Henderson, 'Location, location, location!' for map and description of garden.

25 Potter, *Strange Blooms*.

26 Roy Strong, *The Renaissance Garden in England* (London: Thames & Hudson, 1979), ch. 4; Michael Trapp, 'The Georgian history of the Strand Lane "Roman" bath', *London Journal*, vol. 39, no. 2 (2014), pp. 142–67.

27 E. Beresford Chancellor, *The Private Palaces of London Past and Present* (London: Kegan Paul, Trench, Trübner & Co., 1908); York House: Guerci, *London's 'Golden Mile'*, ch. 10.

28 Thomas Brushfield, 'Britain's Burse, or the New Exchange', *Journal of the British Archaeological Association* vol. 9, no. 1 (1903), pp. 33–48; the best general account remains Lawrence Stone, 'Inigo Jones and the New Exchange', *Archaeological Journal*, vol. 114, no. 1 (1957), pp. 106–21.

29 Croft, *Patronage*, pp. 181–2.

30 'New Exchange', Early Modern Map of London (online), at https://mapoflondon. uvic.ca/NEWE1.htm (accessed 3 September 2023).

31 Lord Mayor cited in Early Modern Map of London (online), at https:// mapoflondon.uvic.ca/NEWE1.htm; Pepys' diary online, 27 June 1668, at https://www.pepysdiary.com/diary/1668/06/27 (accessed 14 January 2024); Detail of traders: Records of London's Livery Companies Online, https://www. londonroll.org (accessed 11 January 2024).

32 Plomer, *A Dictionary*, p. 187; C. Y. Ferdinand, 'Herringman, Henry (bap. 1628, d. 1704), bookseller)' (23 September 2004), *ODNB* (accessed 20 January 2024).

33 Stone, 'Inigo Jones', p. 120; 'Sundry Debaucht Gentry' is from a petition to the House of Lords from inhabitants of New Exchange – see 'House of Lords Journal Volume 10: 3 February 1648', in *Journal of the House of Lords: Volume 10, 1648–1649* (London, 1767–1830), pp. 16–20, at BHO, https://www.british-history. ac.uk/lords-jrnl/vol10/pp16-20 (accessed 10 December 2023).

34 Deborah Harkness, *The Jewel House: Elizabethan London and the Scientific Revolution* (New Haven, CT: Yale University Press, 2007), pp. 108–31; Gloria Clifton and Gerard L'E. Turner, *Directory of British Scientific Instrument Makers, 1550–1851* (1995), pp. 6, 59, 199; Alexandra Rose and Jane Desborough, *Science City* (London: Scala Arts and Heritage Publishers, in association with the Science Museum, 2019), ch. 1, 'A new trade in London'.

35 John Harley, 'Merchants and privateers: a window on the world of William Byrd', *Musical Times*, vol. 147, no. 1896 (autumn 2006), pp. 51–66.

36 Savoy: Guerci, *London's 'Golden Mile'*, p. 83. On French locals: Norman Brett-James, *The Growth of Stuart London* (London: George Allen & Unwin, 1935), p. 48. On Durham House: Henry B. Wheatley, 'Original plan of Durham House and grounds, 1626', *London Topographical Record*, vol. 10 (1916), pp. 160–1. On Somerset House chapel: Leanda de Lisle, *Henrietta Maria: Conspirator, Warrior, Phoenix Queen* (London: Random House, 2023), pp. 128–9, 147–8.

37 Margarette Lincoln, *London and the 17th Century: The Making of the World's Greatest City* (New Haven, CT: Yale University Press, 2022), pp. 69, 93.

38 De Lisle, *Henrietta Maria*, p. 249; Guerci, *London's 'Golden Mile'*, pp. 73, 83, 101. On petitions: Civil War Petitions, at https://www.civilwarpetitions.ac.uk (accessed 1 February 2024).

39 'Mercurius Politicus Redivivus … by Thomas Rugge', *Camden Third Series*, vol. 91 (1961), pp. 1–180.

40 Theofraste Fady, 'London's first taxi rank', June 2021, on the Strandlines website, at https://www.strandlines.london/2021/06/18/londons-first-taxi-rank (accessed 22 September 2024).

41 On the opening of the new maypole see *The cities loyalty display'd* (London, 1661) – Thomason Tract E.1087[12]; William Stukeley, 'Revised memoir of Newton', published by the Newton Project, at https://www.newtonproject.ox.ac.uk/view/ texts/diplomatic/OTHE00001 (accessed 10 October 2023).

42 *The London Gazette*, 3 September 1666, at https://www.thegazette.co.uk/London/issue/85/page/1 (accessed 9 January 2024); T. F. Reddaway, *The Rebuilding of London After the Great Fire* (London: Cape, 1940), p. 263; Guerci, *London's 'Golden Mile'*, pp. 31, 46; 103; Pepys' diary online, at https://www.pepysdiary.com/diary/1666/09 (accessed 20 February 2024); Rebecca Rideal, *1666: Plague, War, and Hellfire* (London: Macmillan, 2016), ch. 7.

43 Frank Kelsall and Timothy Walker, *Nicholas Barbon: Developing London, 1667–1698* (London: London Topographical Society, 2022); 'Southampton Street and Tavistock Street area: the Cecil estate', in F. H. W. Sheppard (ed.), *Survey of London: Volume 36, Covent Garden* (London, 1970), p. 223, at BHO, https://www.british-history.ac.uk/survey-london/vol36/p223 (accessed 11 January 2024).

44 David Allan, *The Adelphi Past and Present: A History and a Guide* (London: Calder Walker, 2001), pp. 26–30; 'Durham Place', in G. H. Gater and E. P. Wheeler (eds), *Survey of London: Volume 18*, pp. 84–98, at BHO, https://www.british-history.ac.uk/survey-london/vol18/pt2/pp84-98 (accessed 10 January 2024). On theatres: Janette Dillon, *Theatre, Court and City, 1595–1610* (Cambridge: Cambridge University Press, 2000); Julian Bowsher, *Shakespeare's London Theatreland: Archaeology, History and Drama* (London: Museum of London, 2012); Brian Dobbs, *Drury Lane: Three Centuries of the Theatre Royal, 1663–1971* (London: Cassell, 1972).

Chapter 4. Eighteenth-century Strand

1 Edward Ward, *The London-spy compleat for the month of July 1699 Part IX* (London: printed and sold by J. How in the Ram-Head-Inn-Yard in Fanchurch Street, 1699), pp. 9–10.

2 John Gwynn, *London and Westminster Improved* (printed for the author, 1766), p. 18.

3 'London, Aug. 11', *Stamford Mercury*, 16 August 1739, p. 2.

4 Richard Burridge, *A New Review of London* (London: printed by W. H. and sold by J. Roberts, at the Oxford Arms in Warwick Lane, 3rd edition, 1722), p. 2.

5 Lynn Hollen Lees, 'World urbanization, 1750 to the present', in J. R. McNeill and Kenneth Pomeranz (eds), *The Cambridge World History* (Cambridge: Cambridge University Press, 2015), p. 53.

6 'Advertisements and notices', *Country Journal of the Craftsman*, 1 June 1728.

7 Derek Howse, 'Sisson, Jeremiah (bap. 1720, d.1783), maker of mathematical instruments' (21 May 2009), *ODNB* (accessed 4 October 2023).

8 Thomas Sandby, *View of Beaufort Buildings, looking towards the Strand*. British Museum Collection, BM 1880,1113.2854.

9 Gloria Clifton, 'Dollond family (per. 1750–1871), makers of optical and scientific instruments' (23 October 2013), *ODNB* (accessed 4 October 2023).

10 Science Museum Group Collection, Trade card: P. Dollond. 1934–121/42.

11 A. D. Morrison-Low, 'Jones, William (bap.1762, d.1831), maker of scientific instruments' (10 February 2022), *ODNB* (accessed 4 October 2023).

12 John Dryden, *The Major Works* (Oxford: Oxford University Press, 2003), p. 21.

13 James Boswell, *The Life of Samuel Johnson, LL.D.* (printed by H. Baldwin and Son, for Charles Dilly, in the Poultry, 1799), vol. II, p. 72.

14 'Temple Bar and the straits of the Strand', *The Builder*, vol. 27, no. 1368 (1869), p. 329.

15 John William Abbott, *A History of London from the Earliest Period to the Present Time: With Some Account of the Present State of Its Most Important Public Buildings* (London: A. K. Newman, 1821), p. 251.

16 Frances Seymour to Lady Luxborough, 17 June 1749, in Helen Sard Hughes, *The Gentle Hertford: Her Life and Letters* (New York: Macmillan, 1940), p. 388.

17 Westminster City Archives, London, Folio 27, Westminster Rate Books, 'J. Sisson', 1726.

18 William Stow, *Remarks on London, being an exact survey* (London: Printed for T. Norris, 1722), p. 13.

19 Acts of the Parliament of Great Britain. Fires Prevention (Metropolis) Act, 1774, 14 Geo. III, c. 78.

20 'Advertisements and notices', *Daily Courant*, 9 April 1722.

21 'News', *Spectator*, 6 March 1711.

22 John Mainwaring, *Memoirs of the life of the late George Frederic Handel* (London: Printed for R. and J. Dodsley, 1760), p. 126; Winton Dean, 'Handel, George Frideric', in Stanley Sadie (ed.), *The New Grove Dictionary of Music and Musicians* (London: Macmillan, 1980), vol. VIII, p. 93.

23 'Bach, Johann [John] Christian', in Sadie (ed.), *The New Grove Dictionary*, vol. I, p. 866.

24 Wilhelm von Archenholtz, *A Picture of England* (London: E. Jeffery, 1789), vol. I, p. 122.

25 César-François de Saussure, *A Foreign View of England in the Reigns of George I and George II*, trans. and ed. Madame van Muyden (London: John Murray, 1902), p. 156.

26 Bird also suffered a kidney complaint: Anita McConnel, 'Bird, John (1709–1776), maker of scientific instruments'(2 January 2008), *ODNB* (accessed 5 October 2023).

27 Pierre-Jean Grosley, *A Tour to London* (1765), trans. T. Nugent (London: Printed for Lockyer Davis, 1772), vol. I, p. 47.

28 de Saussure, *A Foreign View*, pp. 81, 166.

29 John Gay, *Trivia: or, the art of walking the streets of London* (Printed for Bernard Lintott, at the Cross-Keys between the Temple Gates in Fleetstreet, 1716), book 3.

30 de Saussure, *A Foreign View*, p. 127.

31 Pamela Sharpe, 'Population and society 1700–1840', in Peter Clark (ed.), *The Cambridge Urban History of Britain* (Cambridge: Cambridge University Press, 2000), p. 496.

32 Richard Steele, from 'A Discourse upon wenches', *Spectator*, no. 266 (4 January 1712), reproduced in Rick Allen, *The Moving Pageant: A Literary Sourcebook on London Street-Life, 1799–1814* (London: Routledge), p. 41.

33 Edward Ward, *The London-spy compleat* (Printed for, and by J. How, and sold by Eliphal Jaye, at the sign of the candlestick, the lower-end of Cheapside, 1700), p. 12.

34 Grosley, *A Tour to London*, vol. I, p. 91; de Saussure, *A Foreign View*, p. 111.

35 'London, May 5', *Stamford Mercury*, 10 May 1716, p. 223.

36 '48, Report of the Surveyor General (John Pulteney, Esq.) to the Lords of the Treasury' 4 May (1724), in Joseph Redington, Great Britain Public Record Office *Calendar of Treasury Papers, Volume 6, 1720–1728* (London, 1889), pp. 257–76, at BHO, https://www.british-history.ac.uk/cal-treasury-papers/vol6/pp257-276 (accessed 20 October 2023).

37 Gwynn, *London and Westminster Improved*, p. 85.

38 *Ibid.*, p. 93.

39 *Ibid.*, p. vii.

40 Trade card of Twinings, grocer, 1750, Heal Collection, British Museum (Heal, 68.330).

41 Thomas Twining teaman, Devereux Court, Temple, inscribed *c.* 1735 verso. Photograph of the centre part of a tea wrapper on a trade card of Thomas and Daniel Twining, Heal Collection, British Museum (Heal, 68.318).

42 Joseph Jérôme Le Français de Lalande, *Diary of a Trip to England* (1763), ed. Hélène Monod-Cassidy (Kingston: R. Watkins, 2002), p. 6. The equivalent buying power in 2025 for £1 in 1763 is around £250.

43 John Cannon, *Samuel Johnson and the Politics of Hanoverian England* (Oxford, 1994; online edition, Oxford Academic, 3 October 2011), p. 180.

44 de Saussure, *A Foreign View*, p. 162.

45 Citizen of London, *The vices of the cities of London and Westminster* (London: Printed for G. Faulkner in Essex-Street, and R. James in Dame-Street, 1751), p. 22.

46 Philip Rawlings, 'Fielding, Sir John (1721–1780), magistrate' (23 September 2004), *ODNB* (accessed 20 October 2023).

47 John Fielding, *A plan of the Universal register-office, opposite Cecil Street in the Strand, and of that in Bishopsgate-street, the corner of Cornhill. Both by the same proprietors* (London: 1752), p. 9. The Universal Register Office was a one-stop agency that matched enquiries to whatever could be traded: goods and real estate; money-lending; travel arrangements; employment; services. It charged sixpence to register with it and threepence for matches made.

48 Robert Dodsley, James Dodsley and Samuel Wale, *London and Its Environs Described* (London: Printed for R. and J. Dodsley, 1761), p. 205.

49 Charles Whitworth, *A plan for the more easy and speedy execution of the laws relating to the new paving, cleansing and lighting the streets of Westminster* (Printed for J. Walter, at Charing-Cross, 1766), p. 10; 'Advertisements and notices', *Gazetteer and London Daily Advertiser*, 12 March 1764.

50 Whitworth, *A plan*, p. 11.

51 Gwynn, *London and Westminster Improved*, p. 97.

52 Sophie von La Roche, *Sophie in London, 1786: being the diary of Sophie v. La Roche*, transl. Clare Williams (London: J. Cape, 1933), p. 237.

53 The National Archives, London SP 37/8/33, Folios 88–89, A memorandum from Sir John Fielding, 1 July 1771.

54 Reflecting the mutually held antipathy between them: James Gillray, *The Hopes of the Party, prior to July 14th*, British Museum (BM 1868,0808.6086).

55 Country Parson, *Three letters to the tithe association, at the Crown and Anchor in the Strand* (London: Printed for J. Hinton, 1773); Christina Parolin, *Radical Spaces: Venues of Popular Politics in London, 1790–c. 1845* (Acton: ANU Press, 2010).

56 London Corresponding Society, *Address to the nation, from the London Corresponding Society, on the subject of a thorough parliamentary reform: together with the resolutions which were passed at a general meeting of the society; held on Monday, the 8th of July, 1793, at the Crown and Anchor Tavern Strand* (London: Printed by order of the Society, and distributed gratis, 1793).

57 The National Archives, HO 42/29/100, Folios 268–70, Anonymous letter to William Pitt, 31 March 1794; HO 42/29/217, Folios 542–5, Letter to Evan

Nepean, Under-Secretary, Home Office, from George Rose [MP and Joint Secretary to the Treasury], 30 April 1794.

58 John Thelwall, *Prospectus of a course of lectures* (London: H. D. Symonds, 1796), in Robert Lamb and Corinna Wagner, *Selected Political Writings of John Thelwall* (London: Pickering & Chatto, 2009), vol. I, p. 115.

59 John Thelwall, 'The connection between the calamities of the present reign, and the system of borough-mongering corruption' (1796), in *ibid.*, vol. II, p. 197.

Chapter 5. Nineteenth-century Strand

1 George Cruikshank and William Hone, *The Man In the Moon &c. &c. &c.: With Fifteen Cuts*, 22nd edition (London: Printed by and for William Hone, 1820).

2 *The Complete Plays of Gilbert and Sullivan* (New York: Modern Library, 1936), p. 629.

3 Lady Theresa Lewis (ed.), *Extracts of the journals and correspondence of Miss Berry from the year 1783 to 1852* (London: Longmans, Green and Co, 1865), vol. II, p. 309.

4 Frederic G. Stephens, *A Memoir of George Cruikshank* (New York: Scribner & Welford, 1891), p. 10.

5 Lewis, *Extracts of the journals*, vol. III, pp. 103–4.

6 'United Parliament', *Examiner*, 27 June 1830, p. 405.

7 John Robert Day, *The Story of the London Bus: London and Its Buses from the Horse Bus to the Present Day* (London: London Transport Executive, 1973), pp. 8–9.

8 'Miscellaneous', *The Builder*, vol. 1, no. 85 (1844), p. 486.

9 'Table talk', *Leicester Journal*, 31 May 1844, p. 3.

10 'The storm', *Hereford Journal*, 30 July 1806, p. 2.

11 'Failure of wood paving in the Strand', *The Builder*, vol. 3, no. 138 (1845), p. 465.

12 George Augustus Sala, *Gaslight and Daylight, with Some London Scenes They Shine Upon* (London: Chapman & Hall, 1859), pp. 198, 202.

13 'Arcadian traffic', *Punch, or the London Charivari*, 1 June 1844, p. 232.

14 'List of new patents', *The Builder*, vol. 3, no. 119 (1845), p. 238.

15 Brenda Weeden, *The Education of the Eye: History of the Royal Polytechnic Institution* (London: University of Westminster Press, 2008), p. 9.

16 'Advertisements & notices', *Morning Chronicle*, 4 May 1833.

17 Edward Bailey, 'Charles Lyell, founder of modern geology', in Sir Gavin de Beer (gen. ed.), *British Men of Science* (London: Nelson, 1962), p. 123.

18 *Ibid.*, p. 97.

19 Dennis R. Dean, *Gideon Mantell and the Discovery of Dinosaurs* (Cambridge: Cambridge University Press, 1999), p. 87.

20 'Opening of Exeter-Hall', *The Times*, 30 March 1831, p. 6.

21 'Sunday's and Tuesday's posts', *Stamford Mercury*, 20 May 1831, p. 4.

22 'Temperance', *The Times*, 30 June 1831, p. 5.

23 'The end of Exeter-Hall', *The Times*, 23 July 1907, p. 8.

24 'Brother Jacob', 'music', in John Rignall (ed.), *Oxford Reader's Companion to George Eliot* (Oxford: Oxford University Press, 2011), at Oxford Reference, https://www.oxfordreference.com/display/10.1093/acref/9780198604228.001.0001/acref-978 0198604228 (accessed 2 January 2024).

25 Alexander Ireland, *Ralph Waldo Emerson: His Life, Genius and Writings* (London: Simpkin, Marshall & Co., 1882), p. 55.

26 William McDonnell, *Exeter Hall: A Theological Romance* (Boston: William White & Co., 1873), p. 3.

27 Sherlock, 'Miscellaneous intelligence', *Leicestershire Mercury*, 8 April 1837, p. 4.

28 'Poetry', *Northern Star*, 9 March 1850.

29 Charles Haddon Spurgeon, *C. H. Spurgeon's Autobiography Compiled from his diary, letters and records by his wife and his private secretary, Vol. II: 1834–1860* (Cincinnati, OH: Curtis & Jennings, 1899), p. 9.

30 'Hospital', *The Builder*, vol. 8, no. 382 (1850), p. 261.

31 'Building accidents', *The Builder*, vol. 9, no. 416 (1851), p. 60.

32 John Timbs, *Curiosities of London: exhibiting the most rare and remarkable objects of interest in the metropolis; with nearly fifty years' personal recollections* (London: David Bogue, 1855), p. 380.

33 William Hunter, *Historical Account of Charing Cross Hospital and Medical School* (London: John Murray, 1914), p. 159.

34 John Diprose, *Some Account of the Parish of Saint Clement Danes (Westminster): Past and Present* (London: Diprose & Bateman, 1876), vol. II, p. 55.

35 Leonard Huxley, *Life and Letters of Thomas Henry Huxley* (New York: D. Appleton & Co., 1901), vol. I, p. 17.

36 'Increase of buildings', *The Builder*, vol. 9, no. 446 (1851), p. 527.

37 The Institution, *Public Dispensary Carey Street Lincoln's Inn, for the relief of the sick poor, at the dispensary, and at their own homes* (London: Printed by William Stevens, 1862).

38 'Town talk', *Preston Chronicle*, 12 April 1851.

39 'The Great Exhibition', *Leeds Times*, 22 February 1851, p. 7.

40 'Multiple news items', *The Standard*, 19 May 1851.

41 'Our weekly mirror', *Northern Star*, 10 May 1851.

42 'Invaded Strand', *The Times*, 30 April 1851), p. 4.

43 *Ibid.*

44 'John. Mr Dear Peter', *Dundee Courier*, 20 August 1851.

45 'The Great Exhibition', *Dundee Courier*, 15 October 1851, p. 1.

46 *Morning Post*, 24 September 1851, p. 3.

47 *The Lady's Newspaper & Pictorial Times*, 19 April 1851, p. 222.

48 *Newcastle Journal*, 14 June 1851, p. 7.

49 'The Queen's visit to the City', *The Times*, 30 June 1851, p. 5.

50 'The submarine telegraph', *Glasgow Herald*, 17 November 1851.

51 Edwin Clark, 'The Electric Telegraph Company', *The Times*, 8 September 1852, p. 5.

52 Sir Henry Maxwell, *Life and Times of the Right Honourable William Henry Smith* (Edinburgh: Blackwood, 1893), vol. I, p. 81.

53 *Ibid.*, p. 45.

54 'Charing Cross Bridge', *The Builder*, vol. 3, no. 86 (1845), p. 442.

55 'Jottings about railways', *The Builder*, vol. 3, no. 88 (1845), p. 451.

56 'Editorial', *The Builder*, vol. 8, no. 403 (26 October 1850), p. 505.

57 'It is now, we think, pretty nearly eight years', *The Times*, 10 July 1855, p. 9.

58 'The Victoria Embankment. – On Saturday', *The Times*, 10 May 1875, p. 7.

59 Edward G. H. Liveing, *Adventure in Publishing: The House of Ward Lock, 1854–1954* (London: Ward, Lock, 1954), p. 36.

60 A. C. Grayling, 'Illuminating thought', *Financial Times*, 22 May 1993, p. 18.
61 Maxime F. Gendre, 'Two centuries of electric light source innovations' (2003), p. 4, at https://www.einlightred.tue.nl/lightsources/history/light_history.pdf (accessed 12 October 2023).
62 'The opening of the Middle Temple library', *The Times*, 1 November 1861, p. 7.
63 'The electric light', *The Times*, 18 December 1878, p. 3.
64 John Hollingshead, *Footlights* (London: Chapman & Hall, 1883), p. 209.
65 'Editorial: the light of the future', *The Builder*, vol. 36, no. 1863 (19 October 1878), p. 1083.
66 G. D. M. Willoughby, 'Lewis and Lewis: the life and times of a Victorian solicitor', *American Journal of Legal History*, vol. 30, no. 2 (1986), pp. 188–9.
67 Redistribution of Seats Act 1885 (48 & 49 Vict. C 23).

Chapter 6. Edwardian Strand

1 H. Castling and C. W. Murphy, *Let's All Go Down the Strand* (London: Francis, Day & Hunter, 1909).
2 Arthur W. Symons, *London: A Book of Aspects* (London: Privately printed for Edmund D. Brooks and his friends, 1909), p. 14.
3 City of Westminster Archive, London, Sun Insurance Office Ltd, Charing Cross (1884–1965), Staff scrapbook, with enclosures: Illustrated poem by [Eden Phillpotts] of a dinner at the Hotel Cecil 447/1/5.
4 British Library, Western Manuscripts Box 23, 1: Correspondence regarding dinner arrangements from the Earl of Crewe, Literary Fund Anniversary Dinner Papers, A. Judah to R.L.F., 16 October 1899; R.L.F. to B. Sabath, 27 July 1966.
5 'The Hotel Cecil, Limited', *The Times*, 19 May 1896, p. 16.
6 *St. Cecilia, The Official Organ of the Hotel Cecil* (London: Hotel Cecil, 1896), p. 15.
7 Osiah Henry Symon, *Tis Sixty Years Since: An Address Delivered … on May 21st, 1897, … Inaugurating a Course of Public Lectures Arranged by the Chamber of Manufactures, Etc.* (Adelaide: Vardon & Pritchard, 1897), p. 14.
8 Bernard Darwin, *The Lure of London: Being a Treatise on the Historic and Social Features of the Mighty City of the Thames* (London: Hotel Cecil, c. 1920).
9 'Advertisement: Hotel Cecil', *Vogue*, vol. 41, no. 7 (1913), p. 101.
10 The National Archives, Kew, COPY1/520/242, Photograph by Langfiers Studio, Hotel Cecil, 'Mme Tettrazini and her husband', 25 April 1908.
11 'The Strand Palace Hotel', *The Times*, 7 September 1909, p.1 2.
12 Egbert T. Russell, 'The ladies of the chorus', *The Lone Hand*, vol. 1, no.1 (1909), p. 283.
13 National Portrait Gallery, London, x102101, Gladys Cooper, Past Exhibitions – Gaiety Girls exhibition, 1971, at https://www.npg.org.uk/whatson/display/2004/gaiety-girls/past-exhibitions.php (accessed 20 August 2022).
14 'London under Snow', *The Telegraph*, 5 February 1900, p. 7.
15 Wilfred Whitten, *A Londoner's London* (Boston, MA: Maynard, 1913), p. 159.
16 From our special correspondents, 'Return of the CIV', *The Times*, 30 October 1900, pp. 8–9.
17 'A new London', *The Telegraph*, 6 November 1900, p. 5.
18 'Torn-up streets in central London', *The Telegraph*, 28 October 1901, p. 7.

19 'It is a welcome sign of the times', *The Telegraph*, 27 November 1900, p. 9.

20 'Historic Strand tavern', *The Telegraph*, 22 December 1900, p. 9.

21 'Notes from London and thereabouts', *Times of India*, 25 December 1902, p. 4.

22 'Plague in London', *Times of India*, 5 November 1910, p. 8.

23 'The bystander', *The Graphic*, 2 June 1900, p. 786.

24 'Wheels of life', *The Telegraph*, 2 November 1907, p. 7.

25 H. A. Scott, 'The symphony of the London streets', *Pall Mall Magazine*, vol. 46, no. 211 (1910), p. 799.

26 'Adventures of a hansom cab', *The Telegraph*, 22 August 1900, p. 5.

27 'Scene in the Strand', *The Telegraph*, 6 August 1900, p. 6.

28 'A cure for crowded streets', *The Telegraph*, 27 July 1900, p. 5.

29 'Cabs in the Strand', *The Telegraph*, 16 February 1899, p. 7.

30 'The passing of the horsed cab', *The Times*, 5 October 1909, p. 6.

31 'Clearing the Strand', *The Telegraph*, 17 January 1901, p. 7.

32 Special cablegrams, 'Noises in Europe worse than here', *New York Times*, 29 July 1907), p. 4.

33 Elinor Glyn, 'How New York City appears to Elinor Glyn', *New York Times*, 13 October 1907, p. SM1.

34 'The race for a majority: watching the 'Daily Graphic' ladder', *The Graphic*, 6 October 1900, p. 502.

35 'Club comments', *Graphic*, 20 January 1900, p. 71. The *Daily Graphic*, first daily illustrated newspaper in England, was launched following the great commercial success of the weekly *Graphic* illustrated newspaper (issued every Saturday, price 6d).

36 'In the Strand recent great changes', *Times of India*, 31 May 1909, p. 11.

37 'Inquests', *The Times*, 1 September 1906, p. 4.

38 'Scatters money in streets', *New York Times*, 1 May 1912, p. 7.

39 Eileen Chanin, *Capital Designs: Australia House and Visions of an Imperial London* (Melbourne: Australian Scholarly, 2018), p. 170.

40 'We announce to-day a very interesting building scheme', *The Times*, 21 November 1901, p. 9.

41 'Wild flowers on the vacant sites in the Strand', *Illustrated London News*, 27 July 1907, p. 139.

42 'Cabbage patch in Strand: rabbits also, if suggestion to London County Council is adopted', *New York Times*, 12 November 1911, p. 1.

43 'Australian enterprise: N=new London quarters rendezvous for Victorians', *Times of India*, 24 October 1908, p. 11.

44 'The illuminations down the Strand', *Manchester Guardian*, 23 June 1911, p. 11.

45 'John Bull, Limited', *Sunday Times*, 11 October 1908, p. 5.

46 Chanin, *Capital Designs*, plate 37.

47 'Australia's advertisement in the Strand', *Manchester Guardian*, 16 August 1912, p. 5.

48 'Home opinion: the great shout', *Times of India*, 11 July 1908, p. 8.

49 'S. Smith & Son's 'Strand' watches', *Illustrated London News*, 23 April 1910, p. 626.

50 H. Dominic W. Stiles, 'Acoustic instrument makers in the Strand, acoustic "throne" myths, & Frederick Charles Rein & Son', at https://blogs.ucl.ac.uk/library-rnid/2016/11/11/acoustic-instrument-makers-in-the-strand-acoustic-thrones-frederick-charles-rein-son (accessed 20 August 2022).

51 Grace's Guide to British Industrial History, https://gracesguide.co.uk/Villiers-Strand (accessed 20 August 2022).
52 *Western Daily Press*, 12 September 1910, p. 10.
53 A. R. Hope Moncrieff, *London* (London: A. & C. Black, 1916), p. 74.
54 Whitten, *A Londoner's London*, p. 159.
55 Sir Arthur Conan Doyle, *A Treasury of Sherlock Holmes* (New York: Nelson Doubleday, 1955), p. 317.
56 '"Davey", king of London chefs since the days of Dickens', *New York Times*, 17 August 1913, p. SM14.
57 Jacob Epstein, *Let There Be Sculpture* (New York: Putnam's, 1940), p. 27.
58 Richard Cork, 'Jacob Epstein and Charles Holden: a Whitmanesque collaboration in the Strand', *AA Files*, vol. 8 (1985), p. 73.
59 C. Despard, 'Women taxpayers and the franchise', *The Scotsman*, 1 January 1908, p. 9.
60 '"Wireless" school: world centre', *Times of India*, 13 June 1912, p. 8.
61 Marconi Transatlantic Wireless Telegraph, 'Wireless from the Strand', *New York Times*, 25 August 1912, p. 1.
62 'A congress of nations', *Aberdeen Journal*, 12 June 1914, p. 4.
63 'In London Town', *Cheltenham Looker-On*, 17 October 1914) p. 10.
64 *Nottingham Evening Post*, 4 December 1915, p. 1.
65 'Serbian troops in London', *The Telegraph*, 3 March 1916, p. 3.
66 Andrew Reid & Co., Ltd, 50, Grey Street, Newcastle-on-Tyne, Poster showing a dirigible in the night sky over London, illuminated by a searchlight. [London]: Publicity Department, Central Recruiting Depot, [1915].
67 Baseball in the Strand (1918), British Pathé and the Reuters Historical Collection, Film ID 1888.32, at https://www.britishpathe.com/asset/77273 (accessed 1 September 2022).
68 'Beaver hut opened', *The Telegraph*, 31 October 1918, p. 3.
69 'News in brief', *Western Star and Roma Advertiser*, 3 December 1919, p. 2.
70 'London's women police', *The Telegraph*, 17 December 1918, p. 10.
71 'Anzac march', *Daily Mail*, 26 April 1919, p. 3.

Chapter 7. Interwar Strand

1   City of Westminster Archives, St Clement Danes' Parish Records 1868–2013, 2824/18, 'St Clement Danes' Notes made by the Reverend W. Pennington-Bickford 1941, p. 2.
2   'London joy night', *Daily Mail*, 30 June 1919, p. 5.
3   Nancy Price, *Into an Hour-glass* (London: Museum Press, 1953), pp. 116, 155.
4   E. V. Lucas, *A Wanderer in London* (London: Methuen & Co., 1923), p. 15.
5   C. B. Cochran, *Showman Looks On* (London: J. M. Dent & Sons, 1945), p. 253.
6   Arthur Burrows, *The Story of Broadcasting* (London: Cassell & Co., 1924), p. 69.
7   Bill Egan, *Florence Mills: Harlem Jazz Queen* (Lanham, MD: Scarecrow Press, 2004), pp. 196–7.
8   *Ibid.*, p. 191.
9   'At home and abroad', *TES*, 16 August 1930, p. 1.
10 J. L. Fisher, 'Architecture to-day', *Financial Times*, 27 July 1932, p. 8.
11 'Twenty-eight years of the motor-omnibus', *Daily Mail (Atlantic Edition)*, 20 May 1925, p. 18.

12 'Dangerous driving in the Strand', *The Times*, 5 April 1929, p. 11.

13 'Motor-'buses in the Strand', *Daily Telegraph*, 8 September 1910, p. 4.

14 'Armistice Day programme', *Nottingham Evening Post*, 14 October 1925, p. 6.

15 Charles B. Cochran, 'Negro art', *Daily Mail*, 26 July 1926, p. 8.

16 Marie Seton, *Paul Robeson* (London: Dennis Dobson, 1958), p. 42.

17 *Ibid.*, p. 52.

18 'Men and women of to-day', *Dundee Courier*, 3 July 1928, p. 12.

19 Westminster City Archives, London, 2917/1, Geo. Monro Ltd florists and fruit merchants Tavistock Street, Covent Garden, 1913.

20 *Ibid.*, 2370/1/5, Volume containing Royal Commission Scheme for a New Charing Cross Bridge 1926, p. 5.

21 '*Pickwick* centenary celebration', *TES*, 21 May 1927, p. 4.

22 'Oranges and Lemons Day', *TES*, 5 April 1924, p. 1.

23 'All London out again', *Daily Mail*, 3 September 1931, p. 9.

24 Philip S. Foner (ed.), *Paul Robeson Speaks: Writings, Speeches, Interviews, 1918–1974* (London: Quartet, 1978), p. 230.

25 Seton, *Paul Robeson*, p. 41.

26 Paul Robeson, *Here I Stand* (London: Dennis Dobson, 1958), p. 41.

27 Paul Robeson, Jr, *The Undiscovered Paul Robeson: An Artist's Journey, 1898–1939* (New York: John Wiley & Sons, 2001), p. 156.

28 H. R. L. Sheppard, 'The gift of the gab', *Answers*, 5 November 1932, p. 3.

29 'The Peace Army: views of the Rev. "Dick" Sheppard', *Manchester Guardian*, 29 February 1932, p. 12; Our London Staff. 'The Peace Army: "small but real nucleus" enrolled helping China', *Manchester Guardian*, 8 April 1932, p. 13.

30 H. R. L. Sheppard, *Echoes from St Martin-in-the-Fields* (London: Athenaeum Press, 1934), p. 129.

31 *Ibid.*, p. 131.

32 City of Westminster Archive, London, WDP2/1313/05, Gatti's Restaurant, 436 Strand WC2, 1940.

33 William Mundy, 'A night in at Gatti's', *Daily Mail*, 15 March 1941, p. 2.

34 Philip Page, 'Beethoven in revue', *Daily Mail*, 13 March 1940, p. 5.

35 City of Westminster Archive, London, 2238/11, Walter Robert Wallace Bell (23470).

36 'C.E.M.A. in the Shelters', *TES*, 16 November 1940, p. 449.

37 City of Westminster Archive, London, 2824/18, 'St Clement Danes', Notes made by the Reverend W. Pennington-Bickford, 1941.

38 'Obituaries', *The Times*, 14 June 1941, p. 6.

39 'The rector of St Clement Danes', *The Times*, 24 June 1941, p. 7.

Chapter 8. To the twenty-first century

1 Arthur Machen, *Far Off Things* (London: Martin Secker, 1922), quoted on the Strandlines website, at https://www.strandlines.london/2018/01/28/that-strand-which-is-lost-as-atlantis-arthur-machens-memories-of-the-strand-2/ (accessed 5 January 2024).

2 A description of every area affected by the bombing can be found on the Bomb Sight website, at https://www.bombsight.org (accessed 10 November 2023); see also the West End at War website, at https://www.westendatwar.org.uk/page/incident3?path=op28p (accessed 10 November 2023).

3 'Conservation of the Spirit of Gaiety', on the V&A website, at https://www. vam.ac.uk/articles/conservation-of-the-spirit-of-gaiety (accessed 10 November 2023).

4 Caroline Shenton, *National Treasures: Saving the Nation's Art in World War II* (London: John Murray, 2022), pp. 62–3, 112–14.

5 'The Londoner's diary', *Evening Standard*, 5 July 1952.

6 Becky Conekin, *'The Autobiography of a Nation': The 1951 Festival of Britain* (Manchester: Manchester University Press, 2003); Mary Schoeser, 'The appliance of science', in Elai Harwood and Alan Powers (eds), *Festival of Britain* (London: Twentieth Century Society, 2006).

7 Seweryn Chomet (ed.), *DNA: Genesis of a Discovery* (London: Newman-Hemisphere, 1995), pp. 10–14, 138–46.

8 'DNA: the King's story', at https://kingscollections.org/exhibitions/archives/dna/key-individuals/wilkins (accessed 5 November 2023).

9 Maurice Wilkins, *The Third Man of the Double Helix* (Oxford: Oxford University Press, 2003), ch. 5, 'Crystal genes'.

10 Struther Arnott, 'Maurice Hugh Frederick Wilkins', *Biographical Memoirs of Fellows of the Royal Society*, vol. 52 (2006), p. 457; Brenda Maddox, *Rosalind Franklin: The Dark Lady of DNA* (London: Harper Perennial, 2002), ch. 9, 'Joining the circus'; Wilkins, *Third Man*, pp. 127, 130–5, 147.

11 Open University, 'Making Britain. Z. A. Bokhari', at https://www.50open.ac.uk/research-projects/making-britain/content/z-bokhari (accessed 2 January 2024); Marie Gillespie and Alban Webb (eds), *Diasporas and Diplomacy: Cosmopolitan Contact Zones at the BBC World Service (1932–2012)* (London: Routledge, 2013), p. 57.

12 Hamid Ismailov, Marie Gillespie and Anna Aslanyan (eds), *Tales from Bush House* (London: Hertfordshire Press, 2012), pp. 10, 56; John Tusa, *A World in your Ear* (London: Broadside Books, 1992), ch. 5, 'Voices in the dark'; Gillespie and Webb, *Diasporas*, pp. 1, 57, 86–93; Marie Gillespie, 'Diasporic creativity: refugee intellectuals, exiled poets and corporate cosmopolitanism at the BBC World Service', in Kim Knott and Sean McLoughlin (eds), *Diasporas: Concepts, Intersections, Identities* (London: Zed Books, 2010), p. 240.

13 Andrea Thorpe, *South African London: Writing the Metropolis After 1948* (Manchester: Manchester University Press, 2001).

14 For the listing of radio broadcasts, see BBC Programme Index at https://genome.ch.bbc.co.uk (accessed 10 October 2023).

15 Lesley Cowling and Shelley Roberts, 'Ungovernable women of southern Africa', in John Bak and Bill Reynolds (eds), *The Routledge Companion to World Literary Journalism* (Abingdon: Routledge, 2023), pp. 66–9; Sarah Mir, 'People of the Strand: Noni Jabavu', on the Strandlines website, at https://www.strandlines.london/2020/03/16/people-of-the-strand-helen-noni-jabavu-1919-2008/ (asccessed 5 January 2024); Christopher Driver, 'New *Strand*'s new editor', *The Guardian*, 7 September 1961; Athambile Masola, 'Reading Noni Jabavu in 2017', *Mail and Guardian* [South Africa], 10 August 2017; 'New *Strand* editor', *Ebony*, April 1962; 'Bantu woman edits an English magazine', *Sydney Morning Herald*, 21 September 1961; Makhosazana Xaba, 'Noni Jabavu: Black Briton, South African', 2021, on the York Festival of Ideas YouTube channel, at https://youtu.be/k7xv6dLoF7c?si=Yu8lGGvraAh_Cw_k (accessed 10 January 2024).

16 Colin Allen, *Transplanting the Garden* (London, 1998), pp. 31–2; Myfanwy

Boudry, 'Arundel Great Court', 23 May 2020, on the Strandlines website, at https://www.strandlines.london/2020/05/23/arundel-great-court (accessed 24 February 2024).

17 John Davis, *Waterloo Sunrise: London from the Sixties to Thatcher* (Princeton, NJ: Princeton University Press, 2022), pp. 204–6; Peter Mappleston, *St Mary le Strand* (London: CreateSpace, 2019), pp. 259–68; Covent Garden Memories website, at https://www.coventgardenmemories.org.uk/category_id__27. aspx (accessed 13 January 2024); 'London's historic new shopping experience', *Evening Standard*, 19 June 1980.

18 'Do the Strand', Bryan Ferry, 1973, Viva Roxy Music, at https://www. vivaroxymusic.com/songs_118.php (accessed 10 December 2023).

19 Francesca Allfrey, 'India Club continues their fight for survival', 8 February 2021, on the Strandlines website, at https://www.strandlines. london/2021/02/08/save-india-club-2021 (accessed 10 January 2024); Olivia Williams, *The Secret Life of the Savoy* (London: Headline, 2020), pp. 224–53.

20 H. V. Morton, *In Search of London* (London: Methuen, 2013), p. 147.

21 Jerry White, *London in the Twentieth Century: A City and Its People* (London: Viking, 2008), p. 283; 'Police round up the beggar thugs', *Evening Standard*, 26 June 1990; '£5 m facelift for a grand new Strand', *Evening Standard*, 27 May 1994.

22 'Queen opens a new house in the Strand', *Evening Standard*, 25 May 1972; 'The Strand is the noisiest place in London', *Guardian*, 31 July 1962.

23 'The new new thing', *Evening Standard*, 19 December 2000.

24 On tourism: White, *London*, pp. 211–13, 326. On key visitor statistics to London in 2012: London and Partners, 'Key visitor statistics: 2012 fact sheet', at https://cdn.londonandpartners.com/l-and-p/assets/media/london_factsheet_ key_visitor_statistics_2012.pdf (accessed 15 January 2024); Somerset House, 'History', at https://www.somersethouse.org.uk/history (accessed 4 October 2023).

25 Clive Aslet, *Strands of History: Northbank Revealed* (London: Wild Research, 2014).

Conclusion

1 Benjamin Disraeli, *Tancred; or, The New Crusade* (London: Henry Colburn, 1847); Virginia Woolf, *Street Haunting: A London Adventure*, 1930 (London: Penguin, 2005); Arthur Machen, *Far Off Things* (London: Martin Secker, 1922).

2 Samuel Butler, 'Darwin among the machines', *The Press*, 13 June 1863.

3 Ethan Huang, 'How ice-shelf loss drives sea level rise', at https://sealevel.nasa. gov/news/266/how-ice-shelf-loss-drives-sea-level-rise (accessed 2 August 2024); NASA, 'Study predicts more long term sea level rise', at https://climate.nasa. gov/news/2883/study-predicts-more-long-term-sea-level-rise-from-greenland-ice (accessed 10 February 2024).

SELECT BIBLIOGRAPHY

Ackroyd, Peter, *London: The Concise Biography* (London: Random House, 2012)

Alford, Stephen, *Burghley: William Cecil at the Court of Elizabeth I* (New Haven, CT: Yale University Press, 2008)

Allan, David, *The Adelphi Past and Present: A History and a Guide* (London: Calder Walker, 2001)

Arnold, Dana, *Re-presenting the Metropolis: Architecture, Urban Experience and Social Life in London, 1800–1840* (Aldershot: Ashgate, 2000)

Ashton, Rosemary, *142 Strand: A Radical Address in Victorian London* (London: Random House, 2008)

Aslet, Clive, *Strands of History: Northbank Revealed* (London: Wild Research, 2014)

Baer, Marc, *The Rise and Fall of Radical Westminster, 1780–1890* (New York: Palgrave Macmillan, 2012)

Besant, Sir Walter and Mitton, G. E., *The Strand District* (London: A. & C. Black, 1903)

Biddle, Martin, 'The Road to Lundenwic', in Jonathan Cotton *et al.*, *Hidden Histories and Records of Antiquity: Essays on Saxon London for John Clark, Curator Emeritus, Museum of London* (London: London and Middlesex Archaeological Society, 2014)

Birch, Thomas, *Memoirs of the Reign of Queen Elizabeth* (London: A. Millar, 1754)

Boorman, Francis Calvert, with Jonathan Comber and Mark Latham (eds), *The Victoria History of Middlesex: St Clement Danes, 1660–1900* (London: Institute of Historical Research, 2018)

Bradley, Simon and Pevsner, Nikolaus, *London 6: Westminster* (Harmondsworth: Penguin, 2003)

Brayley, Edward Wedlake, *Londiniana; Or, Reminiscences of the British Metropolis* (London: Hurst, Chance, and Co., 1828–29)

Brett-James, Norman, *The Growth of Stuart London* (London: George Allen & Unwin, 1935)

British History Online, https://archive.british-history.ac.uk

Brooke, Christopher, *London 800–1216: The Shaping of a City* (Berkeley, CA: University of California Press, 1975)

Carpenter, David, *Henry III, 1207–1258: The Rise to Power and Personal Rule* (New Haven, CT: Yale University Press, 2020)

Chancellor, E. Beresford, *The Annals of the Strand: Topographical and Historical* (London: Chapman & Hall, 1912)

Chancellor, E. Beresford, *The Private Palaces of London Past and Present* (London: Kegan Paul, Trench, Trübner & Co., 1908)

Clunn, Harold P., *The Face of London* (London: 1970)

Cockburn, J. S., King, H. P. F. and McDonnell, K. G. T. (eds), *A History of the*

County of Middlesex, Volume I: Physique, Archaeology, Domesday, Ecclesiastical Organization, the Jews, Religious Houses, Education of Working Classes to 1870, Private Education from Sixteenth Century (London: Victoria History of the Counties of England, 1969)

Cowie, L. W., 'The Savoy – Palace and Hospital', History Today, vol. 24, issue 3 (1974)

Cowie, Robert and Blackmore, Lyn (eds), Lundenwic: Excavations in Middle Saxon London 1987–2000 (London: Museum of London, 2013)

Croft, Pauline, Patronage, Culture and Power: The Early Cecils (New Haven, CT: Yale University Press, 2002)

Croot, Patricia, Thacker, Alan and Williamson, Elizabeth (eds), A History of the County of Middlesex, Volume XIII: City of Westminster Part 1 (London: Victoria History of the Counties of England, 2009)

Davis, John, Waterloo Sunrise: London from the Sixties to Thatcher (Princeton, NJ: Princeton University Press, 2022)

Day, W. C., Street Nuisances: A Letter to Colonel E. Y. W. Henderson on the Condition of the Strand, and Other Leading Thoroughfares of the Metropolis (London: William Tweedie, 1871)

de Lisle, Leanda, Henrietta Maria: Conspirator, Warrior, Phoenix Queen (London: Random House, 2023)

Dinnis, Robb and Stringer, Chris, Britain: One Million Years of the Human Story (London: Natural History Museum, 2013)

Fox, Celina (ed.), London, World City, 1800–1840 (New Haven, CT: Yale University Press in association with the Museum of London, 1992)

Garrow, Duncan and Wilkin, Neil, The World of Stonehenge (London: British Museum Press, 2022)

Gater, George Henry, Hiorns, Frederick R. and Godfrey, Walter H., Survey of London: Trafalgar Square and Neighbourhood (the Parish of St. Martin-in-the-Fields) (London: London County Council, 1940)

Gelling, Margaret, 'The boundaries of the Westminster charters', Transactions of the London and Middlesex Archaeological Society, vol. 11 (1953), pp. 101–4

Goldring, Elizabeth, Robert Dudley, Earl of Leicester, and the World of Elizabethan Art (New Haven, CT: Yale University Press, 2014)

Gray, Alexander Stuart, Edwardian Architecture: A Biographical Dictionary (London: Duckworth, 1985)

Guerci, Manolo, London's 'Golden Mile': The Great Houses of the Strand, 1550–1650 (New Haven, CT: Yale University Press, 2021)

Halliday, Stephen, The Great Stink of London: Sir Joseph Bazalgette and the Cleansing of the Victorian Capital (Stroud: Sutton, 1999)

Hibbert, Christopher and Weinreb, Ben (eds), The London Encyclopaedia, 3rd edn (London: Pan-Macmillan, 2008)

Hingley, Richard, Londinium: A Biography (London: Bloomsbury, 2018)

Hitchcock, Tim and Shore, Heather (eds), foreword by Roy Porter, The Streets of London: From the Great Fire to the Great Stink (London: Rivers Oram Press, 2003)

Husselby, Jill and Henderson, Paula, 'Location, location, location! Cecil House in the Strand', Architectural History, vol. 45 (2002), pp. 159–93

Ismailov, Hamid, Gillespie, Marie and Aslanyan, Anna (eds), Tales from Bush House (London: Hertfordshire Press, 2012)

Jenkins, Simon, A Short History of London: The Creation of a World Capital (London: Penguin, 2009)

Kelsall, Frank and Walker, Timothy, *Nicholas Barbon: Developing London, 1667–1698* (London: London Topographical Society, 2022)

Lincoln, Margarette, *London and the 17th Century: The Making of the World's Greatest City* (New Haven, CT: Yale University Press, 2022)

McCarthy, Justin and Joseph Pennell, *Charing Cross to St Paul's* (London: Seeley, 1891)

Machen, Arthur, *Far Off Things* (London: Martin Secker, 1922)

Mapplestone, Peter, *St Mary le Strand* (London: CreateSpace, 2019)

Margary, Ivan, *Roman Roads in Britain* (London: Phoenix, 1955)

Mattingly, David, *An Imperial Possession: Britain in the Roman Empire, 54 BC – AD 409* (London: Allen Lane, 2006)

Milne, Gustav, *The Port of Medieval London* (Reading: Tempus, 2003)

Moore, Judith, *A Zeal for Responsibility: The Struggle for Professional Nursing in Victorian England, 1868–83* (Athens,GA: University of Georgia Press, 1988)

Naismith, Rory, *Citadel of the Saxons: The Rise of Early London* (London: Bloomsbury, 2018)

Newman, Ian David, *The Romantic Tavern: Literature and Conviviality in the Age of Revolution* (Cambridge: Cambridge University Press, 2019)

Newnham-Davis, Nathaniel, *Dinners and Diners* (London: Richards, 1899)

Nichols, J. G. (ed.), *The Diary of Henry Machyn, Citizen and Merchant-Taylor of London, 1550–1563* (London: Camden Society, 1848)

Ogborn, Miles, *Spaces of Modernity: London's Geographies, 1680–1780* (New York: Guilford Press, 1998)

Olsen, Donald J., *Town Planning in London: The Eighteenth and Nineteenth Centuries* (New Haven, CT: Yale University Press, 1964)

Oxford Dictionary of National Biography (ODNB, https://www.oxforddnb.com, accessed 22 September 2024)

Pepys, Samuel, The Diary of Samuel Pepys (Pepys' diary online, https://www.pepysdiary.com, accessed 22 September 2024)

Perring, Dominic, *London in the Roman World* (Oxford: Oxford University Press, 2022)

Plomer, Henry Robert, *A Dictionary of the Booksellers and Printers Who Were at Work in England, Scotland and Ireland from 1641 to 1667* (London: Bibliographical Society/Blades, East & Blades, 1907)

Proceedings of the Old Bailey, https://www.oldbaileyonline.org (accessed 22 September 2024)

Pudill, Rainer and Eyre, Clive, *The Tribes and Coins of Celtic Britain* (Ipswich: Greenlight, 2005)

Rapport, Michael, *Rebel Cities: Paris, London and New York in the Age of Revolution* (London: Abacus, 2018)

Ross, Catherine and Clark, John, *London: The Illustrated History* (London: Allen Lane, 2008)

Rosser, Gervase, *Medieval Westminster: 1200–1540* (Oxford: Clarendon Press, 1989)

Saint, Andrew, *London, 1870–1914: A City at Its Zenith* (London: Lund Humphries, 2021)

Shenton, Caroline, *National Treasures: Saving the Nation's Art in World War II* (London: John Murray, 2022)

Shepherd, Robert, *Westminster: A Biography. From Earliest Times to the Present* (London: Bloomsbury Academic, 2012)

Smith, John Thomas. *The Streets of London with Anecdotes of Their More Celebrated Residents* (London: R. Bentley, 1846)

Somerville, Robert, Sir, *The Savoy: Manor, Hospital, Chapel* (London: Duchy of Lancaster, 1960)

Strandlines [blog], https://www.strandlines.london

Summerson, John and Colvin, Howard, *Georgian London* (New Haven, CT: published for the Paul Mellon Centre for Studies in British Art by Yale University Press, 2003)

Tallis, John, *John Tallis's London Street Views, 1838–1840* (London: Nattali & Maurice, 1969)

Tatton-Brown, Tim, 'The medieval and early Tudor topography of Westminster', in *Westminster, Part I: The Art, Architecture and Archaeology of the Royal Abbey* (London: Routledge, 2020)

Thornbury, Walter, *Old and New London, Volume III* (London, 1878)

Thorpe, Andrea, *South African London: Writing the Metropolis After 1948* (Manchester: Manchester University Press, 2001)

Thurley, Simon, *Somerset House: The Palace of England's Queens 1551–1692* (London: Topographical Society, 2009)

Tindall, Gillian, *The Man Who Drew London* (London: Random House, 2013)

Trapp, Michael, 'The Georgian history of the Strand Lane "Roman" bath', *London Journal*, vol. 39, no. 2 (2014), pp. 142–67

Vaughan, Richard (ed.), *Chronicles of Matthew Paris: Monastic Life in the Thirteenth Century* (London: Sutton, 1984)

Vince, Alan, *Saxon London: An Archaeological Investigation* (London: B. A. Seaby, 1990)

West End at War, https://www.westendatwar.org.uk (accessed 10 November 2023)

White, Jerry, *London in the Nineteenth Century – A Human Awful Wonder of God* (London: Vintage, 2008)

White, Jerry, *London in the Twentieth Century: A City and Its People* (London: Viking, 2008)

Williams, Olivia, *The Secret Life of the Savoy* (London: Headline, 2020)

Williams, Thomas, *Viking Britain: A History* (London: Harper Collins, 2017)

Williams, Thomas, *Viking London* (London: Harper Collins, 2019)

Wynne Jones, Robert, *The Flower of All Cities: The History of London from Earliest Times to the Great Fire* (Stroud: Amberley, 2022)

INDEX

Page numbers in **bold** refer to figures.

EU authorised representative for GPSR:
Easy Access System Europe, Mustamäe tee 50,
10621 Tallinn, Estonia
gpsr.requests@easproject.com

www.ingramcontent.com/pod-product-compliance
Lightning Source LLC
Chambersburg PA
CBHW01092315O426
42812CB00068B/3349/J

9 781526 179111